Presidential Places

John F. Blair, Publisher
Winston-Salem, North Carolina

Presidential Places

A Guide to the Historic Sites of U. S. Presidents

by Gary Ferris

★ ★ ★ ★ ★ ★ ★ ★ ★ ★ ★ ★ ★ ★ ★ ★

Second Printing, 1999

DESIGN BY DEBRA LONG HAMPTON

PRINTED AND BOUND BY R. R. DONNELLEY & SONS

*The paper in this book meets the guidelines for
permanence and durability of the Committee
on Production Guidelines for Book Longevity
of the Council on Library Resources.*

Cover photographs, clockwise from top—

Abraham Lincoln Birthplace National Historic Site in Hodgenville, Kentucky

   Courtesy of the Abraham Lincoln Birthplace National Historic Site

Friendship Firehouse in Alexandria, Virginia

   by Brian J. McCormick, Jr.

Ulysses S. Grant Cottage State Historic Site in Saratoga Springs, New York

   by Beverly Clark

Carter Center in Atlanta, Georgia

   Courtesy of Carter Center

Palace Hotel in San Francisco, California

   Courtesy of the Palace Hotel

Library of Congress Cataloging-in-Publication Data

Ferris, Gary W.

   Presidential places : a guide to the historic sites of U. S. presidents / Gary Ferris.

      p.   cm.

   Includes bibliographical references and indexes.

   ISBN 0-89587-176-9 (alk. paper)

      1. Presidents—United States—Homes and haunts—Guidebooks.   2. Historic sites—United
States—Guidebooks.   3. United States—Guidebooks.   I. Title.

E176.1.F49   1999

917.304—dc21   98–50395

To Sue,
my precious wife,
forever the love
of my life

Contents

Preface

★★★★★★★★★★

It was a beautiful morning in late May a few years ago when the idea for this book first came to mind.

My wife and I were living near Albany, New York, and we decided to head to Boston for the day. Our children were in Buffalo for the weekend with relatives, and Boston was only a three- or four-hour drive.

We got there late in the morning. I had attended Boston University but had not been back for a number of years. Sue had been there only once or twice, many years before we met. I pointed out the apartment building in Brookline where I had lived and said that the Kennedy birthplace was just around the corner. Since neither or us had ever visited the historic house on Beals Street, we decided to go.

We were impressed immensely by it. We both remember the Kennedy presidency, even though we were young at the time. True to the stereotype, we recall where we were when we heard that Kennedy was shot. For us, the visit was special. We immersed ourselves in the innocence of an earlier time. The basement of the house has a small visitor center, where we watched a brief video. Two or three families were there, and the children were asking their parents about Kennedy. I was moved by how John F. Kennedy, more than 30 years after his death, could still bring families together. When the video ended, a ranger told us that in honor of Kennedy's birthday, cake was being served in the backyard. What could be a better family event?

When we finished our cake and went back inside, I wanted to get a National Park Service book or at least a handful of brochures about presidential sites. What a wonderful thing it would be for our family to travel to other such sites. Our children were just getting to school age, and American history would be a hot topic in our house for at least the next dozen years. That left us plenty of time to hit the history trail, I reasoned.

I picked up a National Park Service passport book and was stunned to see that only 30 or 40 presidential sites were managed by the service. It seemed to me that there must be many others. I grew up in the Northeast, where it seemed that everywhere I looked, there was a "Washington Slept Here" sign. Just those Washington sites, I figured, would outnumber the entire list of presidential homes maintained by the park service. A perusal through travel guides confirmed that there were indeed many, many more presidential sites, yet I could find no single source listing all of them. This still surprises me, because while compiling this book, a number of park rangers and site curators told me that they constantly talk to visitors who are trying to visit as many presidential sites as possible and who like to record their visits in journals.

With this book, I hope to accomplish three things. First, I want to instill in the reader a deeper understanding of and appreciation for the presidency. Second, I want to help families grow closer by sharing some truly meaningful time together. And finally, I want to have something special that Sue and I can share with our own children. We had two children when I started working on this book. Now, we have five. What fun we will have in the coming years!

The information in this book was correct at the time it was written, but be aware that sites may change their admission prices or hours at any time. It is best to call ahead before making travel plans.

Included in this book are places of historical significance to the presidents—where they were born, lived, went to school, went to church, were married, died, were buried, and are honored. Not included are places that honor presidents in name only, like the George Washington Bridge and the countless John F. Kennedy High Schools that dot our land. Also not generally included are statues of presidents unless they are tied to a presidential visit or some place or event of significance. Many of the presidents lived in a number of different homes for short periods or briefly attended a variety of churches and schools. I do not pretend to offer an exhaustive list of such places.

Note that some of the sites listed here are private property. Please respect the privacy of the residents. Please also note that many sites are owned or operated by small local agencies. They may depend on admission revenue, gift-shop sales, or charitable contributions in order to survive. Please give generously whenever you have the opportunity to support a site, especially ones that are controlled by small nonprofit agencies.

Acknowledgments

There are many who helped to make this book a reality. Among them are Trine Ackelman of the Palace Hotel in San Francisco; J. Michael Adams, dean of Nesbitt College of Design Arts at Drexel University; Bill Arbon of Impeckible Aviaries in Johnson City, Texas; Joan Baillon of the Omaha Parks, Recreation, and Public Property Department; Peter Blankman of Union College; Denise Bollinger of the United States Air Force Museum; Dr. Paul K. Bookman of Bryn Mawr, Pennsylvania, for his crowning encouragement; Fred Boyles of Jimmy Carter National Historic Park; Nancy Brown of Belle Grove Plantation; George Bush; Jimmy Carter; Penny Circle, chief of staff to Gerald R. Ford; Beverly Clark of Ulysses S. Grant Cottage State Historic Site; Deanna Congileo of The Carter Center; Leslie Credit for her photography; Michael C. Dannenhauer, chief of staff to George Bush; Dr. Richard Durschlag of the Museum of the Waxhaws; Frank Donaghue of the American Red Cross in Philadelphia for his encouragement; Linda Duff of Adams National Historic Site; Rita Embry, site administrator of Harry S Truman Birthplace State Historic Site; Ian Ferris for his photography; Shawn M. Fitzpatrick of Whittier College; Gerald R. Ford; Estella Grobe of the Dixon Historical Society; Stephen Handro of the Johnson City Historical Review Board; Carol Hegeman of Eisenhower National Historic Site; K. Hinkle of Andrew Johnson National Historic Site; Dr. Lynn Hoffman for his advice on writing and publishing; Carolyn Holmes of Ashlawn-Highland; John Holtzapple of the James K. Polk Memorial Association; Terri Jones of Mordecai Historic Park; Nancy Kleinhenz of the Rutherford B. Hayes Presidential Center; Dion Lerman of Drexel University for putting up with me as I developed my book idea; Lisa McClatchy of the American Red Cross in Philadelphia for her support; Meredith and Brian McCormick of Chestnut Hill, Pennsylvania; Amy McElhiney of the Tampico Area Historical Society; Karen Myers of the United States Naval Academy; Gary D. Peak of Zachary Taylor National Cemetery; Ernest Platzer of the American Architectural Foundation; Maxine Reese of Plains, Georgia; George Retmeier of the Aurora Historical Society; Ralph Rourke of the Hall of Fame for Great Americans; Nancy Sambets of Andrew Jackson State Park; Mickail Simmons of Duxbury, Massachusetts, for teaching me how to do research; Nancy Steele of Running Press; Hal Walsh of the Harry S Truman Little White

House Museum; Bill Wilcox of Herbert Hoover National Historic Site; Ronald G. Wilson of Appomattox Court House National Historic Park; and John R. Wright of the Elijah Miller House. I especially wish to thank Steve Kirk, Debbie Hampton, and Carolyn Sakowski of John F. Blair, Publisher. Thanks also to Jillian, Kimberly, Daniel, Kathryn, and Abigail for believing in their daddy.

In addition, I would like to acknowledge the men who have held our nation's highest office, the wives and children who supported them, the voters who elected them, and the women and men who will hold the position in years to come.

★ ★ ★ ★ ★

Presidential Places

George Washington
First President of the United States

Birthplace

George Washington Birthplace National Monument
National Park Service
1732 Popes Creek Road
Washington's Birthplace, VA 22443
804-224-1732
www.nps.gov/gewa

George Washington's great-grandfather settled this plantation in 1657. The house in which Washington was born in 1732 (built by his father between 1722 and 1726) was destroyed by fire on Christmas Day 1779. Since its original appearance is not known, a memorial house representing similar buildings of the day has been constructed on the site.

The 538-acre facility replicates an 18th-century tobacco farm. The grounds contain the graves of 32 members of the Washington family, including George Washington's father, grandfather, and great-grandfather. Picnic facilities and a visitor center are on the premises.

Hours
Daily from 9 A.M. to 5 P.M.; closed New Year's and Christmas
Admission
$2 for adults; guests under 17 are free

George Washington Birthplace National Monument

Travelogue

Homes

George Washington's Ferry Farm
Kenmore Plantation and Gardens Association
King's Highway
Stafford County, VA 22554
540-373-3381
www.kenmore.org

The Washington family settled Ferry Farm in 1738; Washington's mother lived here until her death. On his 21st birthday, Washington received an inheritance from his father's estate that included Ferry Farm, property in nearby Fredericksburg, 10 slaves, and other personal property.

George Washington's Ferry Farm

Travelogue

again when he became our first president.

The mansion has been restored to how it looked in 1799. On display are original furnishings and belongings, including the bed in which Washington died, his sword, and a key to the Bastille given to him by the Marquis de Lafayette. The plantation includes numerous outbuildings, as well as the graves of George and Martha Washington.

See also Kenmore Plantation on page 21.

Hours
Monday through Saturday from 10 A.M. to 5 P.M. and Sunday from noon to 5 P.M.
Admission
Free

Hours
Daily from 8 A.M. to 5 P.M. from April to August; from 9 A.M. to 5 P.M. during March, September, and October; and from 9 A.M. to 4 P.M. from November to February
Admission
$8 for adults; $7.50 for guests over 62; $4 for ages four to 11

Mount Vernon
Mount Vernon Ladies' Association
George Washington Memorial Parkway
Mount Vernon, VA 22121
703-780-2000
www.mountvernon.org

Washington acquired Mount Vernon in 1754, two years after the death of his half-brother Lawrence, who had inherited the plantation and who gave it its name. Washington greatly enlarged the property and improved the mansion and lived at Mount Vernon until his death in 1799, leaving it in 1775 to command the Continental Army and

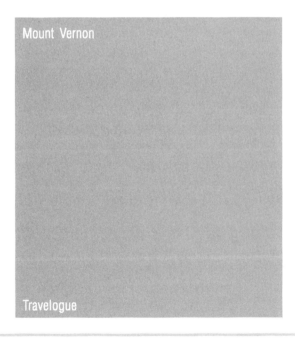
Mount Vernon

Travelogue

George Washington's
Grist Mill Historical State Park
VA 235
Mount Vernon, VA 22121
703-780-3383

The history of the mill is presented on videotape in the restored mill, which sits on its original foundation. Also on display are replicas of mill machinery.

Hours
The grounds are open from dawn to dusk daily. The mill is open on weekends from 10 A.M. to 6 P.M. from Memorial Day to Labor Day.
Admission
Admission to the mill is $1.25 for adults and $1 for ages six to 12. Admission to the grounds is free.

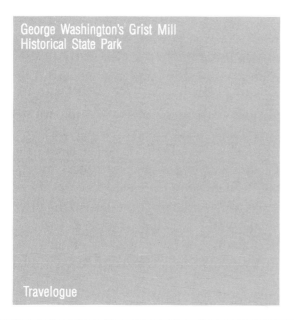

George Washington's Grist Mill Historical State Park

Travelogue

River Farm
American Horticultural Society
George Washington Memorial Parkway
Alexandria, VA 22308-1300
703-768-5700 or 800-777-7931
www.ahs.org/nonmembers/riverfarm.htm

Washington purchased this farm in 1760 and is believed to have planted the many walnut trees that cover the grounds. At the time, it was the northernmost of his five farms.

In 1971, the Soviet embassy tried to buy the property for use as a retreat. Objections arose, however, and the property eventually was purchased by the American Horticultural Society.

The main house (1757) is furnished in period style. The American Horticultural Society offers classes, lectures, and other events on the grounds. Picnic facilities are available.

Hours
Monday through Friday from 8:30 A.M. to 5 P.M.; closed holidays
Admission
Free

River Farm

Travelogue

Deshler-Morris House

National Park Service
5442 Germantown Pike
Philadelphia, PA 19118
215-596-1748
www.nps.gov/htdocs4/inde/morris.htm

Philadelphia merchant David Deshler built this historic home. In October 1777, during the Battle of Germantown, it was headquarters for British general William Howe. In 1793, when Washington was president, he escaped Philadelphia's yellow-fever outbreak by staying here. He and his family returned to the house during the following summer to find relief from the oppressive heat. Four cabinet meetings were held here. The restored 1772 house contains period furnishings.

Hours
Tuesday through Saturday from 1 to 4 P.M. from April to December; call to arrange tours at other times
Admission
$1

Deshler-Morris House

Churches

Christ Church

118 North Washington Street
Alexandria, VA 22314
703-549-1450
www.historicchristchurch.org

Washington was a member here; the pew he purchased for 36 pounds and 10 shillings is preserved in its original configuration. Legend holds that it was in the churchyard that George Washington, age 41, first told friends of his willingness to fight for independence. His ties to the church spared it during the Civil War, when occupying Federal troops confiscated other area churches for use as stables and hospitals but respected the place where Washington had worshiped.

Tours are conducted weekdays from 9 A.M. to 4 P.M. and Sunday from 2 to 4 P.M.

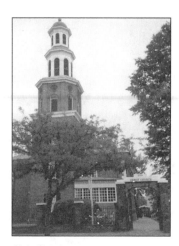

Christ Church
Photo by Brian J. McCormick, Jr.

Bronze plaque at Christ Church commemorating the pallbearers of Washington's funeral
Photo by Brian J. McCormick, Jr.

Christ Church

Travelogue

Pohick Church
9301 Richmond Highway
Lorton, VA 22079-1519
703-550-9449

Washington selected the site for this church, which served Mount Vernon, Gunston Hill, and Belvoir. He served as vestryman for 23 years. During the Civil War, the interior was torn out by Union troops, who used the building as a stable. It was restored between 1902 and 1917. The stone baptismal font was recovered years later, having been used as a trough on a nearby farm.

The church may be visited daily from 9 A.M. to 4:30 P.M.

Pohick Church

Travelogue

Education

Washington's older brothers were sent to England for schooling. Their mother, however, did not want to send young George after his father's death. While it is not known who tutored Washington, he was proficient in reading, writing, and mathematics by the age of 11. He did not attend college.

Marriage

Washington married Martha Dandridge Custis, a widow with two children, at her family's home along the Pamunkey River near Williamsburg, Virginia.

Revolutionary War Sites

Washington Elm
Cambridge Common at Mason Street
Cambridge, MA
hbook.harvard.edu/hbook/v2toc27.htm

On July 3, 1775, Washington officially took command of the Continental Army at ceremonies beneath the tree, which stood at the edge of the training grounds used by the troops. A small bronze plaque marks the spot.

The history of the Washington Elm is included in the "Harvard Book," the electronic history of Harvard and its surroundings, which may be accessed via the above Web address.

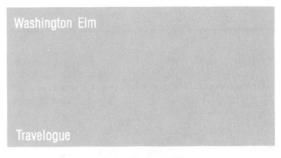

Longfellow National Historic Site
National Park Service
105 Brattle Street
Cambridge, MA 02138
617-876-4491

Washington made his headquarters here during the siege of Boston from July 1775 through April 1776. From 1837 until 1882, it was the home of poet Henry Wadsworth Longfellow while he taught at Harvard. The site's collections deal mainly with Longfellow, but there are some Washington letters as well.

<u>Hours</u>
Wednesday through Sunday from 10 A.M. to 4:30 P.M.; closed New Year's, Thanksgiving, and Christmas
<u>Admission</u>
$2 for adults; guests under 17 are free

Morris-Jumel Mansion

65 Jumel Terrace
New York, NY 10032
212-923-8008
www.ci.nyc.cy.uc/nyclink/html/dpr/html/
housesm_morris.html

Built in 1765, this is the oldest house on Manhattan Island. It served as Washington's headquarters in 1776. Currently a museum set on a 1.5-acre park, it features a decorative-arts collection representing the colonial and Revolutionary War periods. Washington's office is among the 12 restored rooms. The mansion is accessible by the B and C subway lines (163rd Street stop) and by the M2, M3, M100, and M101 buses.

Hours
Tuesday through Sunday from 10 A.M. to 4 P.M.
Admission
$3 for adults; $1 for seniors and students; guests under 12 are free

Morris-Jumel Mansion

Travelogue

Elijah Miller House

Washington's Headquarters Museum
140 Virginia Road
White Plains, NY 10602
914-949-1236 or 914-941-0757

In 1776, during the last phase of the Battle of White Plains, Washington made his headquarters in this humble building, which dates from 1738. The house was also used by General Charles Lee during the battle and served as headquarters for Generals McDougall and Gates during the latter stages of the war.

The structure is a representative 18th-century middle-class farmhouse and includes original furniture and artifacts. Adjacent is Miller Hill, the only preserved battlefield in Westchester County and the site of the conclusion of the Battle of White Plains; you may visit the battlefield after touring the house. The house is noted for its hands-on and

Elijah Miller House
Photo © 1998 by Gray Williams

living-history programs. It is located between NY 22 and the Bronx River Parkway.

Hours
Living-history programs are offered monthly; hands-on programs are offered to groups by appointment.
Admission
Free

Elijah Miller House

Travelogue

Washington Crossing Historic Park
PA 32
Washington Crossing, PA 18977
215-493-4076
www.spiritof76.com/wchp/index.html

This 500-acre park is divided into two sections: the Thompson's Mill section and the Washington Crossing section.

The latter section is the site from which Washington and the Continental Army crossed the Delaware River on December 25, 1776. (A bridge connects this section with New Jersey's Washington Crossing State Park; see below.) The Washington Crossing section features McConkey Ferry Inn, where Washington is believed to have dined prior to the crossing; the Taylor House, home of influential businessman Mahlon Taylor; and the Memorial Building, which has a copy of Emanuel Leutze's painting *Washington Crossing the Delaware*. Each year, the crossing is reenacted on Christmas Day; call for details.

The Thompson's Mill section features Bowman's Hill Tower, a 110-foot tower with a 14-mile view of the Delaware Valley; the Thompson-Neely House, the site of many conferences before the Battle of Trenton; and the Memorial Flagstaff, which marks the graves of Continental Army troops who were the first of our nation's unknown soldiers.

Hours
Monday through Saturday from 9 A.M. to 5 P.M. and Sunday from noon to 5 P.M.
Admission
Guided tours cost $4 for adults and $2 for ages six to 12; there is a $1 toll for the picnic grounds; admission to the visitor center is free.

Washington Crossing Historic Park

Travelogue

Washington Crossing State Park

335 Washington Crossing–Pennington Road
Titusville, NJ 08560
609-737-0623
www.nj.com/outdoors/parks/washington.htm

This park is the site of the historic December 25, 1776, crossing of the Delaware River by Washington and the Continental Army on their way to the Battle of Trenton. Memorial markers have been placed along the length of Continental Lane, over which the troops marched en route to the battle. The crossing is reenacted annually on Christmas Day beginning on the Pennsylvania side of the river (see above). Also within the park is the George Washington Memorial Arboretum, which features an assortment of native trees and shrubs. The visitor center has period exhibits.

Hours
The park is open daily from dawn to dusk. The visitor center is open daily from 9 A.M. to 4:30 P.M. from Memorial Day to Labor Day and Wednesday through Sunday from 9 A.M. to 4:30 P.M. the rest of the year.
Admission
Free, although parking costs $4 from Memorial Day through Labor Day

Washington Crossing State Park

Travelogue

Brandywine Battlefield

Box 202
Chadds Ford, PA 19317
610-459-3342
www.libertynet.org/iha/brandywine

The Battle of Brandywine, fought September 11, 1777, was one of the bloodiest in the region. The park includes Washington's rebuilt headquarters and Lafayette's headquarters.

Hours
Tuesday through Saturday from 9 A.M. to 5 P.M. and Sunday from noon to 5 P.M.
Admission
The battlefield may be toured for free; house tours cost $3.50 for adults, $2.50 for seniors, and $1.50 for children.

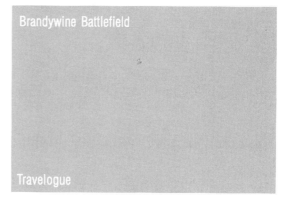

Brandywine Battlefield

Travelogue

Clivenden

6401 Germantown Avenue
Philadelphia, PA 19144-1998
215-848-1777

Clivenden was the scene of the October 2, 1777, battle during which American forces under Washington surprised General Howe's 9,000 troops. The British, however, put up a strong defense and forced the Americans to retreat.

Washington's Valley Forge headquarters

Hours
Thursday through Sunday from noon to 4 P.M.
Admission
$6 for adults; $4 for children

Clivenden

Travelogue

Valley Forge National Historical Park
National Park Service
PA 23
P.O. Box 953
Valley Forge, PA 19481
610-783-7700
www.nps.org/vafo

Washington and the severely depleted Continental Army camped here from December 19, 1777, until June 19, 1778, while British troops were bottled up in Philadelphia. During that time, some 2,000 troops died from disease brought on by the harsh winter, poor sanitation, and short supplies. Despite the setbacks, Baron von Steuben was able to revive the troops. By the time they left the encampment, they were a well-trained and efficient military organization.

Included in the park are Washington's headquarters (the Potts House), which is furnished with period items. Also on the premises is the Washington Memorial Chapel, constructed on the site where Washington is said to have prayed for divine providence during the encampment; a small museum at the chapel features Washington memorabilia, and a 58-bell carillon plays throughout the summer.

Hours
The park is open daily from 6 A.M. to 10 P.M.; the visitor center and Washington's headquarters are open daily from 9 A.M. to 5 P.M.; the facilities are closed Christmas.
Admission
A $2 fee is charged for Washington's headquarters from April through November; admission to the rest of the facilities is free.

Valley Forge National Historical Park

Travelogue

King of Prussia Inn

King of Prussia Historical Society
US 202 and Gulph Road
King of Prussia, PA 19406
610-265-7570

Built in the early 1700s, this former inn was named for Prussia's Prince Frederick; many of the area's earliest settlers came here from Prussia. The surrounding community took its name from the famous tavern.

The inn is said to have been frequented by George Washington during the Valley Forge encampment. It remained a popular restaurant until the 1950s, when the Pennsylvania Department of Transportation planned to demolish it in order to widen US 202. Area residents opposed to the plan blocked demolition crews. This impasse between preservationists and the state ended when the Department of Transportation erected a chain-link fence around the building and cut away its land, leaving the historic structure abandoned on a traffic island. It remains in this condition today, crumbling and totally inaccessible

to the public. Recently, however, the Department of Transportation gave the structure to the King of Prussia Historical Society on the condition that it raise sufficient funds to move and rehabilitate it. A site was selected on South Gulph Road, and a capital campaign is under way. After the building is moved, it will be renovated to include a small museum and other public facilities.

King of Prussia Inn

Travelogue

John Kane House

Pawling Historical Society
126 East Main Street
P.O. Box 99
Pawling, NY 12564
914-855-9316

During the fall of 1778, Washington made this his headquarters. Included today are exhibits of post–Revolutionary War lifestyles and Lowell Thomas memorabilia. The Pawling Historical Society also owns and maintains the Oblong Friends Meeting House, a 1764 building that served as a Revolutionary

War hospital. The meeting house is on Quaker Hill east of the Kane House.

Hours
Saturday and Sunday from 2 to 4 P.M.
from May 15 to October 15; other times
by appointment
Admission
Donations are accepted.

John Kane House

Travelogue

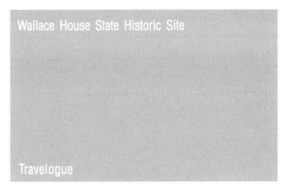

Wallace House State Historic Site

Travelogue

Wallace House State Historic Site
38 Washington Place
Somerville, NJ 08876
908-725-1015

During the encampment of the Continental Army in the winter of 1778–79, Washington made his headquarters in this 1778 house. It contains period furnishings.

Hours
Wednesday through Saturday from 10 A.M. to 5 P.M. and Sunday from 1 to 5 P.M.; closed New Year's, Thanksgiving, and Christmas
Admission
Free

Morristown National Historical Park
National Park Service
Washington's Place
Morristown, NJ 07960
973-539-2085
www.nps.gov/morr

Washington's headquarters, the Ford Mansion, was built between 1772 and 1774 for Colonel Jacob Ford, Jr. Washington selected this defensible site as the main encampment for the Continental Army in early 1777 and again in 1779–80. During the latter period, it served as the home of George and Martha. Washington's leadership was greatly tested during this encampment, as troops resorted to mutiny due to starvation and cold.

Hours
Daily from 9 A.M. to 5 P.M.; closed New Year's, Thanksgiving, and Christmas. Guided tours depart the nearby historical museum and library hourly between 10 A.M. and 4 P.M.
Admission
$4

Morristown National Historical Park

Travelogue

Colonial National Historic Park

National Park Service
Colonial Parkway
Yorktown, VA 23690-0210
757-898-3400
www.nps.gov/colo

This park includes two important sites: the Jamestown settlement, site of the first permanent English colony in this country, and the Yorktown Battlefield, site of the final battle of the Revolutionary War. As such, it includes both the beginning and the end of English settlement in what is now the United States.

On September 14, 1781, Washington, aided by French allies, arrived to fight General Cornwallis; intense bombardment into early October forced Cornwallis to surrender.

Washington's headquarters are located on the nine-mile Encampment Drive. The visitor center includes numerous artifacts and exhibits.

Hours
Daily from 9 A.M. to 5 P.M.; call for

information about extended hours in the spring, summer, and fall
Admission
Free

Colonial National Historic Park

Travelogue

Washington's Headquarters State Historic Site

84 Liberty Street
Newburgh, NY 12551
914-562-1195

This 1750 stone house, the home of Jonathan Hasbrouck, was Washington's headquarters in 1782 and 1783. It was from this place that he ordered the end of the Revolutionary War.

The six-acre park includes the 1887 Tower of Victory monument and a museum related to the Continental Army. Special celebrations are held each year on Presidents' Day weekend and on the first Sunday in June, the latter to celebrate Martha Washington's birthday. Tours are offered in Braille. Nearby is

New Windsor Cantonment, the site of a Continental Army encampment (see below).

(see below)

Hours
Wednesday through Saturday from 10 A.M. to 5 P.M. and Sunday from 1 to 5 P.M.
Admission
Free

Washington's Headquarters State Historic Site

Travelogue

New Windsor Cantonment State Historic Site

Travelogue

New Windsor Cantonment State Historic Site

Temple Hill Road
New Windsor, NY 12550
914-561-1765

This was the site of the last encampment of Washington's army. It features military drills, the firing of artillery, and camp-life exhibits.

Hours
Wednesday through Saturday from 10 A.M. to 5 P.M. and Sunday from 1 to 5 P.M.
Admission
Free

Inaugural Sites

Federal Hall National Memorial

National Park Service
26 Wall Street
New York, NY 10005
212-264-8711
www.cr.nps.gov/feha/index.htm

This Greek Revival structure, reminiscent of a Doric temple, is on the site of New York's second city hall, which was enlarged in 1788 to become Federal Hall, the nation's first capital. Washington was inaugurated here in 1789.

The present structure dates from 1842 and was the United States Custom House and later the Sub Treasury Building before becoming part of the National Park Service in 1955. Exhibits about Washington, his inauguration (including the Bible on which he took the

Federal Hall National Memorial
Photo by Ian Ferris

oath of office), and the Constitution are featured.

Hours
Daily from 9 A.M. to 5 P.M.
Admission
Free

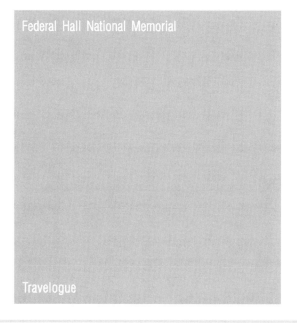

Federal Hall National Memorial

Travelogue

Independence Hall

Independence National Historic Park
National Park Service
Independence Mall South
Philadelphia, PA 19106
215-597-8787
www.cr.nps.gov/htdocs4/inde/exindex.htm

At only 135 words, Washington's inaugural address of March 4, 1793, was the shortest ever given. He took the oath in Congress Hall within Independence Hall.

Independence Hall, one of the country's best-known historic sites, was built to house the Pennsylvania legislature. Instead, it became the home of the Continental Congress and later the United States Congress. It is part of Independence National Historic Park (*see* Sites Related to Multiple Presidents).

Hours
Daily from 9 A.M. to 5 P.M.
Admission
Free

Independence Hall

Travelogue

Place of Death

Mount Vernon
Mount Vernon, VA

See page 4.

Funeral

Old Presbyterian Meeting House
321 South Royal Street
Alexandria, VA 22314-3716
703-549-6670

Built in 1774, this church was a gathering place for patriots during the Revolution. On December 29, 1799, a memorial service for Washington was held here.

The church may be visited daily from 9 A.M. to 5 P.M.

Old Presbyterian Meeting House

Travelogue

Burial Site

Mount Vernon
Mount Vernon, VA

See page 4.

Other Sites

Colonial Williamsburg
Colonial Williamsburg Foundation
P.O. Box 1776
Williamsburg, VA 23187-1776
757-220-7654
www.colonialwilliamsburg.org

Colonial Williamsburg is recognized as the nation's leading living-history museum. Within its historic area are approximately 500 restored or reconstructed buildings set amid streams and gardens. The interpreters here are not merely costumed museum guides; many are scholars who have studied their characters for years.

Although Colonial Williamsburg is not strictly a George Washington site, its DeWitt Wallace Gallery houses Charles Willson Peale's well-known portrait of Washington. Additionally, Colonial Williamsburg celebrates Washington's birthday by holding its "Celebration of George Washington." This three-day program celebrates Washington's arrival in Williamsburg in 1781, while he was on his way to Yorktown. Included are reenactments, military events, and a chance for visitors to talk with the general.

Colonial Williamsburg is open year-round and has numerous hotels on its grounds. Visitors should plan to spend at least two days. One-day passes and suggested itineraries are available for those wishing to spend only a day.

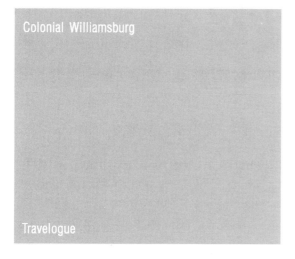

Colonial Williamsburg

Travelogue

Dumbarton House
Washington, DC

See Sites Related to Multiple Presidents on page 256.

See Sites Related to Multiple Presidents on page 256.

Fort Necessity National Battlefield
National Park Service
1 Washington Parkway
Farmington, PA 15437
724-329-5512
www.nps.gov/fone

The 22-year-old George Washington, then a lieutenant, built this palisade fort in two days. On July 3, 1754, the opening battle of the French and Indian War was fought here. For the first and only time in Washington's military career, he was forced to surrender to an enemy.

The visitor center features a 10-minute slide show and tours of the reconstructed fort. At the site are Mount Washington Tavern, which features period exhibits; Jumonville Glen, the site of Washington's first encounter with the French; and British general Braddock's grave. In summer, there are regular musket firings, during which visitors can talk to interpreters. Calendars of summer events are available.

Hours
Daily from 8:30 A.M. to 5 P.M.; the fort is open until sunset
Admission
$2 for adults (maximum of $4 per family); visitors under 16 and over 62 are free

Fort Necessity National Battlefield

Travelogue

Friendship Firehouse
Photo by
Brian J. McCormick, Jr.

Friendship Firehouse

Office of Historic Alexandria
107 South Alfred Street
Alexandria, VA 22314-3001
703-838-4994
alexandriacity.com/friendship.htm

The Friendship Fire Company was established in 1774 with George Washington as one of its founding members. The current building was constructed in 1855, remodeled in 1871, and restored in 1991. On display are hand-drawn fire apparatus, Victorian furnishings, and ceremonial objects. Images of Washington are displayed throughout the museum.

Hours
Friday and Saturday from 10 A.M. to 4 P.M.
and Sunday from 1 to 4 P.M.; closed New
Year's, Thanksgiving, and Christmas
Admission
Free

George Washington Masonic Historic Site

20 Livingston Avenue
Tappan, NY 10983
914-359-1359

The DeWint House, built around 1700, now houses Washington and Masonic memorabilia and period furnishings.

Hours
Daily from 10 A.M. to 4 P.M.
Admission
Free

George Washington Masonic National Memorial

101 Callahan Drive
Alexandria, VA 33301-2751
703-683-2007
www.georgewashington.org

High atop Shooter's Hill, this memorial is modeled after the ancient lighthouse of Alexandria, Egypt. The Replica Room contains original furnishings from Alexandria Lodge #22, over which Washington served as Worshipful Master. Also on display are Washington's family Bible and numerous objects of Masonic significance. The massive building contains numerous elegantly decorated rooms. The observation tower offers an impressive view of the surrounding area. Although historically significant to Masons, the memorial and its museum are geared toward and open to the general public.

Hours
Daily from 9 A.M. to 5 P.M.; closed New Year's, Thanksgiving, and Christmas
Admission
Free

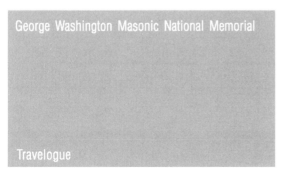

George Washington Masonic National Memorial

Travelogue

George Washington Masonic National Memorial
Photo by Brian J. McCormick, Jr.

Hall of Fame for Great Americans

Bronx, NY

See Sites Related to Multiple Presidents on page 258.

Kenmore Plantation and Gardens

Kenmore Plantation and Gardens Association
1201 Washington Avenue
Fredericksburg, VA 22401
540-373-3381
www.kenmore.org

In 1752, George Washington surveyed this land. Just prior to the Revolution, his sister Betty and her husband, Fielding Lewis, built one of the area's most lavishly decorated homes here. *See also* George Washington's Ferry Farm on page 3.

Monday through Saturday from 10 A.M. to
5 P.M. and Sunday from noon to 5 P.M.;
open on weekends only during January
and February
Admission
Free

Kenmore Plantation and Gardens

Travelogue

Mount Rushmore National Memorial
Keystone, SD

See Sites Related to Multiple Presidents on
pages 254–55.

Powell House
244 South Third Street
Philadelphia, PA 19106
215-627-0364

Built in 1765, the Powell House was regarded as one of Philadelphia's finest homes.
George and Martha Washington were friends
of the Powells and frequent visitors here.
Washington was so impressed by the "pret-
zel-back" chairs Powell had that he ordered

two dozen for himself. A blue-and-white
china crock on display in the house was a
gift from the Washingtons.

Hours
Tuesday through Saturday from 10 A.M. to
4 P.M. from May to July; Thursday through
Saturday from 10 A.M. to 4 P.M. the rest of
the year
Admission
$3 for adults; $2 for seniors and students

Powell House

Travelogue

Rising Sun Tavern
1306 Caroline Street
Fredericksburg, VA 22401-3704
540-371-1494

This building was constructed around 1760
by Charles Washington, brother of George
Washington, as a private home. It later served
as a stagecoach stop and was an important gathering place for patriots during the Revolution.

Hours
Daily from 9 A.M. to 5 P.M. from March to

November and from 10 A.M. to 4 P.M. the rest of year; closed New Year's, Thanksgiving, Christmas Eve, and Christmas

Admission
$3 for adults; $1 for ages six to 18

Rising Sun Tavern

Travelogue

State House
State Circle
Annapolis, MD 21411
410-974-3400

The oldest continuously used statehouse in the nation, this building dates from 1772. It served as the United States Capitol from November 26, 1783, until August 13, 1784. It was here, in the Old Senate Chamber, that Washington resigned his commission with the Continental Army on December 23, 1783. Over the fireplace in the chamber is a 1784 painting by Charles Willson Peale, *Washington, Lafayette, and Tilghman at Yorktown*. On the landing of the marble staircase leading to the second floor is a 1859 Edwin White painting, *Washington Resigning His Commission*.

Hours
Daily from 9 A.M. to 5 P.M.; closed New Year's, Thanksgiving, and Christmas. Guided tours are available from 11 A.M. to 3 P.M.

Admission
Free

State House

Travelogue

Sulgrave Manor
Sulgrave
Banbury
Oxon, England OX17 2SG
www.stratford.co.uk/sulgrave

Sulgrave is the ancestral home of the Washington family. It was acquired by Lawrence Washington in 1539 and occupied by the family until 1659. The museum on the site focuses on the connection to George Washington and offers numerous educational and interpretive programs about him.

Hours
Weekends from 10:30 A.M. to 4:30 P.M.

during November, December, and March and from 10:30 A.M. to 5:30 P.M. the rest of the year. Weekday hours are offered in the summer. The manor is closed during January.
Admission
3.75 pounds sterling

Sulgrave Manor

Travelogue

Washington Monument
National Park Service
National Mall
Washington, DC 20242
202-426-6841
www.nps.gov/wamo

The national monument to Washington was authorized in 1833. Although construction started in 1848, the monument was not opened to the public until 1888 due to financial, managerial, and political problems.

The 555-foot monument provides an impressive view of Washington from its observation level. Access to the observation deck is by elevator only, as the monument's 897-step staircase is closed to the public. During

peak tourist times, the lines around the monument can be long. Admission, although free, is by ticket; tickets may be obtained from the 15th Street kiosk near the base of the monument. A snack bar and a souvenir stand are also at the base.

Hours
Daily from 8 A.M. until midnight from April 1 to Labor Day and from 9 A.M. to 5 P.M. the rest of the year
Admission
Free

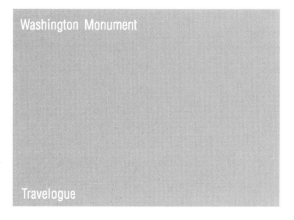

Washington Monument

Travelogue

Washington Square Park
Walnut Street between Sixth and Seventh Streets
Philadelphia, PA 19106
215-597-8787

This is one of the original parks from William Penn's design. It served as a drill ground during the Revolution. An estimated 2,000 Continental Army soldiers were buried here, making this the largest Revolutionary War cemetery. In 1955, city officials built a monument to honor Washington. An eternal flame was installed in 1976.

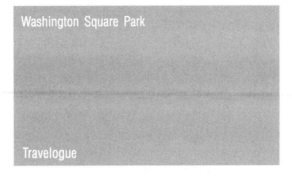
Washington Square Park

Travelogue

Hours
Always open
Admission
Free

John Adams

Second President of the United States

Birthplace/Homes

Adams National Historic Site

National Park Service
Visitor Center
1250 Hancock Street
Quincy, MA 02169
617-770-1175
www.nps.gov/adam

This site includes three historic Adams homes and the church the family attended. All tours start at the visitor center.

The John Adams Birthplace is the oldest presidential birthplace in the country. Adams was born October 30, 1735, and spent his youth here. It was also here that he first began writing letters to Abigail Smith.

The John Quincy Adams Birthplace was the home of John and Abigail Adams until after the Revolution. John Quincy Adams was born here July 11, 1767. Within this house, John Adams maintained a law office and launched his political career. John Adams, Samuel Adams, and James Bowdoin wrote the Constitution of Massachusetts here. That document, still in use today, became the model for the national constitution and those of numerous other states as well.

The Old House, built in 1731, was the home of four generations of the Adams family between 1788 and 1927. The house contains 78,000 artifacts, including a 14,000-volume library and an 18th-century garden. The 1873 carriage house is also open for self-guided tours.

United First Parish Church, built in 1828, was designed by Alexander Parris. John Adams donated the land on which it stands. John Adams, John Quincy Adams, and their wives are interred in the crypt beneath the sanctuary. The church remains active today.

Hours
Daily from 9 A.M. to 5 P.M.; the last tour departs the visitor center at 3:15 P.M.
Admission
$2 for adults; guests under 16 are free. The church requests an additional $2 donation per person.

Adams National Historic Site

Travelogue

Churches

United First Parish Church
Quincy, MA

See previous page.

New York Avenue Presbyterian Church
Washington, DC

See Sites Related to Multiple Presidents on page 243.

Education

Adams attended Mrs. Belcher's one-room schoolhouse and Joseph Cleverly's Latin school, neither of which exists today.

Harvard University
Cambridge, MA

See Sites Related to Multiple Presidents on pages 246–47.

After his graduation from Harvard, Adams studied law under James Putnam of Worcester. He was admitted to the Massachusetts Bar in 1758.

Marriage

Adams married Abigail Smith on Octo-

ber 25, 1764, at the bride's family's home in Weymouth, Massachusetts.

Inaugural Site

Independence Hall
Independence National Historic Park
National Park Service
Independence Mall South
Philadelphia, PA 19106
215-597-8787
www.cr.nps.gov/htdocs4/inde/exindex.htm

Adams took the oath of office on March 4, 1797, before Washington—then known as Federal City—became the nation's capital. Adams served here as a member of the Continental Congress.

Hours
Daily from 9 A.M. to 5 P.M.
Admission
Free

Independence Hall

Travelogue

Place of Death

Adams died at his home (see page 26) on July 4, 1826. He had been invited to participate in the nation's 50th birthday celebration but was confined to bed due to failing health.

In the last years of his life, he rekindled his friendship with Thomas Jefferson, the two having grown apart due to political and philosophical differences. The last words Adams uttered were "Thomas Jefferson survives." Adams thus died not knowing that Jefferson had died hours earlier.

Burial Site

Adams National Historic Site
Quincy, MA

See page 26.

Other Sites

Abigail Adams Birthplace
North and Norton Streets
Weymouth, MA 02188-4203
781-335-4205

The birth of Abigail Smith Adams, the only woman to be the wife of one president and the mother of another, took place here in 1744. The restored portion of the house, which dates to 1685, is furnished in period style with items that belonged to the Smith family.

Hours
Tuesday through Sunday from 1 to 4 P.M. from July 1 to Labor Day; by appointment during June and from Labor Day until October 15
Admission
$1 for adults; $.25 for guests under 13

Abigail Adams Birthplace
Courtesy of Abigail Adams Historical Society

Abigail Adams Birthplace

Travelogue

Abigail Adams Smith Museum

421 East 61st Street
New York, NY 10021-8736
212-838-6878

This is the former home of Abigail Adams Smith, daughter of John and Abigail Adams. It has been restored to its 19th-century condition and now serves as a museum depicting hotel life during that time. There are no John Adams artifacts except for a few letters he wrote to his daughter.

Hours
Tuesday through Sunday from 11 A.M. to 4 P.M.; closed New Year's, the Fourth of July, the month of August, Thanksgiving, and Christmas
Admission
$3 for adults; $2 for seniors and students; guests under 12 are free

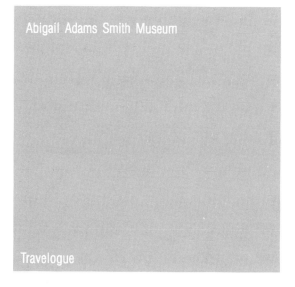

Abigail Adams Smith Museum

Travelogue

Conference House

7455 Hylan Avenue
Tottenville, NY 10307-2119
718-984-6046

Billopp House, as this home was known when it was built in 1680, was the site of a 1776 meeting that attempted to forestall the Revolutionary War. The Continental Congress was represented by John Adams, Benjamin Franklin, and Edward Rutledge; the British were represented by Admiral Richard Howe.

The house is located on beautifully rolling grounds near the southern tip of Staten Island and features a working 17th-century kitchen and period furnishings.

Hours
Friday through Sunday from 1 to 4 P.M.
Admission
$2

Conference House

Travelogue

Hall of Fame for Great Americans
Bronx, NY

See Sites Related to Multiple Presidents on page 258.

Thomas Jefferson
Third President of the United States

Birthplace

Thomas Jefferson was born April 13, 1743, at Shadwell Plantation in Virginia. His birthplace was destroyed by fire in 1770.

Home

Monticello
Thomas Jefferson Memorial Foundation
VA 53
Charlottesville, VA 22902
804-977-1783
www.monticello.org

Jefferson began building Monticello in 1769 and moved in the following year. In 1773, he brought his bride here; they lived in the south pavilion. Jefferson did not complete the massive home until 1809, after 40 years of additions and alterations. He died here on July 4, 1826, exactly 50 years after the signing of the Declaration of Independence. He and his family are buried in the cemetery on the premises.

Ten rooms on the main floor have been preserved and are open to the public. On display are many of Jefferson's possessions, including some of his inventions. A visitor center on VA 20 features exhibits of Jeffersonian objects and the film *Thomas Jefferson: Pursuit of Liberty*. In 1987, the United Nations Educational, Scientific, and Cultural Organization included Monticello on a list of worldwide treasures to be protected at all costs; other sites on the list include the Great Wall of China and the Taj Mahal. The surrounding community includes buildings that reflect Jefferson's architectural influence.

Hours
The visitor center is open daily from 9 A.M. to 5:30 P.M. from March to October and from 9 A.M. to 5 P.M. the rest of the year. The house is open daily from 8 A.M. to 5 P.M. from March to October and from 9 A.M. to 4:30 P.M. the rest of the year. The entire complex is closed Christmas.
Admission
$9 for adults; $5 for ages six to 11; guests under six are free

Monticello

Travelogue

Education

Jefferson boarded at St. James Parish in Northam, Virginia, where he studied under the Reverend William Douglas. He later studied at the Reverend James Maury's school in Fredericksville. Neither of these sites exists today.

College of William and Mary
Williamsburg, VA

See Sites Related to Multiple Presidents on page 245.

After his graduation from William and Mary, Jefferson apprenticed under attorney George Wythe for five years. He was admitted to the Virginia Bar in 1767.

Marriage

Jefferson married Martha Wayles Skelton on January 1, 1772, at the home of the bride's father in Charles City County, Virginia.

Inaugural Site

The Capitol
Washington, DC

March 4, 1801
March 4, 1805

Place of Death/Burial Site

Monticello
Charlottesville, VA

See page 31.

Other Sites

Dumbarton House
Washington, DC

See Sites Related to Multiple Presidents on page 256.

Graff House

Graff House
National Park Service
Seventh and Market Streets
Philadelphia, PA 19106
215-597-8974
www.cr.nps.gov/htdocs4/inde/declaration-house.html

The original house on this site was built in 1775 by bricklayer Jacob Graff, Jr. During the summer of 1776, Jefferson rented two rooms on the second floor while he served in the Continental Congress. It was here that he wrote the Declaration of Independence.

The present re-creation was built in 1975. Jefferson's two-room suite is furnished in period style and includes his swivel chair and the lap desk on which he wrote the famous document. Exhibits and a film are offered on the first floor.

Hours
Daily from 9 A.M. to 5 P.M.; closed New Year's and Christmas
Admission
Free

Graff House

Travelogue

Hall of Fame for Great Americans
Bronx, NY

See Sites Related to Multiple Presidents on page 258.

Jefferson National Expansion Memorial
National Park Service
11 North Fourth Street
St. Louis, MO 63102-1882
314-425-6010
www.nps.gov/jeff/

This park consists of three components: the Gateway Arch, the Museum of Western Expansion, and the Old St. Louis Courthouse.

The 630-foot stainless-steel Gateway Arch marks the site of the original St. Louis village, which was thought of as the gateway to the West. The national movement to settle the West gained in popularity during Jefferson's administration, due to the consummation of the Louisiana Purchase. A unique elevator system takes visitors to an observation deck atop the arch.

At the base is the Museum of Westward Expansion, which features a variety of displays dealing with our nation's westward expansion.

The Old St. Louis Courthouse, just two blocks from the arch, is the oldest building in St. Louis. It was the site of Dred Scott's two trials (in 1847 and 1850). Today, it interprets local history.

Hours
The arch and the museum are open daily from 8 A.M. to 10 P.M. and the Old St. Louis Courthouse from 8:30 A.M. to 4 P.M. The entire complex is closed New Year's, Thanksgiving, and Christmas.
Admission
$2 for individuals and $4 for families;

admission to the Old St. Louis Courthouse is free

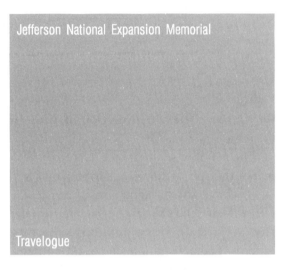

Jefferson National Expansion Memorial

Travelogue

Mount Rushmore National Memorial
Keystone, SD

See Sites Related to Multiple Presidents on pages 254–55.

Natural Bridge
P.O. Box 57
Natural Bridge, VA 24578
800-533-1410
www.naturalbridgeva.com

Discovered by Indians, Natural Bridge became a favorite curiosity of Jefferson's. In fact, he called it "undoubtedly one of the sublimest curiosities in nature." The natural rock bridge is 90 feet long, ranges in width from 50 to 150 feet, and is 245 feet high. Cedar Creek runs beneath it.

In July 1774, Jefferson purchased Natural Bridge from King George III in order to keep it accessible to the public. During the Revolutionary War, Continental Army soldiers used it as a natural shot tower, dropping molten lead from the span into the frigid creek below. Perfectly shaped bullets resulted. Jefferson eventually built a two-room cabin on the site to accommodate visitors. During his lifetime, the site earned worldwide renown.

In 1833, the property passed from the hands of Jefferson's descendants. Today, it includes a large resort hotel and conference center, a wax museum, caverns, a tavern, a fudge shop, and one of the largest gift shops in the state.

Hours
Daily from 8 A.M. to 6 P.M.
Admission
$8 for adults and $4 for children; guests may also purchase tickets for visiting the wax museum and the caverns

Natural Bridge

Travelogue

Thomas Jefferson Memorial and Tidal Basin

National Park Service
National Mall
Washington, DC 20242
202-426-6821
www.nps.org/htdocs4/thje

The memorial, reminiscent of Monticello, is a marble-domed structure supported by Ionic columns. Jefferson is credited with bringing this architectural style to this country. Inside is a bronze sculpture of Jefferson by Rudolph Evans surrounded by panels inscribed with some of his best-known writings. A gift shop and rest rooms are on the lower level.

Hours
Daily from 8 A.M. to 11:45 P.M.
Admission
Free

Thomas Jefferson Memorial and Tidal Basin

Travelogue

University of Virginia
Charlottesville, VA

See Sites Related to Multiple Presidents on page 247.

Notable Buildings Designed by Jefferson

Brandon Plantation Farm
23105 Brandon Road
Spring Grove, VA 23881
757-866-8486

Brandon has been a working plantation since the 17th century. Its principal crops today include corn, soybeans, wheat, and barley. In the mid-18th century, proprietor Nathaniel Harrison built the main house, which was designed by Jefferson. The Harrison family owned the property until 1926. It was a significant site during both the Revolutionary War and the Civil War.

Hours
The grounds and the garden are open daily from 9 A.M. to 5 P.M. The house is open during Garden Week (late April to early May) and by appointment.
Admission
$5

Brandon Plantation Farm

Travelogue

Belle Grove Plantation
Middleburg, VA

See Sites Related to Multiple Presidents on page 251.

Farmington Historic Home
3033 Bardstown Road
Louisville, KY 40205-3019
512-452-9920

John Speed built this magnificent 14-room Federal-style home in 1810 from Jefferson's design. It is furnished with 1820s pieces and has a garden of native plants and a working blacksmith shop. The original deed, signed by Patrick Henry, hangs on the wall. The gift shop offers unusual Kentucky items.

<u>Hours</u>
Monday through Saturday from 10 A.M. to 4:30 P.M. and Sunday from 1:30 to 4:30 P.M.; closed New Year's, Easter, the day of the Kentucky Derby, Thanksgiving, Christmas Eve, and Christmas
<u>Admission</u>
$4 for adults; $3 for guests over 60; $2 for students and children ages six to 12; children under six are free

Farmington Historic Home

Travelogue

James Madison
Fourth President of the United States

Birthplace

James Madison was born March 16, 1751, in the home of his maternal grandparents in Port Conway, King George County, Virginia.

Homes

Montpelier

National Trust for Historic Preservation
11407 Constitution Highway
Montpelier Station, VA 27957
540-672-2728
www.montpelier.org

Built between 1755 and 1765 by James Madison's father, Montpelier stayed in the family until 1844. Madison and his wife are buried on the 2,700-acre estate.

Marion DuPont Scott eventually acquired the estate and enlarged the grounds and the main building. The main building now has 55 rooms and features changing exhibits; the estate has more than 130 buildings. Montpelier Hunt Race Day, a tradition begun by the DuPonts, is held annually on the first Saturday in November.

<u>Hours</u>
Daily from 10 A.M. to 4 P.M. from March to December and from 11 A.M. to 3 P.M. the rest of the year; closed New Year's, Thanksgiving, and Christmas
<u>Admission</u>
$7.50 for adults; $3.50 for ages six to 11

Montpelier

Travelogue

Todd House

National Park Service
Fourth and Walnut Streets
Philadelphia, PA 19106
215-597-8974
www.libertynet.org/iha/tour/_todd.htm

Built in 1775, the Todd House was home to attorney John Todd, his wife, Dolley, and their children. After Todd died of yellow fever in 1793, his widow faced hard economic times and began renting rooms to earn money. One of her tenants was James Madison, then serving in Congress. Less than a year after John Todd's death, Dolley Todd and James Madison were wed.

Today, the restored home interprets middle-class life in 18th-century Philadelphia. The home, near Independence Hall, is part of Independence National Historic Park. Before the building was restored by the National Park Service, a soda shop that served Dolley Madison Ice Cream operated here.

Hours
Daily from 9 A.M. to 5 P.M.; closed New Year's and Christmas
Admission
Though there is no charge, tickets must be obtained from the visitor center for Independence National Historic Park, located at Third and Chestnut Streets.

Todd House

Travelogue

Todd House

Church

St. John's Lafayette Square
Washington, DC

See Sites Related to Multiple Presidents on pages 243–44.

Education

Madison was tutored by Donald Robertson and the Reverend Thomas Martin.

Princeton University
Princeton, NJ

See Sites Related to Multiple Presidents on pages 247–48.

After he left Princeton, Madison studied law sporadically but was never admitted to the bar.

Marriage

Madison married Dorothy "Dolley" Payne Todd on September 15, 1794, at Harewood, the West Virginia estate of the bride's sister.

Inaugural Site

The Capitol
Washington, DC

March 4, 1809
March 4, 1813

Place of Death/Burial Site

Montpelier
Montpelier Station, VA

Madison died at his home (see page 37) on June 28, 1836.

Other Sites

Dumbarton House
Washington, DC

See Sites Related to Multiple Presidents on page 256.

Hall of Fame for Great Americans
Bronx, NY

See Sites Related to Multiple Presidents on page 258.

James Madison Museum
129 Caroline Street
Orange, VA 22960-1532
540-672-1776
www.gemlink.com/~jmmuseum.home2.htm

The permanent exhibits at this site include a fine collection of Madison objects, including a chair given to Madison by his friend Thomas Jefferson. Madison the farmer is interpreted through a collection of agricultural equipment. The museum also features a wide variety of exhibits highlighting the Orange County area.

Hours
Open weekdays from 9 A.M. to 4 P.M. and weekends from 1 to 4 P.M. from March to November; open weekdays only the rest of the year; closed New Year's, Memorial Day, the Fourth of July, Labor Day, Thanksgiving, and Christmas
Admission
$4 for adults; $3 for guests over 60; $1 for ages six to 16

James Madison Museum

Travelogue

The Octagon, 1801, Washington, D.C.
Photo by Robert C. Lautman

The Octagon

Museum of the American Architectural Foundation
1799 New York Avenue NW
Washington, DC 20006-5292
202-638-3221
www.amerarchfoundation.com

After the White House was burned by the British during the War of 1812, this magnificent house served as the temporary home of James and Dolley Madison. It was in the upstairs parlor that the Treaty of Ghent ending that same war was signed by Madison.

Designed by William Thornton, the first architect of the United States Capitol, this National Historic Landmark, built between 1799 and 1801, was home to Colonel John Tayloe III and his family. Today, visitors to The Octagon may explore architecture, design, preservation, and the early history of Washington through tours, exhibitions, and programs for adults and children.

Hours
Tuesday through Sunday from 10 A.M. to 4 P.M.; closed New Year's, Thanksgiving, and Christmas
Admission
$3 for adults; $1.50 for seniors and students

The Octagon

Travelogue

Scotchtown

16120 Chiswell Lane
Beaverdam, VA 23015-1726
804-227-3500

This is the restored childhood home of Madison's wife, the former Dolly Payne Todd. It has living quarters on the first floor and a jerkinhead roof, both uncommon features for the time. From 1771 until 1778, this was the home of Patrick Henry.

The tour of the house includes information on the Todds, the Henrys, the other families that lived here, and the home's architecture.

<u>Hours</u>
Wednesday through Saturday from
10:30 A.M. to 4 P.M. and Sunday from 1:30
to 4:30 P.M. from April to October;
Christmas tours are offered in November
<u>Admission</u>
$5 for adults; $4 for guests over 65; $2
for ages six to 12

Belle Grove Plantation
Middleburg, VA

See Sites Related to Multiple Presidents on
page 251.

James Monroe
Fifth President of the United States

Birthplace

James Monroe was born April 28, 1758, in Westmoreland County, Virginia.

Home

Ash Lawn-Highland
College of William and Mary
James Monroe Parkway
Charlottesville, VA 22902-8722
804-293-9539
monticello.avenue.gen.va.us/ashlawn

The site for Monroe's mansion was selected by Thomas Jefferson while Monroe was serving as minister to France. With Jefferson's help at home, Monroe purchased the property—then called Highland—in 1793 but did not move to the plantation until his return to the United States in 1799. He furnished his "cabin-castle" with elegant French objects obtained during his diplomatic service; many of these are still on display. Following his retirement from the presidency in 1825, Monroe faced hard financial times, due in large part to his years of public service. He was forced to sell Highland in 1826. During the 1830s, the new owner renamed the estate Ash Lawn.

In the 1920s, the property was purchased by Jay W. Johns, who bequeathed it to the College of William and Mary (Monroe's alma mater) in 1974. The college uses the estate to perpetuate Monroe's memory, to interpret his life and presidency, and to promote the arts and sciences. The property has been restored to its early-1800s appearance. On display are many of Monroe's possessions. A statue of Monroe by Attillio Piccirilli is in the boxwood garden, as is an oak tree 20 feet in diameter believed to date from Monroe's days.

Hours
Daily from 9 A.M. to 6 P.M. from March to October and from 10 A.M. to 5 P.M. the rest of the year; closed New Year's, Thanksgiving, and Christmas
Admission
$7 for adults; $6.50 for guests over 60; $3 for ages six to 11

Ash Lawn-Highland

Travelogue

Church

St. John's Lafayette Square
Washington, DC

See Sites Related to Multiple Presidents on pages 243–44.

Education

Monroe studied under the Reverend Archibald Campbell in Washington Parish, Virginia.

College of William and Mary
Williamsburg, VA

See Sites Related to Multiple Presidents on page 245.

Marriage

Monroe married Elizabeth Kortright in New York City on February 16, 1786.

Inaugural Site

The Capitol
Washington, DC

March 4, 1817
March 5, 1821

Place of Death

Three of the first five presidents died on the Fourth of July. Adams and Jefferson both died July 4, 1826. Monroe died July 4, 1831, in New York City from heart failure. Eulogies were offered at New York City Hall before the funeral service.

Funeral

St. Paul's Episcopal Church
Photo by Ian Ferris

St. Paul's Episcopal Church
415 West 59th Street
New York, NY 10019-1104
212-265-3209

Following Monroe's funeral, thousands of mourners followed the hearse procession up Broadway to Marble Cemetery on Second

Street, where the body was temporarily interred in the Gouverneur family vault.

St. Paul's Episcopal Church

Travelogue

Burial Site

Hollywood Cemetery
Richmond, VA

See Sites Related to Multiple Presidents on page 241.

Other Sites

Hall of Fame for Great Americans
Bronx, NY

See Sites Related to Multiple Presidents on page 258.

James Monroe Museum and Memorial Library
908 Charles Street
Fredericksburg, VA 22401-5810
540-654-1043
www.flstarweb.com/museum/tour/jmuseum.htm

Standing at the site of the law office Monroe used from 1786 to 1789, this museum contains the nation's largest collection of Monroe objects. Included are the desk on which he wrote what later became known as the Monroe Doctrine and costumes worn by him and his wife in the court of Napoleon.

Hours
Daily from 9 A.M. to 5 P.M. from March to November and from 10 A.M. to 4 P.M. the rest of the year; closed New Year's, Thanksgiving, Christmas Eve, and Christmas
Admission
$3 for adults; $1 for ages six to 18

James Monroe Museum and Memorial Library

Travelogue

Monroe-Adams-Abbe House

Arts Club of Washington
2017 I Street NW
Washington, DC 20006-1804
202-331-7282

Monroe-Adams-Abbe House

Travelogue

This building, also known as the Timothy Caldwell House in honor of its builder, served as Monroe's residence after the White House was burned by the British during the War of 1812. It is currently the headquarters of the Arts Club of Washington and is not open to the public. In honor of Monroe's residence here, a small city park across the street is named for him.

John Quincy Adams
Sixth President of the United States

Birthplace/Homes

Adams National Historic Site
National Park Service
Visitor Center
1250 Hancock Street
Quincy, MA 02169
617-770-1175
www.nps.gov/adam

This site includes three historic Adams homes and the church the family attended. All tours start at the visitor center.

The John Adams Birthplace is the oldest presidential birthplace in the country. John Adams was born October 30, 1735, and spent his youth here.

The John Quincy Adams Birthplace was the home of John and Abigail Adams until after the Revolution. John Quincy Adams was born here July 11, 1767.

The Old House, built in 1731, was the home of four generations of the Adams family between 1788 and 1927. The house contains 78,000 artifacts, including a 14,000-volume library and an 18-century garden. The 1873 carriage house is also open for self-guided tours.

United First Parish Church, built in 1828, was designed by Alexander Parris.

John Adams, John Quincy Adams, and their wives are interred in the crypt beneath the sanctuary.

Hours
Daily from 9 A.M. to 5 P.M.; the last tour departs the visitor center at 3:15 P.M.
Admission
$2 for adults; guests under 16 are free. The church requests an additional $2 donation per person.

Adams National Historic Site

Travelogue

The Old House
Photo courtesy of National Park Service

Church

All Souls Church (Unitarian)
Washington, DC

See Sites Related to Multiple Presidents on pages 241–42.

Education

When the Revolution broke out, regular school in Massachusetts was suspended. Adams was tutored by law clerks John Thaxter and Nathan Rice. His first formal education was in France, where he studied with Benjamin Franklin's grandsons at Passy Academy. He later studied at Leyden University in Amsterdam. Adams returned to the United States in 1785 and entered Harvard.

Harvard University
Cambridge, MA

See Sites Related to Multiple Presidents on pages 246–47.

Marriage

Adams married Louisa Catherine Johnson, the only foreign-born first lady, in London on July 26, 1797.

Inaugural Site

The Capitol
Washington, DC

March 4, 1825

Place of Death

The Capitol
Washington, DC

Following Adams's retirement from the presidency, he was elected to the United States House of Representatives, thereby becoming the only president to return to the House. On February 21, 1848, after casting a loud no vote against a proposal to decorate Mexican War generals, Adams suffered a massive stroke and slumped into the arms of Representative David Fisher of Ohio. He was immediately attended by five physicians, four of whom were members of Congress. Adams was moved to the office of the Speaker, where a bed was set up for him. He died there two days later.

Funeral

The Capitol
Washington, DC

After Adams's body lay in state for two days in the United States House of Representatives Committee Room, a funeral service was conducted in the House chamber by House chaplain R. R. Gurley.

Burial Site

Adams National Historic Site
Quincy, MA

See page 46.

Other Site

Hall of Fame for Great Americans
Bronx, NY

See Sites Related to Multiple Presidents on page 258.

Andrew Jackson
Seventh President of the United States

Birthplace

Andrew Jackson was born March 15, 1767, in the Waxhaws, a region straddling the border between the Carolinas. Legend holds that following the death of Jackson's father, the pregnant Mrs. Jackson moved in with a sister in Lancaster County, South Carolina, where she delivered baby Andrew. But some historians have argued that while en route to Lancaster County, Mrs. Jackson stopped off at the home of another sister in Union County, North Carolina, where she gave birth. Although Andrew Jackson often claimed he was born in South Carolina, the matter has never been resolved.

In 1979, officials in the North and South Carolina counties in question agreed to a unique settlement. Each year, high-school football teams from each county compete in the Old Hickory Football Classic. The winning county gets to claim Jackson as a native son for the coming year.

**Andrew Jackson Memorial
Museum of the Waxhaws**
NC 75E
P.O. Box 7
Waxhaw, NC 28173
704-843-1832

This regional history museum, opened in 1996, pays tribute to Jackson and celebrates the fact that he was born in the region. Its collections interpret life in the Waxhaws from the 1500s to the early 1900s.

Hours
Wednesday through Saturday from 10 A.M. to 5 P.M. and Sunday from 1 to 5 P.M.
Admission
$1

Andrew Jackson Memorial
Museum of the Waxhaws

Travelogue

Andrew Jackson State Park

196 Andrew Jackson Park Road
Lancaster, SC 29720
803-285-3344

Included in this park is a replica of a frontier blockhouse typical of those in the region at the time of Jackson's birth. The house is filled with antiques, including some items that belonged to Jackson. Also on the grounds are an Anna Hyatt Huntington statue of Jackson on a horse, a one-room schoolhouse, and a Jackson monument, as well as camping, fishing, and picnicking facilities.

The old James Crawford plantation is within the park's 360 acres, although historians are not certain of the exact location. Jackson lived his boyhood on the Crawford plantation.

Hours
The museum is open on weekends
from 1 to 5 P.M.
Admission
Free

Andrew Jackson State Park

Travelogue

Homes

Jackson was born fatherless and lost his mother and brothers during the Revolution. Much of his youth was spent living with relatives or with a local saddler, under whom he was an apprentice. At the age of 15, he received a sizable inheritance from his grandfather Hugh Jackson, but he spent the entire sum gambling, drinking, and chasing women, rather than investing it to ensure a stable home and future.

The Hermitage

4580 Rachel's Lane
Hermitage, TN 37076
615-889-2941
www.thehermitage.com

The Hermitage is the country's most authentically restored home of an early president. It reflects the period of Jackson's retirement (1837–45).

Jackson purchased the 625-acre estate in 1804. He built his mansion in the Federal style in 1821. Following its partial destruction by fire in 1834, he rebuilt it in the current Greek Revival style. At the time of his death, the plantation totaled 1,000 acres. Nearly all of the personal belongings of the Jacksons have been preserved. Jackson and his wife, Rachel, are buried in the estate's garden.

Adjacent is Tulip Grove, the home of Jackson's nephew Andrew Jackson Donelson. Donelson served as the president's secretary; his wife, Emily, was the White House hostess following the death of Rachel Jackson.

Hours
Daily from 9 A.M. to 5 P.M.; closed the third
week of January, Thanksgiving, and
Christmas
Admission
$9.50 for adults; $8.50 for guests over 62;
$4.50 for ages six to 12. Admission is
free to all on January 8; reduced
admission is offered on March 15.

The Hermitage
Photo by Carolyn Brackett

The Hermitage

Travelogue

Church

St. John's Lafayette Square
Washington, DC

See Sites Related to Multiple Presidents on pages 243–44.

Education

Jackson was tutored by Dr. William Humphries and the Reverend James W. Stephenson. He studied law under Spruce McCay and John Stokes, doing only what was expected of him, as he preferred to spend his time drinking, gambling, and dancing. He was admitted to the North Carolina Bar in 1787.

Marriage

During their marriage, Lewis Robards frequently accused his wife, the former Rachel Donelson, of infidelity, charges she always denied. The frustrated Robards finally sent her home to Tennessee to live with her family.

Andrew Jackson was boarding with Rachel's widowed mother, and he and Rachel fell in love. Nonetheless, Rachel dutifully returned to Kentucky with Robards when he came to reclaim her. Knowing of Rachel's unhappiness with her marriage, Andrew went to Kentucky to rescue his love. In December 1790, Robards was able to get the Kentucky legislature to issue an enabling act to permit him to divorce his wife. Thinking this action was a divorce decree, Jackson and Rachel married in Natchez, Mississippi, in August 1791. Knowing that his wife was living with Jackson, Robards then sued for divorce on the grounds of adultery, and Jackson and Rachel's marriage was declared invalid. Andrew and Rachel finally were legally wed on January 17, 1794, in Nashville, Tennessee.

The scandal surrounding their marriage haunted the Jacksons for the rest of their lives. Jackson blamed the 1828 death of his ailing wife on the stress caused by his political opponents and the national press, who continued to taunt the couple.

Inaugural Site

The Capitol
Washington, DC

March 4, 1829
March 4, 1833

Place of Death/Burial Site

The Hermitage
Hermitage, TN

Jackson was ill the last few years of his life. On June 8, 1845, six days after surgery to drain water from his abdomen, Jackson fell unconscious at The Hermitage (see page 50). He died in the company of his daughter-in-law.

Other Sites

B & O Railroad Station Museum
Photo by David Shackleford

B & O Railroad Station Museum
2711 Maryland Avenue at Main Street
Ellicott City, MD 21043-4661
410-461-1944

This was the first terminal of the famed B&O Railroad outside Baltimore. Opened in 1830, it was the destination of the nation's first steam engine, the Tom Thumb. Jackson became the first president to travel by train when he boarded here in 1833.

The museum includes the restored ticket office, the stationmaster's quarters, the waiting room, and the freight house, which includes a model of the first 13 miles of the railroad and a restored 1927 caboose.

Wednesday through Monday from 11 A.M. to 4 P.M. from Memorial Day to Labor Day; Friday through Monday from 11 A.M. to 4 P.M. the rest of year; closed major holidays

<u>Admission</u>

$3 for adults; $2 for guests over 64; $1 for ages five to 12

Hall of Fame for Great Americans

Hall of Fame for Great Americans
Bronx, NY

See Sites Related to Multiple Presidents on page 258.

Horseshoe Bend National Military Park
National Park Service
11288 Horseshoe Bend Road
Daviston, AL 36256
205-234-7111
www.nps.gov/hobe/index.htm

General Andrew Jackson led nearly 3,000 Tennessee frontier troops in a victorious battle against Creek Indians on March 27, 1814. This battle signaled the end of the Creek In-

dian War and added three-fifths of present-day Alabama and one-fifth of present-day Georgia to the United States.

The site includes a visitor center; a museum containing military artifacts, a diorama, and an electric map of the battle; a three-mile battlefield auto tour; hiking trails; picnic areas; and a boat ramp.

<u>Hours</u>

Daily from 8 A.M. to 5 P.M.; closed Christmas

<u>Admission</u>

Free, though permits and fees are required for special uses

Horseshoe Bend National Military Park

Travelogue

Lafayette Square
National Park Service
Washington, DC 20006

The central monument in this famous park is the Andrew Jackson statue by Clark Mills. The park is directly across Pennsylvania Avenue from the White House. Because of its proximity to the executive mansion, it has been the site of numerous protests and demonstrations.

Hours
Always open
Admission
Free

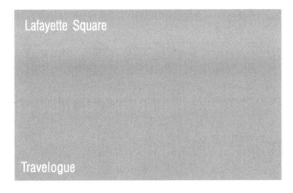

Lafayette Square

Travelogue

The Three Presidents Statue
Raleigh, NC

See Sites Related to Multiple Presidents on page 255.

Martin Van Buren
Eighth President of the United States

Birthplace

Martin Van Buren was the first president born a United States citizen; all prior presidents were born before the signing of the Declaration of Independence and were therefore British subjects at birth.

Van Buren was born December 5, 1782, in the living quarters over the tavern his father operated on Hudson Street in Kinderhook, New York. The building burned years ago, and numerous other structures have since occupied its spot. A state historic marker identifies the location, which is between NY 9H and Broad Street north of Martin Van Buren National Historic Site (see below).

Homes

Decatur House
National Trust for Historic Preservation
748 Jackson Place NW
Washington, DC 20006-4912
202-842-0915
www.decaturhouse.org

Built in 1818 by naval hero Stephen Decatur, this, the first structure on Lafayette Square, was Van Buren's home from 1829 to 1831, while he was serving as secretary of state. Decatur House is one of the few remaining structures designed by Benjamin Henry Latrobe. It is currently operated as a historic house museum. The National Trust for Historic Preservation offers numerous public programs and rents the home and carriage house for private events.

Hours
Tuesday through Friday from 10 A.M. to 3 P.M. and weekends from noon to 4 P.M.
Admission
$4 for adults; $2.50 for seniors and students

Decatur House

Travelogue

"Lindenwald"
Photo by Patricia West

Martin Van Buren National Historic Site
National Park Service
NY 9H
P.O. Box 545
Kinderhook, NY 12106
518-758-9689
www.nps.gov/mava

This 1797 mansion, known as Lindenwald, was built by wealthy judge Peter Van Ness. Van Ness left the property to his son William, a friend of Van Buren's. The younger Van Ness eventually lost the home to creditors. For the following 14 years, the property was neglected. In 1839, Van Buren purchased the run-down estate for $14,000 and began a productive and profitable farm. By 1845, Lindenwald boasted 220 acres of crops and formal gardens. In later years, Van Buren's son Smith made numerous decorative changes, including the addition of a tower, a central gable, and a porch.

Following Van Buren's death, the home changed hands many times, serving as a private residence, a teahouse, a nursing home, and an antiques shop. In the 1970s, it came under the control of the National Park Service and was restored to the era of Van Buren's occupancy.

Guided tours are available. A gift shop is on the premises. Call for a schedule of the numerous special events held at the site.

<u>Hours</u>
Daily from 9 A.M. to 4:30 P.M. from May through October; weekends only from November through December 5; closed from December 6 through April
<u>Admission</u>
$2 for adults; guests under 17 are free

Martin Van Buren National Historic Site

Travelogue

Churches

Kinderhook Reformed Church
Church Street at US 9
Kinderhook, NY 12106
518-758-6401

Although Van Buren's brother and son were founding members of St. Paul's Episcopal Church, Van Buren was a member here. The original church burned in 1867 and was replaced by the current structure.

Kinderhook Reformed Church

Travelogue

St. John's Lafayette Square
Washington, DC

See Sites Related to Multiple Presidents on pages 243–44.

Education

Van Buren studied in a one-room schoolhouse in Kinderhook and later at Kinderhook Academy. Neither of these exists today. He began studying law at age 14 in the Kinderhook office of Francis Sylvester, a well-known Federalist attorney. He gave his first summation before a jury at the age of 15. Van Buren spent his seventh and final year of apprenticeship in the New York City office of William P. Van Ness, friend and attorney of Aaron Burr. Van Ness later served as a second in Burr's infamous duel with Alexander Hamilton. Van Buren was admitted to the New York Bar in 1803.

Marriage

Van Buren married Hannah Hoes, his childhood sweetheart, on February 21, 1807, in the Catskill home of the bride's sister. Mrs. Van Buren died of tuberculosis in 1819. Van Buren never remarried.

Inaugural Site

The Capitol
Washington, DC

March 4, 1837

Place of Death

Van Buren died of heart failure at Lindenwald (see page 56) on July 24, 1862.

Funeral Site

Kinderhook Reformed Church
Kinderhook, NY

At Van Buren's request, no bells tolled at his funeral, which was officiated by Alonzo Potter, the Episcopal bishop of Pennsylvania, and the Reverend Benjamin Van Zandt, the retired pastor of Kinderhook Reformed Church (see page 57). The procession from the church to the cemetery was escorted by the Kinderhook Fire Department and included 80 carriages.

Burial Site

Kinderhook Village Cemetery
Albany Avenue
Kinderhook, NY 12106

Van Buren was buried beside his wife in his family's enclosed plot. A ceremony is held each year on his birthday, December 5.

William Henry Harrison

Ninth President of the United States

Birthplace

Berkeley Plantation

12602 Harrison Landing Road
Charles City, VA 23030
804-829-6018
www.berkeleyplantation.com

William Henry Harrison's birthplace traces its roots back to 1619, when it was settled by 38 families from Berkeley Parish, England. The settlers arrived on December 4, 1619, and immediately thanked God for their safe passage: "Wee ordain that the day of our ships arrivall at the place assigned for plantacon in the land of Virginia shall be yearly and perpetually keept holy as a day of thanksgiving to Almighty God." Berkeley Plantation was, then, the site of the first official Thanksgiving. The current manor house was built in 1726.

Harrison, born February 9, 1773, was the last president born a British subject. Until Ronald Reagan, he also was the oldest man ever elected president.

When Harrison was eight years old, Berkeley Plantation was invaded by Hessian troops and American loyalists under the command of Brigadier General Benedict Arnold. Knowing an attack was imminent, the Harrisons fled. The property was stripped of its furnishings, livestock, and slaves by the attacking troops. Later that year, the Harrisons settled in Richmond, where Harrison's father served as governor.

The plantation later played a role in the Civil War, when it served as the headquarters of General George B. McClellan, who was visited here by President Lincoln. During that same time, General Daniel Butterfield composed "Taps" at the plantation.

The Coach House Tavern serves lunch and Sunday brunch.

Hours
Daily from 8 A.M. to 5 P.M.
Admission
$8.50 for adults; $4 for ages six to 12

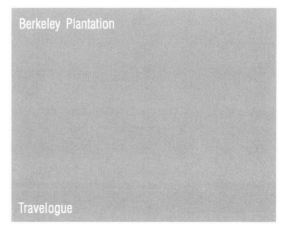

Berkeley Plantation

Travelogue

Home

Grouseland
Harrison Mansion
3 West Scott Street
Vincennes, IN 47591-1433
812-882-2096

Grouseland
Photo by Lorethea Hamke

Harrison built this mansion in 1803–4 while he was serving as the first governor of the Indiana Territory. He and his family lived here for about 10 years.

The home subsequently served as a private residence, a storehouse, and a hotel. A presidential museum today, it is furnished in period style. Its genealogical library is open Thursdays from 10 A.M. to 4 P.M.

Hours
Daily from 9 A.M. to 5 P.M. from March to December and from 11 A.M. to 4 P.M. the rest of the year
Admission
$3 for adults; $2 for high-school and college students; $1 for children. A $1 fee is charged for visiting the library.

Church

St. John's Lafayette Square
Washington, DC

See Sites Related to Multiple Presidents on pages 243–44.

Education

Harrison and his siblings were tutored in an outbuilding on Berkeley Plantation.

Hampden-Sydney College
Hampden-Sydney, VA 23943
804-223-6000

Harrison enrolled at the age of 14 for pre-medical education. He was a founder of the campus literary society and a member of the

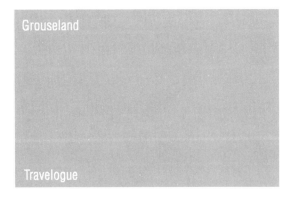

Grouseland

Travelogue

Union-Philanthropy Society, the country's second-oldest debating society. In the yard of the college's Atkinson Hall (the main administration building) is a mounting block that belonged to Harrison. It is on display at the base of a historical marker sent to the college from Harrison's home in North Bend, Ohio. The block was used by Mrs. Harrison for getting into and out of their carriage.

In 1790, Harrison apprenticed in the medical offices of Dr. Andrew Leiper in Richmond before enrolling the following year in the University of Pennsylvania Medical School. There, he studied under Dr. Benjamin Rush. Shortly after arriving in Philadelphia, Harrison learned of his father's death. In keeping with his father's wishes, he remained at the school. Money soon ran out, however, and he abandoned the idea of becoming a physician.

Hampden-Sydney College

Travelogue

Marriage

Harrison married Anna Tuthill Symmes on November 25, 1795, at the home of Dr. Stephen Wood in North Bend, Ohio.

Inaugural Site

The Capitol
Washington, DC

On March 4, 1841, a cold and rainy day, Harrison delivered the longest inaugural address ever—one hour and 40 minutes. The address was written by Daniel Webster.

Place of Death

The White House
Washington, DC

Harrison refused to wear a hat and coat during his inauguration. Following the ceremony, he was caught in a downpour while strolling outside the White House. He came down with a cold that grew progressively worse. By April 3, he began slipping into and out of consciousness. On April 4, he died in bed in the White House.

Funeral Site

The White House
Washington, DC

An Episcopal funeral service was held April 7, 1841, in the East Room. Following the funeral, Harrison's body lay in state in the Capitol before being temporarily buried in Washington. In June of that year, it was moved to its final resting place in Ohio.

Burial Site

Harrison Tomb
Cliff Road
North Bend, OH 45052
www.oplin.lib.oh.us/OHS2/site/sites/southwest/harto.html

Harrison's tomb, with its 60-foot Bedford limestone obelisk, is on the summit of Mount Nebo. Its numerous vaults contain Harrison family members. The terrace provides a panoramic view of the Ohio River Valley. The cemetery is maintained by the Ohio Historical Society (614-294-2630).

Hours
Open during daylight hours
Admission
Free

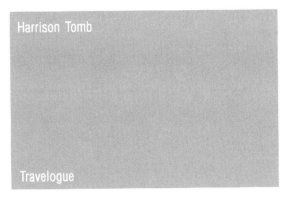

Harrison Tomb

Travelogue

Other Sites

Fort Megis
29100 West Reber Road
Perrysburg, OH 43552
419-874-4121
www.oplin.lib.oh.us/OHS2/site/sites/northwest/ftmei.htm

General Harrison built this fort in 1813 to protect Ohio and Indiana from the British. British and Canadian forces assisted by Tecumseh attacked the fort in May 1813 and again that July, but they were defeated both times.

The reconstructed Fort Megis is the largest log fort in the country. It encompasses 10 acres and has seven blockhouses and five emplacements. Displays interpret the War of 1812 and life in the fort. Many artifacts from the fort are on display.

Hours
Monday through Saturday from 9:30 A.M. to 5 P.M. and Sundays and holidays from

noon to 5 P.M. from Memorial Day to Labor Day; Saturday from 9:30 A.M. to 5 P.M. and Sunday from noon to 5 P.M. from Labor Day through March; closed from April through Memorial Day
Admission
$4 for adults; $1 for ages six to 12

Fort Megis

Travelogue

Tippecanoe Battlefield
Tippecanoe County Historical Society
909 South Street
Lafayette, IN 47901-1414
317-742-8411
jupiter.wvec.k12.in.us/battle/associat.htm

This 90-acre park includes a monument marking the site of the 1811 battle in which General Harrison defeated the Indians led by Prophet, the brother of Tecumseh. A series of exhibits and audiovisual presentations brings the action to life.

Hours
Daily from 10 A.M. to 5 P.M. from March to November and from 10 A.M. to 4 P.M. the rest of the year
Admission
$3 for adults; $2 for students and guests over 59; $1 for ages four to 12

Tippecanoe Battlefield

Travelogue

John Tyler
Tenth President of the United States

Birthplace

John Tyler was born March 29, 1790, at Greenway, his family's plantation on the James River between Williamsburg and Richmond.

Home

Sherwood Forest Plantation
14501 John Tyler Highway
P.O. Box 8
Charles City, VA 23030
804-829-5377
www.sherwoodforest.org

Following his term as president, Tyler and his young bride, Julia, retired to Sherwood Forest, a plantation worked by slaves. There, they raised Tyler's second family, which grew to seven children. Tyler loved to dance the Virginia reel and therefore had a 68-foot ballroom added to the building, which made his home the world's longest wood-frame building.

The Tylers summered at a cottage in Hampton, Virginia.

Sherwood Forest Plantation traces its roots to a 1616 land grant. The current home was built in 1730 and remains the property of the Tyler family. Sherwood Forest is a popular spot for weddings and other social events.

Hours
Daily from 9 A.M. to 5 P.M.; closed Thanksgiving and Christmas
Admission
Call for rates.

Sherwood Forest Plantation

Travelogue

Church

St. John's Lafayette Square
Washington, DC

See Sites Related to Multiple Presidents on pages 243–44.

Education

College of William and Mary
Williamsburg, VA

See Sites Related to Multiple Presidents on page 245.

Following his graduation from William and Mary, Tyler returned to Charles City County, where he studied law with his father and his cousin Samuel Tyler. He also studied in the Richmond office of Edmund Randolph, the country's first attorney general. Tyler was admitted to the Virginia Bar in 1809.

Marriages

Tyler married Letitia Christian at her home on March 29, 1813. While she was first lady, Mrs. Tyler suffered a stroke that left her paralyzed. She remained in the upstairs living quarters of the White House, venturing downstairs only once, for the 1842 marriage of daughter Elizabeth. She died of a stroke in September of that year.

Church of the Ascension (Episcopal)
Fifth Avenue at 10th Street
New York, NY 10003
212-254-8620

Tyler met Julia Gardiner, a woman 30 years younger than he, at a White House reception in early 1842. They began dating a few

months after the death of Letitia Tyler and wed quietly and without celebration on June 26, 1844. The only persons attending were the bride's brother and sister and Tyler's son John Jr. Tyler was so concerned about secrecy that he did not discuss his plans with his other children until after the wedding. His sons accepted the new Mrs. Tyler, but his daughters rejected their new stepmother, who was five years younger than Tyler's eldest daughter, Mary.

Julia Tyler died in 1889 and was buried beside her husband in Hollywood Cemetery in Richmond.

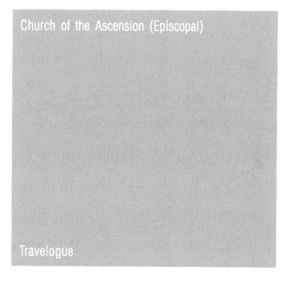

Church of the Ascension (Episcopal)

Travelogue

Inaugural Site

Tyler took the oath of office on April 6, 1841, at the Indian Queen Hotel in Washington, being sworn in by Chief Justice William Cranch of the United States Circuit

Court of the District of Columbia. The hotel no longer exists.

Place of Death

In January 1862, Tyler checked into the Exchange Hotel in Richmond, Virginia, in preparation for taking a seat in the Confederate House of Representatives. When he became ill, his physician diagnosed his condition as biliousness and recommended he return home. He died on January 18, before he was able to leave Richmond. The hotel no longer exists.

Funeral

St. Paul's Episcopal Church
815 East Grace Street
Richmond, VA 23219-3409
804-643-3589

Tyler's body lay in state in the Confederate Capitol, draped with the Confederate flag, before his funeral on January 20, 1862. The service was officiated by the Reverend Charles Minnegrode and the Reverend John Johns. A 150-carriage procession brought Tyler's body to the cemetery.

In the North, Tyler was considered a traitor for joining the Confederacy. No mention of his death was reported in the Washington press. Congress finally acknowledged his death in 1915 when it erected a memorial at his grave site.

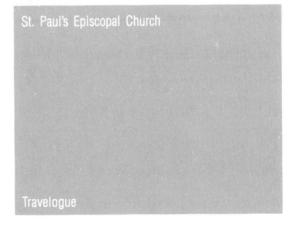
St. Paul's Episcopal Church

Travelogue

Burial Site

Hollywood Cemetery
Richmond, VA

See Sites Related to Multiple Presidents on page 241.

James Knox Polk

Eleventh President of the United States

Birthplace

James K. Polk Memorial State Historic Site

North Carolina Department of Cultural Resources
US 521
P.O. Box 475
Pineville, NC 28134
704-889-7145
www.plcmc.lib.nc.us/branch/main/carolina/polk.htm

James Knox Polk was born November 2, 1795, on his family's farm, where he spent his first 11 years. The visitor center at the site has exhibits and a film depicting Polk's life and times. Guided tours are conducted through the reconstructed log buildings.

Hours
Monday through Saturday from 9 A.M. to 5 P.M. and Sunday from 1 to 5 P.M. from April to October; Tuesday through Saturday from 10 A.M. to 4 P.M. and Sunday from 1 to 4 P.M. from November to March
Admission
Free

James K. Polk Memorial State Historic Site

Travelogue

Home

James K. Polk Ancestral Home

301 West Seventh Street
Columbia, TN 38401-3132
931-388-2354

Polk began his legal and political career while living in this Federal-style house built by his father in 1816. Aside from the White House, this is the only surviving Polk home. Many personal possessions, including artwork and jewelry that belonged to the Polks, are

James K. Polk Ancestral Home
Photo by John Holtzapple

on display. Also in the home are some of the furnishings the Polks used in the White House. Political and Mexican War memorabilia are exhibited in the adjacent Sister's House.

<u>Hours</u>
Monday through Saturday from 9 A.M. to 5 P.M. and Sunday from 1 to 5 P.M. from April to October; Monday through Saturday from 9 A.M. to 4 P.M. and Sunday from 1 to 5 P.M. the rest of the year
<u>Admission</u>
$5 for adults; $4 for guests over 60; $2 for ages six to 18. These fees cover admission to the home, museum, and gardens.

James K. Polk Ancestral Home

Travelogue

Church

First Presbyterian Church
801 South High Street
Columbia, TN 38401-3277
615-388-1985

Polk's parents brought their young son to be baptized here. But because Polk's father refused to join the church, the minister would not perform the baptism.

During James's youth, Mrs. Polk brought him regularly to Presbyterian services. Out of respect for his mother, Polk continued Presbyterian worship into his adulthood. Liking the Methodist church better, he frequented Methodist services whenever he went to church alone. He was baptized a Methodist a week before his death.

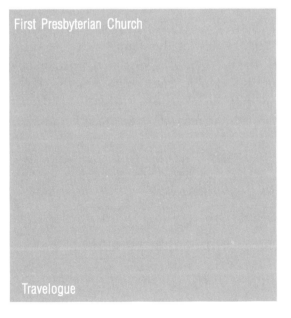
First Presbyterian Church

Travelogue

Education

At 17, Polk enrolled in a Presbyterian school near Columbia, Tennessee; the school was run by the Reverend Robert Henderson.

University of North Carolina
Chapel Hill, NC 27514
919-962-2211
www.unc.edu

In 1816, Polk entered the University of North Carolina. He roomed in South Building, then a dormitory and classroom building and now the administration building. His roommate was William D. Moseley, who eventually became governor of North Carolina; Polk and Moseley occupied the room on the southwest corner of the third floor. Polk was known for his dependability. A skilled debater, he was twice elected president of the Dialectic Society. Minutes from the society show that on one occasion, "Hamilton C. Jones was fined ten cents for threatening language to James K. Polk, and Polk was fined the same for replying to Jones." Polk graduated with honors in 1818. At graduation, he delivered the Latin welcoming address.

In 1847, during his presidency, Polk returned to campus to participate in commencement exercises. His portrait hangs in the DiPhi Senate Room of South Building.

After his days at the University of North Carolina, Polk studied law in the Nashville office of Felix Grundy, who later served as attorney general under Martin Van Buren.

University of North Carolina

Travelogue

Marriage

Polk married Sarah Childress on January 1, 1824, at the home of the bride's parents in Murfreesboro, Tennessee.

Inaugural Site

The Capitol
Washington, DC

March 4, 1845

Place of Death

Polk died at home on June 15, 1849, after becoming ill during a trip through the South.

Burial Site

State Capitol

Travelogue

State Capitol
Capitol Square
Nashville, TN 27603
615-741-1621

Polk and his wife were originally buried in a family plot. In 1893, they were moved to their current resting place on the grounds of the State Capitol.

Hours
Always open
Admission
Free

Other Site

The Three Presidents Statue
Raleigh, NC

See Sites Related to Multiple Presidents on page 255.

Zachary Taylor
Twelfth President of the United States

Birthplace

Historians believe that Zachary Taylor was born November 24, 1784, at Montebello, the Orange County, Virginia, home of maternal relatives; the Taylors were visiting while en route from Hare Forest, the family's former Orange County home, to its new home in Louisville, Kentucky. It is possible that Taylor was born at Hare Forest prior to the move.

Home

The Taylors lived on Beargrass Creek, just east of Louisville.

Church

St. John's Lafayette Square
Washington, DC

See Sites Related to Multiple Presidents on pages 243–44.

Education

Taylor received a basic education from private tutors and never attended college. He is said to have been a poor speller his entire life.

Marriage

Taylor married Margaret "Peggy" Mackall Smith on June 21, 1810, at the home of the bride's sister near Louisville, Kentucky.

Inaugural Site

The Capitol
Washington, DC

March 5, 1849

Place of Death

The White House
Washington, DC

In 1850, Taylor attended the lengthy Fourth of July festivities in the nation's capital, after which he went for a long walk in the hot sun. It is believed that upon his return to the White House, the hot and tired president ate a large bowl of cherries and drank iced milk, after which he fell ill with severe cramps. He was diagnosed with cholera, a common malady in Washington, where it was risky to eat fresh fruit and dairy products during the heat of summer. A team of doctors attended the president, whose health declined steadily until his death on July 9.

Funeral

The White House
Washington, DC

Taylor lay in state in the East Room, where a funeral service officiated by the Reverend Smith Pyne was held on July 13. Taylor's body was temporarily interred in the Congressional Burial Ground before being moved to his childhood home near Louisville, Kentucky.

Burial Site

Zachary Taylor National Cemetery
4701 Brownsboro Road
Louisville, KY 40207-1746
502-893-3852

After being temporarily interred in the Congressional Burial Ground, Taylor's body was reinterred in a private family cemetery. In 1926, it was moved again, to its current resting place.

Zachary Taylor National Cemetery, listed on the National Register of Historic Places, contains the graves of numerous veterans.

Hours
Daily from 8 A.M. to 4:30 P.M.
Admission
Free

Zachary Taylor National Cemetery

Travelogue

Zachary Taylor National Cemetery
Photo by Gary Peak
Courtesy of the Department of Veterans Affairs
and the National Cemetery System

Other Sites

Palo Alto Battlefield

National Park Service
1623 Central Boulevard
Brownsville, TX 78520
210-541-2785
www.nps.gov/paal/paal.htm

The Battle of Palo Alto marked an important point in the Mexican War. On July 8, 1846, General Taylor led 2,300 Americans against 3,400 Mexican troops to liberate Fort Texas. Nine Americans died and 43 were injured; the Mexicans suffered 200 dead and 125 wounded.

The park was established in 1991 and dedicated two years later. It is still under development and is not yet open to the public. The National Park Service intends to develop the battlefield to pay honor to both the American and Mexican forces.

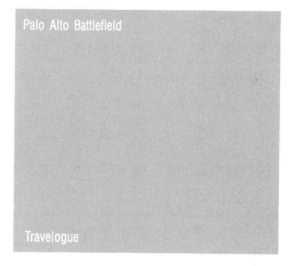

Lincoln Monument State Memorial
Dixon, IL

See Sites Related to Multiple Presidents on page 254.

Millard Fillmore

Thirteenth President of the United States

Birthplace

Millard Fillmore Birthplace
Fillmore Glen State Park
NY 38
Moravia, NY 13118
315-497-0130
nysparks.state.ny.us/maps

In 1799, Millard Fillmore's father, Nathaniel, grew frustrated by his failure as a farmer in Bennington, Vermont. He caved in to the sales pitch of an unscrupulous land speculator, who sold the family a faulty title to property in the Finger Lakes community of Moravia, New York. The elder Fillmore failed at farming the dense clay on his new property, and when the faults in his title were exposed, he was forced to move the family to present-day Niles, near Lake Skaneateles. There, the family farmed rented land for 17 years, then moved southwest to Montville and eventually to Aurora.

A replica of the Fillmores' cabin is at the edge of a meadow in the state park. Its furnishings suggest the family's rugged life. Neither the cabin nor its location nor its furnishings are authentic. Millard Fillmore was born January 7, 1800; his actual birthplace is four miles northwest of the park on Skinner Hill Road. That desolate site, on a dirt road, is poorly marked and maintained. A historical marker installed in 1932 commemorates the site, located on a gently sloping hillside. The original cabin was destroyed in 1851. Today, only a few old picnic tables and a broken flag-pole accompany the historical marker behind a rail fence. Due to the poor markings and road conditions, visitors should inquire at the state park for directions to the site.

Hours
The state park is open daily from 7 A.M. to dusk year-round. The cabin is open Wednesday through Sunday from 8 A.M. to dusk from May to October.
Admission
Free, though parking costs $4 during the summer season and $3 the rest of the year

Millard Fillmore Birthplace

Travelogue

Millard Fillmore birthplace

Homes

Millard Fillmore House
Aurora Historical Society
24 Shearer Avenue
East Aurora, NY 14052
716-652-8875
www.home.earthlink.net/~pock/home_mf.htm

Fillmore built this house in the early 1820s; he and his first wife, Abigail, lived here from 1826 to 1830. The house was originally on Main Street but was moved in the 1930s to make way for a movie theater. The house has been restored to its 1830s appearance. Among the exhibits are five Hitchcock chairs that belonged to Fillmore, the key to his Buffalo mansion, his watch, a lock of his hair, and the desk he used in his East Aurora law office.

Hours
Open weekends from 2 to 4 P.M. from Memorial Day to October 15

Admission
$2

Fillmore and his second wife, Caroline, bought a mansion at Niagara Square in Buffalo, where they settled following their 1858 wedding. While living there, Fillmore was active in numerous causes, among them the establishment of the University of Buffalo and Buffalo General Hospital. He served as the first chancellor of the university, now the State University of New York at Buffalo. In 1861, the Fillmores hosted President-Elect Abraham Lincoln at their home while Lincoln was en route to his inauguration. Following Lincoln's assassination, the exterior of the Fillmores' home was vandalized by an angry mob. The mob criticized Fillmore's Southern sympathies—he supported the Fugitive Slave Act—and demanded that he drape the house in black. When Fillmore refused, the mob splashed ink on the house.

The mansion no longer exists. At the site is the Statler Building, once the flagship Statler Hotel and now one of the city's most fashionable office addresses.

The Fillmores also owned a brownstone home within the city. That home no longer exists.

Millard Fillmore House

Travelogue

Church

Fillmore attended a Unitarian church in Buffalo. The church no longer exists.

Education

Fillmore received basic instruction during his youth. At 19, he enrolled in a newly constructed academy at New Hope, New York, where he was a student of his future wife, Abigail Powers. In 1819, he began studying law in the office of Judge Walter Wood. In 1822, he left Wood's office and moved to Aurora with his parents. There, he accepted a teaching position in nearby Buffalo and spent his spare time studying law in the offices of Asa Rice and Joseph Clary. He was admitted to the New York Bar in 1823.

Marriages

Fillmore married his former teacher Abigail Powers on February 5, 1826, at the Moravia home of the bride's brother, Judge Powers. Frequently ill during Fillmore's presidency, Abigail caught a cold during the outdoor inauguration of Franklin Pierce in 1853 and died a few weeks later of pneumonia.

Fillmore married Caroline Carmichael McIntosh on February 10, 1858, in Albany, New York. They settled in Buffalo, where they remained for the rest of their lives.

Inaugural Site

The Capitol
Washington, DC

Fillmore was inaugurated in the United States House of Representatives Chamber on July 10, 1850, the day after Zachary Taylor's death.

Place of Death/Funeral

Fillmore suffered a stroke on February 13, 1874, while shaving at his home in Buffalo. He fell unconscious during the evening of March 8 and died at home a few hours later. His funeral was held March 10 in his Buffalo house.

Burial Site

Forest Lawn Cemetery and Garden
1411 Delaware Avenue
Buffalo, NY 14209-1110
716-885-1600

The Fillmore plot is on a shady hillside near the middle of the cemetery. Forest Lawn is noted for its exquisite statuary. The cemetery offers trolley tours on weekends during

Millard Fillmore grave in Forest Lawn Cemetery and Garden

warm weather. Occasional Victorian picnics are also held. Call for details.

<u>Hours</u>
Open during daylight hours
<u>Admission</u>
Free

Forest Lawn Cemetery and Garden

Travelogue

Franklin Pierce

Fourteenth President of the United States

Birthplace

Franklin Pierce Homestead

Hillsborough Historical Society
NH 31
P.O. Box 896
Hillsborough, NH 03244
603-478-3165
www.conknet.com/~hillsboro/pierce/contents.html

Franklin Pierce was born November 23, 1804, in a log cabin on the 50-acre plot his father, Benjamin, had bought in 1786. The cabin no longer exists. The family moved to the existing home shortly after Franklin's birth. Pierce's father operated a tavern on the ground floor and later trained county militia in an upstairs ballroom.

Over the years, the guests at the Pierce home included Daniel Webster and Nathaniel Hawthorne, a friend of Franklin's from college. In 1827, Franklin returned home after attending law school and established a practice in a shed across the street from the homestead. It was about that time that the elder Pierce became governor of New Hampshire.

The homestead was restored by the New Hampshire Federation of Women's Clubs and now operates as a historical museum. Included are original stenciling, wallpaper dating to 1824, and many items that belonged to the Pierce family.

Hours
Monday through Saturday from 10 A.M. to 4 P.M. and Sunday from 1 to 4 P.M. during July and August; open weekends only from Memorial Day weekend through June and from September through Columbus Day weekend
Admission
$2.50

Franklin Pierce Homestead

Travelogue

Home

Pierce Manse

14 Penacook Street
P.O. Box 425
Concord, NH 03302-0425
603-225-2068, 603-224-7668, or 603-224-0094
newww.com/free/pierce/pierce.htm

Following James Buchanan's inauguration, Pierce and his wife retired to Concord, where they lived out the balance of their lives.

In later years, Pierce voiced his opposition to the Civil War. Although he was sympathetic to the Confederate cause and denounced Lincoln's war policies, he carefully expressed his support of the Union and his opposition to the secession of the Southern states. Needless to say, his sentiments made him vastly unpopular among local residents. In fact, many neighbors and former friends denounced Pierce as a traitor. When Lincoln was assassinated, an angry mob threatened Pierce's home. It was during these later years of his retirement that Pierce began drinking heavily.

In 1971, the house, originally located at 18 Montgomery Street, was on the verge of being demolished. The Pierce Brigade, a group dedicated to preserving Pierce's legacy, bought it and moved it to its current location within the Concord Historic District. The Greek Revival house is full of Pierce artifacts.

Hours
Open weekdays from 11 A.M. to 3 P.M. from
June to Labor Day
Admission
$2 for adults; $.50 for children and students

Pierce Manse

Travelogue

Church

St. Paul's Episcopal Church

Park Street
Concord, NH 03301
603-224-2523

Although a man of faith since his college days, Pierce never joined a church until his retirement from the presidency. He was baptized in 1865 and confirmed the following year.

Pierce attended the existing St. Paul's, but he wouldn't recognize its interior, which was completely renovated following a fire in the

1980s. The pew Pierce used has been pre-served and is marked by a plaque.

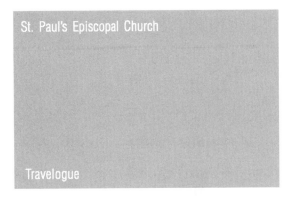
St. Paul's Episcopal Church

Travelogue

Education

Pierce studied in a brick schoolhouse in Hillsborough before enrolling at Hancock Academy and then at Francestown Academy, neither of which exists today.

Bowdoin College
Brunswick, ME 04011
207-725-3000
www.bowdoin.edu

As a sophomore at Bowdoin College, Pierce befriended freshman Nathaniel Hawthorne, with whom he would have a life-long friendship. He also met Hawthorne's classmate Henry Wadsworth Longfellow. During his junior year, Pierce had the dubious distinction of being at the bottom of his class. He applied himself, however, and graduated 14th in the class of 1824. At commence-

ment, he delivered an address entitled "The Influence of Circumstances on the Intellectual Character."

Following his graduation from Bowdoin, Pierce studied law in the offices of John Burnham, Levi Woodbury, Samuel Howe, and Edmund Parker. He was admitted to the bar in 1827.

Bowdoin College

Travelogue

Marriage

Pierce married Jane Means Appleton on November 19, 1834, at the home of the bride's grandparents in Amherst, New Hampshire.

Inaugural Site

The Capitol
Washington, DC

Pierce was inaugurated March 4, 1853. He

and his wife witnessed the death of their son Benny in a train accident before they arrived in Washington. So distraught was Mrs. Pierce that she did not attend the inauguration and was rarely seen outside the White House during the next two years. In fact, she was nicknamed "The Shadow of the White House."

Place of Death

Pierce died at his Concord home on October 8, 1869, following months of steadily deteriorating health.

Funeral

St. Paul's Episcopal Church
Concord, NH

Following Pierce's funeral at St. Paul's (see page 79) on October 11, 1869, his body lay in state in the New Hampshire State Capitol.

Burial Site

Old North Cemetery
North State Street and Keane Avenue
Concord, NH

Pierce is buried in a fenced plot. A historical marker is located near the cemetery entrance.

Old North Cemetery

Travelogue

Other Site

Quartermaster Museum
Fort Lee, VA

See Sites Related to Multiple Presidents on pages 260–261.

James Buchanan
Fifteenth President of the United States

Birthplace

Buchanan Birthplace State Park
Pennsylvania Department of Conservation and Natural Resources
Cowans Gap State Park
HCR 17266
Fort Loudon, PA 17224-9801
717-485-3948
www.dcnr.state.pa.us/stateparks/parks/buchanan.html

James Buchanan's father bought this site, then known as Tom's Trading Place, in 1789. At the time, it included cabins, barns, stables, storehouses, a store, and an orchard. The senior Buchanan renamed it Stony Batter, after the family's ancestral home in Northern Ireland. James Buchanan was born here April 23, 1791. His father continued to operate a business on the site until the family moved to Mercersburg in 1796.

The birthplace is marked by a 38-foot-square, 31-foot-high rock pyramid consisting of 50 tons of American gray granite over 250 tons of rubble and mortar. Work on the monument began in October 1907 in accordance with the terms of the will of Buchanan's niece, Harriet Lane Johnston. The 18.5-acre park features two picnic pavilions and numerous picnic tables. Union and Confederate forces battled on the site on June 24, 1863.

Hours
Open daily from dawn to dusk
Admission
Free

Buchanan Birthplace State Park
Travelogue

Mercersburg Academy
300 East Seminary Street
Mercersburg, PA 17236-1551
717-328-6173
www.mercersburg.edu

In 1953, the cabin where Buchanan was born was moved to the Mercersburg Academy campus, where it stands adjacent to the football stadium today. The cabin may be viewed during daylight hours.

Mercersburg Academy

Travelogue

Homes

Buchanan Home
17 North Main Street
Mercersburg, PA 17236

When Buchanan was five, his family moved to this Mercersburg home, where he lived for the remainder of his childhood. His father built the house in 1796; it was later converted to a hotel. Currently, it is a private home not open to the public. A historic marker is located in front of the house.

Across the street at 14 North Main Street is the home in which Buchanan's niece, Harriet Lane, lived. Lane served as White House hostess during the Buchanan administration. This, too, is a private home not open to the public.

Nearby on the southwest corner of the town square is the Mansion House, a popular gathering place where Buchanan gave an address in 1852.

Mercersburg was frequented by Confederate raiders during the Civil War. On the first Chambersburg raid (October 10, 1862), 1,500 men under General J. E. B. Stuart passed through. During the Gettysburg campaign, bands of Confederates foraged the town. On July 5, 1863, nearly 700 wounded Confederates were brought here from Gettysburg by Union soldiers; they were held in makeshift hospitals throughout the town.

Buchanan Home

Travelogue

Wheatland
James Buchanan Foundation
1120 Marietta Avenue
Lancaster, PA 17603-2550
717-392-8721
www.wheatland.org

Buchanan bought this estate for $9,000 in 1848, while he was serving as secretary of state. He described Wheatland as "a beau ideal of a statesman's abode." And indeed it was. Ever the statesman, Buchanan used his home to its fullest political advantage. It was common for him to receive Southern visitors at the front entrance, where the facade had the appearance of a plantation mansion. Northern visitors were greeted at the rear, where the appearance was that of a New England home. Buchanan conducted his entire 1856 presidential campaign from the home's office, which was dominated by a large wood-and-leather desk still on display. Following his presidency, he retired to Wheatland, where he led a very private life, rarely speaking publicly.

The house was one of the first in the region to have a central heating system. In addition to guided tours of the estate, special programs—such as Christmas candlelight tours, "Murder at the Mansion," and "Old-Fashioned Sunday"—are offered. Call for details.

Wheatland

Hours
Daily from 10 A.M. to 4 P.M. from April through November; closed Easter and Thanksgiving
Admission
$5.50 for adults; $4.50 for seniors; $3.50 for students; $1.75 for children

Churches

First Presbyterian Church
140 East Orange Street
Lancaster, PA 17602-2844
717-394-6854

Buchanan accepted his faith while serving as president but delayed joining a church until his term ended, for fear of being branded a hypocrite. He joined First Presbyterian Church in 1865, shortly after leaving Washington. The current building dates from 1851 and has nine Tiffany windows.

Visitors may take self-guided tours on weekdays from 9 A.M. to 4 P.M. Guided tours are offered following the 11 A.M. Sunday service.

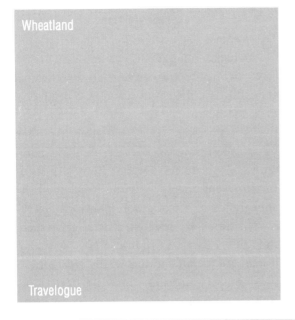
Wheatland

Travelogue

First Presbyterian Church

Travelogue

First Presbyterian Church

St. John's Lafayette Square
Washington, DC

See Sites Related to Multiple Presidents on pages 243–44.

Education

Dickinson College
P.O. Box 1773
Carlisle, PA 17013
717-243-5121
www.dickinson.edu

Buchanan studied hard but evidently played just as hard, as he was a serious discipline problem throughout his time at Dickinson College. Historians are not clear on exactly what he did, but Buchanan's behavior led college officials to withhold an academic honor he had earned. Although he threatened boycotting commencement, he eventually recanted and received his baccalaureate degree in 1809 with the rest of his class.

Buchanan then studied law in the Lancaster office of James Hopkins and was admitted to the Pennsylvania Bar in 1812.

Dickinson College

Travelogue

Marriage

Buchanan was the only president who never married. As a young man, he was engaged to Anne Coleman, but Coleman broke off the engagement upon hearing false reports of Buchanan's philandering. Before Buchanan could right the situation, Coleman became ill and died. It is said that Buchanan was never interested in any other woman.

During his administration, his orphaned

niece, Harriet Lane, whom Buchanan raised, served as official White House hostess.

Inaugural Site

The Capitol
Washington, DC

March 4, 1857

Place of Death

Wheatland
Lancaster, PA

Buchanan died at Wheatland (see page 83) on June 1, 1868, of pneumonia and inflammation of the lining of the heart.

Funeral

Wheatland
Lancaster, PA

The Reverend John W. Nevin of First Presbyterian Church officiated at Buchanan's funeral on June 4, 1868. Although Buchanan wanted a simple funeral without pomp or pageantry, thousands lined the streets from Wheatland (see page 83) to the cemetery.

Burial Site

Woodward Hill Cemetery
South Queen Street
Lancaster, PA 17603

Woodward Hill Cemetery is an old, poorly maintained facility in the middle of Lancaster. Buchanan's grave, located atop a hill and marked by an American flag, is humble but stately.

To reach the cemetery from Wheatland's driveway (located on the west side of the mansion), turn right onto Marietta Avenue, then right onto President Avenue. Turn left at the light onto PA 462, then right onto US 222 in the center of town. Turn left onto Sycamore Street, then left onto Queen Street. The cemetery is on the right.

Woodward Hill Cemetery

Travelogue

Other Sites

Blair House
Washington, DC

See Sites Related to Multiple Presidents on pages 251–52.

James Buchanan Memorial
Meridian Hill Park
16th Street at W Street NW
Washington, DC 20010

In her will, Harriet Lane Johnston left $100,000 for the erection of two monuments to her famous uncle: one at his birthplace (see page 82) and one in Washington. The will stated that if the monuments were not authorized within 15 years of her death, the funds would pass to the Harriet Lane Home for Invalid Children (now Johns Hopkins Children's Hospital). Numerous delays—and World War I—ensued. Finally, on June 18, 1918, six days before the 15th anniversary of Johnston's death, the Senate gave its approval to the Washington project. Meridian Hill Park was chosen the site, Hans Schuler was selected the sculptor, and William Beecher was chosen the architect.

The memorial is a 9.5-foot bronze statue atop a granite base in front of an 82-foot panel with carvings representing law and diplomacy. On June 26, 1939, President Herbert Hoover accepted the monument on behalf of the American people.

Hours
Always open
Admission
Free

James Buchanan Memorial

Travelogue

Abraham Lincoln

Sixteenth President of the United States

Birthplace

Marble memorial building of the Abraham Lincoln Birthplace National Historic Site
Courtesy of the Abraham Lincoln Birthplace National Historic Site

Abraham Lincoln Birthplace National Historic Site
National Park Service
2995 Lincoln Farm Road
Hodgenville, KY 42748-9707
502-358-3137
www.nps.gov/abli

This elaborate memorial opened in 1911 on the site of Sinking Spring Farm, where Abraham Lincoln was born February 12, 1809. He lived here for two and a half years. The large marble memorial building contains a log cabin once believed to have been the actual cabin where Lincoln was born. Subsequent research, however, indicated otherwise. The 56 steps leading to the building's entrance represent the 56 years of Lincoln's life. Over the six columns are inscribed his words, "With malice toward none, with charity for all." The visitor center features a diorama and a film. Nature trails and picnic areas are on the premises.

Hours
Daily from 8 A.M. to 6:45 P.M. from Memorial Day to Labor Day and from 8 A.M. to 4:45 P.M. the rest of the year; closed Thanksgiving and Christmas
Admission
Free

Sinking Spring
Courtesy of the Abraham Lincoln Birthplace National Historic Site

Log cabin once believed to have been where Lincoln was born
Courtesy of the Abraham Lincoln Birthplace National Historic Site

Abraham Lincoln Birthplace National Historic Site

Travelogue

Homes

Lincoln's Boyhood Home
US 31E
Hodgenville, KY 42748
502-549-3741

The Lincoln family lived here at Knob Creek Farm for two and a half years before moving to Indiana (see page 90) when Lincoln was eight years old. It was here that Lincoln first saw slave traders moving their slaves along the public roads. Markers along US 31E lead to the site.

<u>Hours</u>
Open daily from 9 A.M. to 7 P.M. from Memorial Day through Labor Day; open daily from 9 A.M. to 5 P.M. from April 1 to Memorial Day and from the day after Labor Day to October 31; closed the rest of the year
<u>Admission</u>
$1

Lincoln's Boyhood Home

Travelogue

Lincoln Boyhood Home National Memorial

National Park Service
IN 162
Lincoln City, IN 47552
812-937-4541
www.nps.gov/libo

This memorial park includes a visitor center offering various exhibits on Lincoln's 14-year residency in Indiana, interpretive materials, and audiovisual presentations. A living-history museum at the southwest corner of the original Thomas Lincoln farm features costumed interpreters and a reconstruction of the buildings, gardens, and fields that influenced Lincoln. Nancy Hanks Lincoln, Lincoln's mother, died when the future president was nine years old; her burial site is on the grounds.

Hours
Daily from 8 A.M. to 5 P.M.; closed New Year's, Thanksgiving, and Christmas
Admission
$2 per person; maximum of $4 per family

Lincoln Boyhood Home National Memorial

Travelogue

Lincoln Trail Homestead State Park

US 36
Harristown, IL 62537
www.isbe.state.il.us/dachelpo/home1/index.htm

Thomas Lincoln brought his family here in 1830 but moved the following year after going through a difficult winter. It was at this time that young Abraham Lincoln set out on his own. While his family headed back toward Indiana, Lincoln hopped a boat and went down the Mississippi, eventually settling in New Salem in 1831.

It is not known exactly where the Lincoln family built its cabin. Markers in the park indicate the possible location, but historians believe it may have been closer to the river.

Hours
Open from dawn to dusk
Admission
Free

Lincoln Trail Homestead State Park

Travelogue

Lincoln's New Salem Historic Site

IL 97
RR1, Box 244A
Petersburg, IL 62675
217-632-4000
www.state.il.us/HP/II.HIM

This 600-acre site includes a reconstruction of New Salem, the town in which Lincoln lived from 1831 to 1837. When he arrived here, he had no definite plans. By the time he left New Salem, he was a determined young man destined to greatness.

Lincoln never owned a home here; he lived in several log cabins. Among his occupations at New Salem were store clerk, wood chopper, postmaster, and deputy surveyor. He ran unsuccessfully for the Illinois General Assembly in 1832 but was elected in 1834.

Shortly after Lincoln left town, the county seat was moved to the nearby town of Petersburg, leaving New Salem in decline. In 1906, William Randolph Hearst became interested in preserving the town. He purchased the land and conveyed it to the New Salem Chautauqua Association. In 1919, the association deeded the property to the state of Illinois.

Much of the site's reconstruction was done by the Civilian Conservation Corps. The Onstot Cooper Shop, where Lincoln studied at night, is the only original building. The Rutledge Tavern, a gristmill, a sawmill, a school, a carding mill, shops, and houses were constructed to look as the originals did in the 1830s. The visitor center features changing exhibits and an orientation film on Lincoln's life in New Salem.

Hours
Daily from 9 A.M. to 5 P.M. from April to October and from 8 A.M. to 4 P.M. the rest of the year
Admission
Free; donations are accepted

Lincoln's New Salem Historic Site

Travelogue

Lincoln Home National Historic Site

National Park Service
413 South Eighth Street
Springfield, IL 62701-1950
217-492-4241, ext. 221
www.nps.gov/liho

In 1844, Abraham and Mary Todd Lincoln bought this home—the only one they ever owned—for $1,200 from the Reverend Charles Dresser, the man who had married them two years earlier. Three of their four sons were born here; their son Edward died here at the age of four. When the Lincolns left for Washington in 1861, they rented out the house, sold most of the furnishings, and gave their dog to a neighbor.

The Greek Revival home has been restored to its 1860 appearance. The National Park Service is currently restoring the four-block area around the Lincoln home. Although many of the buildings are not yet open to the public, visitors are welcome to stroll the neighborhood. Homes in the park area have signs telling their significance. Some of the sites are listed elsewhere in this section of the book.

Hours
Daily from 8:30 A.M. to 5 P.M.
Admission
Free, although visitors must have a ticket to tour the house; tickets are available from the visitor center at 426 South Seventh Street on a first-come, first-served basis

Lincoln Home National Historic Site

Travelogue

Lincoln Log Cabin State Historic Site
RR1, Box 175
Lerna, IL 62400
217-345-6489
www.state.il.us/HPA/LINCLOG.HTM

Disheartened by the long, hard winter of 1830–31, Lincoln's father, Thomas, packed his family and began moving back to Indiana. En route, the family visited friends in Coles County, who persuaded the Lincolns to settle there and give Illinois one more try. After living on three area farms, Thomas Lincoln finally purchased this site, called Goosenest Prairie Farm, in 1840.

The structure in which the family lived was a "saddlebag" cabin, having two rooms and a central chimney. At one point in the mid-1840s, there were 18 people living in the cabin. Thomas Lincoln died here in 1851; Sarah Lincoln (Abraham's stepmother) died here in 1869. At that time, Sarah's grandson John Hall took possession of the farm. He lived here until 1892, when the cabin was dismantled for transport to the World's Columbian Exposition in Chicago, where it was displayed. Today, the site operates as a museum and living-history farm.

Hours
Daily from 9 A.M. to 5 P.M.
Admission
Free

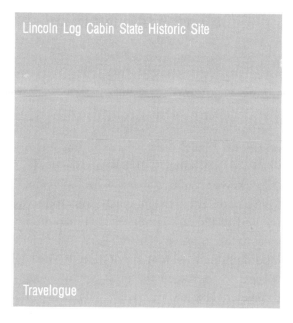
Lincoln Log Cabin State Historic Site

Travelogue

Churches

First Presbyterian Church
Seventh and Capitol Streets
Springfield, IL 62701
217-528-4311
www.netins.net/showcase/creative/lincoln/sites/pew.htm

Following the death of their son in 1850, Abraham and Mary Lincoln began attending First Presbyterian Church, then located at Third and Washington Streets, because they admired the pastor, Dr. James Smith, who had conducted the funeral service. Mary joined the church; Abraham, although deeply spiritual, was not a religious man and never joined any church.

The present building dates from 1868; it was the site of the funerals for Mary Lincoln and son Tad Lincoln. The pew the Lincolns rented for 10 years is in front of the pulpit. It may be seen during church office hours; call ahead to make arrangements. The church office is open daily from 10 A.M. to 4 P.M.

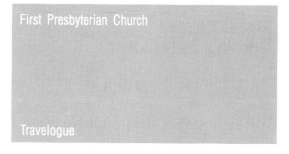
First Presbyterian Church

Travelogue

New York Avenue Presbyterian Church
Washington, DC

See Sites Related to Multiple Presidents on page 243.

St. John's Lafayette Square
Washington, DC

See Sites Related to Multiple Presidents on pages 243–44.

Education

Lincoln estimated that he had perhaps the equivalent of one year of formal education. During his boyhood, frontier schoolhouses operated only when a teacher could be persuaded to stay around long enough to offer instruction.

Marriage

Lincoln married Mary Todd on November 11, 1842, in the home of the bride's sister in Springfield, Illinois.

Places Related to Lincoln's Early Career

Bank One Main

1 East Old State Capitol Plaza
Springfield, IL 62701
217-525-9600
www.bankone.com

The Lincoln financial records from the Marine and Fire Insurance Company have been preserved by Bank One. They may be viewed during normal banking hours. Visitors should call ahead to make arrangements.

Hours
Open weekdays from 8:30 A.M. to 5 P.M.
and Saturdays from 9 A.M. to noon
Admission
Free

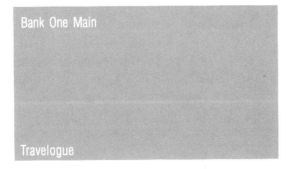

Bank One Main

Travelogue

Beardstown Courthouse

Third and State Streets
Beardstown, IL 62618
217-323-3110
www.beardstown.org

Here, just two years before being elected president, Lincoln won an acquittal for 24-year-old William "Duff" Armstrong. The case—known as the "Almanac Case"—stemmed from a midnight brawl in which Armstrong was accused of killing his opponent. Lincoln used an almanac to prove that there was insufficient moonlight on the night in question for the key witness to have seen the fight clearly enough to give credible testimony.

This is the only Lincoln courtroom still in use, and it looks just as it did in his day. The building now serves as Beardstown's city hall. On August 12, 1858, Lincoln returned to Beardstown as the Republican candidate for the United States Senate and delivered a speech in a park directly across from the courthouse. A small plaque commemorates the speech.

Hours
Open weekdays from 9 A.M. to 5 P.M.
Admission
Free

Beardstown Courthouse

Travelogue

Lincoln-Herndon Law Offices State Historic Site

Illinois Historic Preservation Agency
Sixth and Adams Streets
Springfield, IL 62701
217-785-7961
www.state.il.us/HPA/Linchern.htm

Lincoln and law partner Stephen T. Logan, with whom he had been practicing since 1841, moved into the third floor of this building in 1843. It was an ideal location for law offices, directly above the second-floor federal courtroom. After Logan left the partnership in 1844, Lincoln took in William Herndon as a junior partner. During the ensuing years, Lincoln frequently traveled the Eighth Judicial Circuit while Herndon worked in the offices. When Lincoln left Springfield for Washington in 1861, he wrote Herndon, "If I live I'm coming back some time, and then we'll go right on practising law as if nothing had ever happened."

Hours
Daily from 9 A.M. to 5 P.M. from March to October and from 9 A.M. to 4 P.M. the rest of the year
Admission
$2

Lincoln-Herndon Law Offices State Historic Site

Travelogue

Metamora Courthouse State Historic Site

Illinois Historic Preservation Agency
113 East Partridge Street
Metamora, IL 61548
309-367-4470
www.state.il.us/HPA/METAMORA.HIM

This is one of the few remaining courthouses in which Lincoln argued cases while traveling the Eighth Judicial Circuit from 1845 to 1856. The courtroom still has its original furnishings. Among the unusual artifacts here is a table Lincoln used in his 1860 campaign; a portion of it was cut away to make room for his long legs. The building was constructed in 1845 of local brick and timber.

Hours
Tuesday through Saturday from 9 A.M. to 5 P.M.; closed major holidays
Admission
Free; donations are accepted

Metamora Courthouse State Historic Site

Travelogue

Mount Pulaski Courthouse State Historic Site

Town Square
P.O. Box 355
Lincoln, IL 62656
217-792-3919
www.state.il.us/HPA/MPULASKI.HTM

Mount Pulaski is one of the two remaining courthouses frequented by Lincoln during his days on the Eighth Judicial Circuit. It served as a courthouse from 1848 to 1855. Because of an 1857 fire, most of the records related to Lincoln's cases were destroyed. From 1857 to 1878, the building was a school. It has also housed the town's post office, its jail, and offices. It has now been restored to its 1850s appearance.

Hours
Tuesday through Saturday from noon to
5 P.M.; closed New Year's, Thanksgiving,
and Christmas
Admission
Free

Mount Pulaski Courthouse State Historic Site

Travelogue

Old State Capitol State Historic Site

Springfield, IL

See Sites Related to Multiple Presidents on page 260.

Postville Courthouse State Historic Site

Illinois Historic Preservation Agency
914 Fifth Street
Lincoln, IL 62656
217-732-8930
www.state.il.us/HPS/POSTV.HTM

Postville Courthouse operated from 1840 until the county seat was moved to Mount Pulaski in 1848. Postville then began to decline and was eventually absorbed by the municipality of Lincoln. The building was used briefly as a post office and later as a private home. In 1929, Henry Ford bought it and moved it to Dearborn, Michigan, where it was reassembled as an exhibit at the new Greenfield Village. In 1956, the state of Illinois opened the current replica of the courthouse. It is furnished in the style of the Lincoln years.

Hours
Tuesday through Saturday from noon to
5 P.M.
Admission
$2

Postville Courthouse State Historic Site

Travelogue

Vandalia Statehouse
Illinois Historic Preservation Agency
315 West Gallatin
Vandalia, IL 62471
618-283-1161
www.state.il.us/HPA/VANDALIA.HTM

Vandalia served as the capital of Illinois from 1820 to 1839. During that time, there were three capitol buildings; this is the only one that survives. The first capitol was destroyed by fire in 1823. The second was hastily built in 1824 so Vandalia would remain the capital, but shoddy construction led to that building's eventual abandonment and demolition; when Lincoln arrived in Vandalia as a freshmen legislator, he had an office in that dilapidated structure. The current building was constructed in 1836. Following the legislature's departure for Springfield in 1839, the building was used as a school and a county courthouse. In 1918, the state took possession of the structure to ensure its preservation. County offices were moved from the building during the ensuing years. The structure has since been restored to its Lincoln-era appearance.

Hours
Daily from 9 A.M. to 5 P.M.
Admission
Free

Vandalia Statehouse

Travelogue

Inaugural Site

The Capitol
Washington, DC

March 4, 1861
March 4, 1865

Place of Death

Ford's Theatre National Historic Site
National Park Service
511 10th Street NW
Washington, DC 20004
202-426-6924 or 202-347-4833 (box office)

Lincoln was fatally shot at Ford's Theatre on April 14, 1865. The theater has been restored to its 1860s appearance. Short talks about the Lincoln era and the assassination are presented. A museum in the basement includes exhibits related to the assassination, including the gun used by John Wilkes Booth. Theater performances are offered Tuesday through Sunday at 7:30 P.M.; matinees are presented Thursday at 1 P.M. and Sunday at 3 P.M. The theater typically closes one hour prior to performances. Please call to check performance times and theater closings.

After being shot, Lincoln was carried to the Peterson House, located across the street from the theater. He died there the next day. It was in that house that Secretary of War Edwin Stanton is said to have uttered the words, "Now he belongs to the ages," although historians continue to debate this. The house, built in 1849, has been restored to its 1860s appearance.

Hours
Daily from 9 A.M. to 5 P.M.; closed Christmas
Admission
Free, though there is a charge for theater performances

Ford's Theatre National Historic Site

Travelogue

Funeral

The White House
Washington, DC

After lying in state in the East Room, Lincoln's body lay in state in 14 different cities during the two and a half weeks it took it to be transported to Springfield, Illinois, for burial.

The funeral procession was aboard a private Pullman railroad car that had been made for Lincoln a few years earlier. Thinking the car too elaborate, Lincoln had refused to use it during his time in office. The car was accidentally destroyed in the early 1900s.

Burial Site

Lincoln's Tomb State Historic Site
Oak Ridge Cemetery
Springfield, IL 62701
217-782-2717

This site contains Lincoln's tomb and the crypts of Mrs. Lincoln and three of their four children. Lincoln's career is depicted on statuettes. Bronze tablets contain the Gettysburg Address, Lincoln's second inaugural address, and his Springfield "Farewell Address."

Hours
Daily from 9 A.M. to 5 P.M. from March to October and from 9 A.M. to 4 P.M. the rest of the year; closed major holidays. The

114th Infantry Regiment demonstrates Civil War drills and ceremonies Tuesdays at 7 P.M. from June through August.
Admission
Free

Lincoln's Tomb State Historic Site

Travelogue

Other Sites

Lincoln Memorial
National Park Service
National Mall
Washington, DC 20242
202-426-6841
www.nps.gov/linc

One of Washington's best-known landmarks, this massive edifice stands at the extreme western edge of the National Mall, facing both the Washington Monument and the Capitol. The marble structure's 36 columns represent the 36 states in the Union during Lincoln's presidency. Dominating the interior is Daniel Chester French's statue of Lincoln seated. The text of Lincoln's Gettysburg Address and his second inaugural address are carved into the interior walls. The lower level contains murals by Jules Guerin and "Lincoln's Legacy," a permanent exhibit signed by students.

Hours
Daily from 8 A.M. to midnight from April 1 to Labor Day and from 8 A.M. to 5 P.M. the rest of the year. Interpretive tours are given daily beginning at 8 A.M. upon request.
Admission
Free

Lincoln Memorial

Travelogue

Lincoln Monument State Memorial
Dixon, IL

See Sites Related to Multiple Presidents on page 254.

Blair House
Washington, DC

See Sites Related to Multiple Presidents on pages 251–52.

Lincoln Trail

Lincoln Trail Area Development District
613 College Street Road
Elizabethtown, KY 42702
502-769-2393
www.ltadd.org

The Lincoln Trail is a trade association to which most Lincoln sites belong.

Lincoln Trail

Travelogue

Gettysburg National Military Park

National Park Service
97 Taneytown Road
Gettysburg, PA 17325
717-334-1124
pigpen.itd.nps.gov/gett

The Battle of Gettysburg, which lasted three days during July 1863, was simultaneously the high-water mark of the Confederacy and the battle that signaled the end of General Lee's hope of assaulting the North. By the time it ended, more than 51,000 were dead, the largest number in any North American battle before or since.

Lincoln delivered the Gettysburg Address in November 1863 at the dedication of the national cemetery here. The original address, on loan from the Library of Congress, is displayed during the summer. The site features a visitor center with a cyclorama, ranger-led tours, a book shop, battlefield guides, and numerous outdoor activities. In addition, the surrounding community offers numerous attractions centered on the Civil War and Abraham Lincoln.

Hours
Daily from 8 A.M. to 6 P.M. during the summer and from 8 A.M. to 5 P.M. the rest of the year; closed New Year's, Thanksgiving, and Christmas
Admission
Free, although there is a charge for the cyclorama and special programs

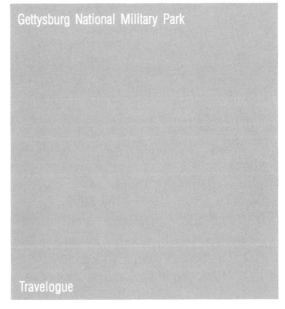

Gettysburg National Military Park

Travelogue

Hall of Fame for Great Americans

Bronx, NY

See Sites Related to Multiple Presidents on page 258

Abraham Lincoln Museum

Lincoln Memorial University
Cumberland Gap Parkway
Harrogate, TN 37752-1901
423-869-6235
www.lmunet.edu/musfront1.htm

This museum has an extensive collection of Lincoln artifacts and publications. Included are the silver-topped case Lincoln carried on the night he was assassinated, a lock of his hair clipped as he lay on his deathbed, two life masks, numerous personal belongings, and more than 20,000 books, photos, and other printed items. The museum's collection is used extensively for educational and research programs.

Hours
Open weekdays from 9 A.M. to 4 P.M.,
Saturdays from 11 A.M. to 4 P.M., and
Sundays from 1 to 4 P.M.
Admission
$2 for adults; $1.50 for guests over 60;
$1 for ages six to 12

Abraham Lincoln Museum

Travelogue

Executive Mansion

Fifth and Jackson Streets
Springfield, IL 62701
217-782-6450
www.netins.net/showcase/creative/lincoln/sites/
mansion.htm

This has been the home of the governor of Illinois since 1855. The Lincolns were frequent guests while living in Springfield.

The mansion was completely restored in 1971. On display are portraits of the Lincolns, some of their White House china, and a table given to Lincoln that contains more than 20,000 pieces of inlaid wood. A portion of the mansion is open for public tours.

Hours
Tuesday and Thursday from 9:30 A.M. to
3:15 P.M. and Saturday from 9:30 to
11 A.M.
Admission
Free

Executive Mansion

Travelogue

Lincoln Depot

National Park Service
10th and Monroe Streets
Springfield, IL 62701
217-544-8695
www.nps.gov.liho/depot/depot.htm

When Lincoln left Springfield on February 11, 1861, en route to his inauguration, he gave his "Farewell Address," an emotional speech to friends who had gathered here.

Today, the depot interprets Lincoln's trip to Washington. It is located two blocks from his Springfield home.

Hours
Daily from 10 A.M. to 4 P.M. from April through August
Admission
Free

Lincoln Depot

Travelogue

Lincoln Museum

66 Lincoln Square
Hodgenville, KY 42748
502-358-3163

Twelve significant episodes in Lincoln's life are presented in wax tableaux here. Also on display are Lincoln and Civil War objects and period art objects.

Hours
Monday through Saturday from 8:30 A.M. to 5 P.M. and Sunday from 12:30 to 5 P.M.; closed New Year's, Thanksgiving, and Christmas
Admission
$3

Lincoln Museum (Kentucky)

Travelogue

Lincoln Museum

200 East Berry Street
Fort Wayne, IN 46802
219-455-3864
www.thelincolnmuseum.org

This museum offers an impressive collection of Lincoln's possessions, letters, photographs, and paintings. An interactive computer system allows visitors to decorate the White House as Mrs. Lincoln did, fight Civil War battles, read Lincoln's mail, and take a history quiz. The museum includes reconstructions of Lincoln's log cabin, the Lincoln-Herndon law offices, and a War Department telegraph room.

Hours
Tuesday through Saturday from 10 A.M. to 5 P.M. and Sunday from 1 to 5 P.M.; closed New Year's, Easter, Thanksgiving, and Christmas
Admission
$2.99 for adults; $1.99 for guests over 60 and for ages five to 12

Lincoln Museum (Indiana)

Travelogue

Lincoln Room Museum

Historic Gettysburg-Adams County, Inc.
Wills House
Lincoln Square
Gettysburg, PA 17325
717-334-8188

This museum preserves the room in which Lincoln stayed on the eve of the dedication of Gettysburg National Cemetery. Lincoln completed the Gettysburg Address in this room. The address is presented in stereo. The furnishings are original.

Hours
Daily from 9 A.M. to 7 P.M. from Memorial Day through Labor Day; open reduced hours the rest of the year
Admission
$3

Lincoln Room Museum

Travelogue

Mary Todd Lincoln House

578 West Main Street
Lexington, KY 40507-1642
606-233-9999
www.uky.edu/LCC/HIS/sites/todd.html

This restored 1803 Georgian house was the childhood home of Mary Todd Lincoln. On display are personal artifacts of the Lincoln and Todd families, as well as pieces from Mrs. Lincoln's Meissen china collection.

Hours
Tuesday through Saturday from 10 A.M. to 4 P.M. from March 15 to November 30
Admission
$5 for adults; $2 for ages six to 12

Mary Todd Lincoln House

Travelogue

Bryant Cottage State Historic Site

146 East Wilson Street
Bement, IL 61813-1250
217-678-8184
www.bement.com/bryant.htm

Built in 1856, this four-room cottage is believed to be the site where Lincoln and Stephen Douglas met in July 1858 to plan their debates. The cottage was built by Bement businessman Francis Bryant, who is believed to have been a mutual friend of Lincoln and Douglas. It is furnished in period style.

Hours
Daily from 9 A.M. to 5 P.M. from March to October and from 8 A.M. to 4 P.M. the rest of the year
Admission
Free; donations are accepted

Bryant Cottage State Historic Site

Travelogue

National Museum of Health and Medicine

Walter Reed Army Medical Center, Building 54
6825 16th Street NW
Washington, DC 20306-6000
202-782-2200

Established in Civil War days as the United States Army Medical Museum, this facility interprets various aspects of medicine and health. Included in its vast collections are locks of Abraham Lincoln's hair and fragments of the bullets that killed him.

The museum will eventually be moved to the south side of the National Mall.

Hours
Daily from 10:30 A.M. to 5 P.M.
Admission
Free

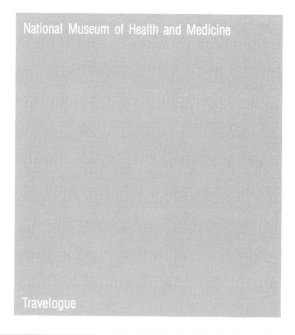

National Museum of Health and Medicine

Travelogue

National Portrait Gallery

Washington, DC

See Sites Related to Multiple Presidents on pages 259–60.

Mount Rushmore National Memorial

Keystone, SD

See Sites Related to Multiple Presidents on pages 254–55.

Surratt House and Tavern

9110 Brandywine Road
P.O. Box 427
Clinton, MD 20735
301-868-1121
www.clark.net/pub/surratt/surratt.html

Even though Lincoln never visited this place, it is one of the most fascinating historical sites related to his life. The 1852 home of Mary Surratt was the first stop of John Wilkes Booth after he fatally shot the president. Surratt, the mother of one of Booth's friends, was accused of having a major role in the assassination and as such was the first woman to be executed in this country. Debate over her role continues to this day.

The museum presents programs and exhibits related to 19th-century life and the fascinating web of conspiracy surrounding Lincoln's assassination. A popular event is the John Wilkes Booth Escape Route Tour, a 12-hour bus tour from Washington, D.C., to Garrett's Farm in Virginia. The tour follows many of the same roads Booth traveled and stops at many of the sites he visited on his 12-day journey as a fugitive. The tour costs $45 and is offered numerous times throughout the year, call for details.

Hours

Thursday and Friday from 11 A.M. to 3 P.M. and Saturday and Sunday from noon to 4 P.M. from March 1 to December 15

Admission

$3 for adults; $2 for seniors; $1 for ages five to 18

Surratt House and Tavern

Travelogue

Andrew Johnson

Seventeenth President of the United States

Birthplace

Mordecai Historic Park
Capital Area Preservation, Inc.
1 Mimosa Street
Raleigh, NC 27604-1297
919-834-4844
www.visitnc.com/cat/visitnc/record/TPN733.htm

Andrew Johnson was born December 29, 1808, in the loft of one of the two kitchens serving Peter Casso's inn; both of Johnson's parents worked at the inn. By the time Johnson was three, his father had died while trying to save a drowning swimmer. His mother raised the future president and his older brother, William, in extreme poverty.

When Johnson was 14, his mother indentured both boys to a local tailor, who provided them food, clothing, and lessons in the tailoring trade in return for work. After two years, however, the boys ran away. The tailor placed an ad in the local newspaper offering a $10 reward to anyone who would return the boys or $10 to Andrew Johnson if he would return alone. The two fled to Carthage, North Carolina, and later to Laurens, South Carolina. A year later—in 1826—Andrew Johnson returned to Raleigh, where he joined his mother and stepfather in a move to Greeneville, Tennessee. Upon arriving in Greeneville, they found that the local tailor was retiring. Johnson, then 17 years old, opened his own tailor shop.

Johnson's birthplace was moved four times before coming to its current site in 1976. Today, Mordecai Historic Park includes the Johnson birthplace; Mordecai House, an antebellum plantation home complete with outbuildings; St. Mark's Chapel, constructed in 1847; and the Badger-Iredell law offices, which date from 1810. The park is about 150 yards from the North Carolina State Capitol, on the grounds of which a Charles Keck statue entitled *The Three Presidents* honors Johnson, Andrew Jackson, and James Knox Polk, the three presidents born in North Carolina.

Hours
Monday, Wednesday, Thursday, Friday, and Saturday from 10 A.M. to 4 P.M. and Sunday from 1 to 4 P.M.
Admission
Free

Mordecai Historic Park

Travelogue

Home

Andrew Johnson National Historic Site
National Park Service
College and Depot Streets
P.O. Box 1088
Greeneville, TN 37744
423-638-3551
www.nps.gov/anjo

Andrew Johnson's first home in Greeneville

This site includes Andrew Johnson National Cemetery, a visitor center, a museum, a tailor shop, and two houses that Johnson occupied—an early home and his later homestead. On the grounds of the homestead is a willow tree that Johnson planted from a shoot taken from the island of St. Helena, where Napoleon was exiled. Johnson's devotion to democracy is communicated on the marker over his grave on the crest of Monument Hill in Andrew Johnson National Cemetery. The visitor center and the early home have interpretive exhibits.

One of the favorite local stories about Johnson concerns his homecoming after he refused to attend the inauguration of Ulysses S. Grant. He returned to find a banner hung over Greeneville's main street that read, "Andrew Johnson, Patriot." It was only eight years earlier that Johnson's loyalty to the Union during the Civil War had led the townspeople to hang a banner reading, "Andrew Johnson, Traitor."

Johnson remained active in Democratic politics during his retirement. He remains the

Andrew Johnson's second home in Greeneville

only former president to return to service in the United States Senate.

Hours
Daily from 9 A.M. to 5 P.M.; closed New Year's, Thanksgiving, and Christmas. Tours of the homestead are offered hourly between 9:30 A.M. and 4:30 P.M.; tickets are available at the visitor center and must be purchased no later than 15 minutes prior to the tour.

Admission
$2 for adults; guests over 61 and under 18 are free

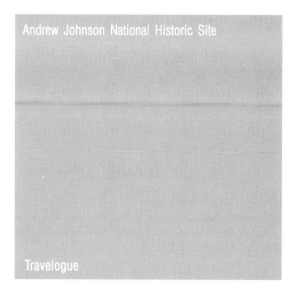
Andrew Johnson National Historic Site

Travelogue

Education

Johnson never attended school. While the future president was an apprentice tailor, two men—the shop foreman, James Litchfield, and a Dr. Hill—would read aloud to the workers as they labored. Johnson was fascinated by the great orations he heard. Recognizing the young man's appetite for knowledge, Dr. Hill gave him a book as a present. Johnson leafed through it late into the night at home and taught himself to read.

Marriage

Johnson wed Eliza McCardle on May 17, 1827, at the bride's home in Greeneville. Age 16 at the time, she married younger than any other future first lady. Ill with "slow consumption" by the time they moved into the White House, Mrs. Johnson was confined to her room and left social responsibilities to their daughter. She attended only two social events during her husband's presidency: an 1866 reception for Queen Emma of the Sandwich Islands (Hawaii) and a birthday party for her husband in 1867.

Inaugural Site

Johnson took the oath of office on the morning of April 15, 1865, in his room at Kirkwood House shortly after Lincoln's death. Chief Justice Salmon Chase administered the oath in the presence of most of the cabinet.

A co-conspirator of John Wilkes Booth's had been assigned to murder Johnson at Kirkwood House at the same time Lincoln was shot. The plan, however, was foiled.

Kirkwood House no longer exists.

Place of Death

On the afternoon of July 28, 1875, Johnson suffered a stroke while on a visit to the home of his daughter in Carter Station, Tennessee. The stroke left him partially paralyzed. He regained consciousness and ordered that no doctor be called. The following day, he suffered a second stroke. He died two days later, on July 31.

Funeral

A Masonic funeral service was held for Johnson on August 3, 1875, at the old Greeneville Court House, which no longer exists. At Johnson's request, his body was wrapped in an American flag and his head rested upon a copy of the United States Constitution. The casket was closed, however, because the body had begun to decompose.

Burial Site

Andrew Johnson National Historic Site
Greeneville, TN

See page 108.

Other Sites

Blair House
Washington, DC

See Sites Related to Multiple Presidents on pages 251–52.

The Three Presidents Statue
Raleigh, NC

See page 107; *see* Sites Related to Multiple Presidents on page 255.

Ulysses S. Grant

Eighteenth President of the United States

Birthplace

Grant Birthplace
Ohio Historical Society
P.O. Box 2
New Richmond, OH 45157
513-553-4911
www.ohiohistory.org/places/grantbir/

Grant was born Hiram Ulysses Grant on April 27, 1822, in a three-room cabin adjacent to the tannery where his father worked. In his teenage years, he unofficially changed his name to Ulysses H. Grant, thinking it would not be good to have the initials *H. U. G.* on his trunk at West Point. Representative Thomas Hammer, who had arranged for Grant to attend West Point, erroneously wrote his name as Ulysses Simpson Grant. Grant liked it and so retained it.

His birthplace is just off US 52 about five miles east of New Richmond. The restored cabin is furnished in period style. It once toured nationwide on a railroad car and was exhibited at the Ohio State Fair.

Hours
Wednesday through Saturday from 9:30 A.M. to 5 P.M. and Sunday from noon to 5 P.M. from April to October

Admission
$1 for adults; $.75 for senior citizens; $.50 for ages six to 12

Grant Birthplace

Travelogue

Homes

Ulysses S. Grant National Historic Site
National Park Service
7400 Grant Road
St. Louis, MO 63123
314-842-1867
www.nps.gov/ulsg/index.htm

Grant lived in this home, known as White Haven, in the years before the Civil War. The site includes five buildings: the main house, a stone building, a barn, a chicken house, and an icehouse.

Hours
Daily from 9 A.M. to 5 P.M.; closed New Year's, Thanksgiving, and Christmas
Admission
Free

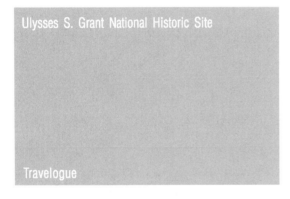

Ulysses S. Grant National Historic Site

Travelogue

Ulysses S. Grant Home State Historic Site

Illinois Historic Preservation Agency
500 Bouthillier Street
Galena, IL 61036
815-777-0248
www.state.il.us/hps/GRANT.HTM

The citizens of Galena, Illinois, presented this handsome Italianate home, built in 1860, to Grant in 1865 upon his return from the Civil War. After his election as president in 1868, Grant spent little time here. He once said, "Although it is probable I will never live much time among you, but in the future be only a visitor as I am at present . . . I hope to retain my residence here. . . . I expect to cast my votes here."

Ulysses S. Grant Home State Historic Site
Courtesy of Illinois Historic Preservation Agency

In 1904, Grant's children left the home to the city of Galena to be preserved as a memorial. In 1931, the city deeded the property to the state of Illinois. In 1955, the home was refurbished to its 1868 appearance. Ninety percent of the furnishings are original.

Hours
Daily from 9 A.M. to 5 P.M.; closed major holidays
Admission
Free; donations are accepted

Ulysses S. Grant Home State Historic Site

Travelogue

Ulysses S. Grant Cottage State Historic Site
Photo by Beverly Clark

Ulysses S. Grant Cottage State Historic Site

Mount McGregor
Wilton, NY
Mailing Address:
Friends of Grant Cottage
P.O. Box 990
Saratoga Springs, NY 12866
518-587-8277

Here, at the summit of Mount McGregor, Grant spent the last weeks of his life completing his memoirs. He died on July 23, 1885, surrounded by his family in the parlor of this Adirondack cottage.

To reach the site, take Exit 16 off I-87 and follow the markers. The furnishings and personal effects remain as they were when Grant was here.

Hours

Wednesday through Sunday from 10 A.M. to 4 P.M. from Memorial Day to Labor Day; weekends only from 10 A.M. to 4 P.M. from Labor Day to Columbus Day

Admission

$2.50 for adults; $2 for senior citizens; $1 for ages six to 16; members and children five and under are free

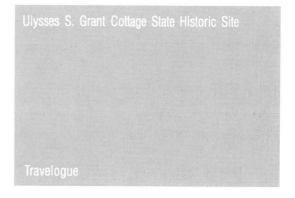

Ulysses S. Grant Cottage State Historic Site

Travelogue

Education

Grant Schoolhouse

Grant Homestead Association
Water Street
Georgetown, OH 45121
937-378-4222
www.ohiohistory.org/places/grantsch

Grant was six years old when his family moved to Georgetown, Ohio. He attended this school until he was 13. His teacher, John White, was so impressed with Grant that he included him in his memoirs. The schoolhouse was built in 1829. At the time of Grant's attendance, it had one room.

The schoolhouse may be visited today by appointment.

Grant Schoolhouse

Travelogue

Grant attended Maysville Seminary in 1836 and 1837 and Presbyterian Academy in 1838 and 1839. Neither exists today.

United States Military Academy
West Point, NY

See Sites Related to Multiple Presidents on page 248.

Marriage

Grant married Julia Boggs Dent on August 22, 1848, at the bride's St. Louis home.

Significant Civil War Sites

Vicksburg National Military Park
National Park Service
3201 Clay Street
Vicksburg, MS 39180
601-636-0583
www.nps.gov/htdocs4/vick

In 1862, General Grant and the Federal troops cleared Confederate resistance at Vicksburg and nearby Port Hudson. This was a vital stretch of the 1,000-mile Mississippi River front between the forces. During the 47-day siege of Vicksburg, area residents sought safety by living in caves.

The site includes a visitor center, programs, and exhibitions. Also within the park is the USS *Cairo* Gunboat and Museum, which interprets the service of a Union ironclad gunboat sunk by torpedoes in December 1862.

Hours
Daily from 9:30 A.M. to 6 P.M. from April to October and from 8:30 A.M. to 5 P.M. from November to March; closed Christmas
Admission
$4 per vehicle; $2 per noncommercial bus passenger

Vicksburg National Military Park

Travelogue

Fort Donelson National Battlefield

National Park Service
US 79
Dover, TN 37058-0434
615-232-5706
www.nps.gov/fodo

This was the site of the first Union victory in the Civil War. Grant's plan was to gain control of the Mississippi Valley, thereby bisecting the South. The initial battle took place on February 13, 1862, and had no clear outcome. The following day, reinforcements arrived that increased the Union force from 15,000 to 27,000 troops. After some Confederates escaped under cover of darkness, Grant issued his order: "No terms except unconditional and immediate surrender." As a result, 13,000 Confederates were taken as prisoners of war.

Among the restored sites in the park is the Dover Hotel, in which Confederate general Simon Buckner surrendered to Grant. Also on the premises are Fort Donelson National Cemetery, Fort Donelson, and a visitor center.

Hours
Daily from 8 A.M. to 4:30 P.M.; closed Christmas
Admission
Free

Fort Donelson National Battlefield

Travelogue

Shiloh National Military Park

National Park Service
Route 1, Box 9
Shiloh, TN 38376
901-689-5696
www.nps.gov/shil

Following their defeat at Fort Donelson, Confederates under General Albert Johnston surprised General Grant's Union forces, pushing them back two miles. Once Union reinforcements arrived, Grant led them in an assault that drove the Confederates into Mississippi. Following the Battle of Shiloh, Grant stated that he "gave up all idea of saving the Union except by complete conquest."

A 25-minute film is shown in the visitor center. Rental audiotapes are available for self-guided auto tours.

Hours
Daily from 8 A.M. to 6 P.M.; closed Christmas
Admission
$2 per individual; $4 per family

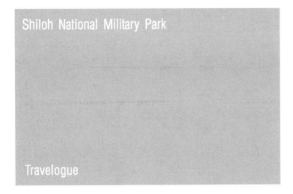

Shiloh National Military Park

Travelogue

Hours
Daily from 8 A.M. to 4:45 P.M.; closed
Christmas
Admission
$3 for adults; $1.50 for guests under 17
and over 62

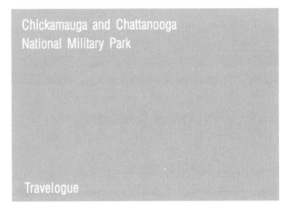

Chickamauga and Chattanooga
National Military Park

Travelogue

Chickamauga and Chattanooga National Military Park

National Park Service
3370 Lafayette Road
P.O. Box 2128
Fort Oglethorpe, GA 30742
706-866-9241
www.nps.gov/chch

Most of this 8,113-acre park, the oldest and largest administered by the National Park Service, is in Georgia; the balance is in Tennessee. Several areas within the park commemorate Civil War battles that occurred around Chattanooga, a major transportation hub of the day. Orchard Knob, General Grant's headquarters during the Battle of Chattanooga, has been restored.

The Battle of Chattanooga began on November 23, 1863, when Union forces under General Grant forced the Confederates back to Missionary Ridge. On the third day of the battle, the Federals dislodged the Confederates, opening the way for the Union assault on Atlanta.

Petersburg National Battlefield

National Park Service
1539 Hickory Hill Road
Petersburg, VA 23803
804-732-3531
www.nps.gov/htdocs4/pete

Early in the war, Dr. Richard Eppes left Appomattox Manor, his plantation home, to become a Confederate surgeon in Petersburg, leaving his wife and children at the plantation. In 1862, however, Union gunboats on the James River forced the Eppes family to evacuate to the safety of Petersburg. In subsequent years, Appomattox Manor was repeatedly shelled and vandalized.

During General Grant's push to take Richmond in 1864, he moved his headquarters from Washington to Appomattox Manor, setting up his tent on the east lawn. As winter set in and it appeared that taking Petersburg and Richmond would require more time than anticipated, the Army of the Potomac built log cabins on the property. President Lincoln visited Grant at this site at least twice.

Upon his return to Appomattox Manor following the war, Dr. Eppes was forced to borrow money in order to pay the United States government before he could dismantle and remove the Union army warehouses and cabins from his land.

Hours
Daily from 8 A.M. to 5 P.M.; closed New Year's and Christmas
Admission
$5 during the summer months; $4 the rest of the year; admission to Appomattox Manor is $1

Petersburg National Battlefield

Travelogue

Appomattox Court House National Historical Park
National Park Service
VA 24
P.O. Box 218
Appomattox, VA 24522
804-352-8987
www.nps.gov/apco

Before the Civil War, Wilmer McLean lived on a farm at Bull Run, Virginia. Frustrated by the devastation of his home during the opening days of the war, he moved to Appomattox Court House, where he thought he could live in peace. On April 9, 1865, General Robert E. Lee's weakened Confederate forces were overcome by Union troops under General Grant. Grant and Lee met that afternoon in the parlor of McLean's house at Appomattox Court House, where Lee surrendered. McLean's homes were thus the settings for both the start and the end of the war.

Memorial tablets note the headquarters of both Grant and Lee at Appomattox, the sites from which Confederate troops fired their last

Appomattox Court House
Courtesy of Appomattox Court House National Historical Park

shots, and the locations where arms were laid down. The courthouse burned in 1892; a replica was built on the site in 1964. The McLean House was dismantled in 1893 by a group of speculators, who planned to move it to the nation's capital and rebuild it there. The plan failed, and the materials fell prey to the weather and souvenir hunters. The National Park Service has since built a replica on that site, too. The 1,694-acre site now includes 27 restored or rebuilt buildings, including Meeks' Store, the Woodson law office, Clover Hill Tavern, the county jail, the Kelly House, the Mariah Wright House, Surrender Triangle, the Isbell House, the Peers House, and many outbuildings. During the summer months, historical reenactors interact with visitors.

Hours
Daily from 9 A.M. to 5:30 P.M. from June to August and from 8:30 A.M. to 5 P.M. the rest of the year; closed New Year's, Martin Luther King Day, Presidents' Day, Thanksgiving, and Christmas
Admission
$4 from Memorial Day through Labor Day; $2 the rest of the year; guests under 17 are free

Appomattox Court House National Historical Park

Travelogue

Inaugural Site

The Capitol
Washington, DC

March 4, 1869
March 4, 1873

Place of Death/Funeral

Ulysses S. Grant Cottage State Historic Site
Mount McGregor, NY

See page 113.

Burial Site

General Grant National Memorial (Grant's Tomb)
National Park Service
122nd Street at Riverside Drive
New York, NY 10003
212-666-1640
www.nps.gov/gegr

Although most of his funeral plans were completed years before his death, Grant was undecided on his place of burial. He ruled out West Point because his wife could not be buried there with him. He finally accepted the invitation of New York's mayor, W. R. Grace, to be buried in a city park. Grant selected the location.

Following funeral services at the Mount McGregor cottage on August 4, 1885, a special train took Grant's body to the New York State Capitol and then to New York City Hall, where it lay in state. On August 8, an estimated million people lined the route to the site of Grant's Tomb, where a temporary brick structure had been built to hold Grant's body until the palatial mausoleum could be completed two years later.

This is the largest mausoleum in North America, rising 150 feet from its Hudson River bluff location. Its construction required hundreds of workers and more than 8,000 tons of granite. An extensive collection of Grant artifacts is on display in the museum. A small gift shop is open daily.

Grant's Tomb
Photo by Ian Ferris

Hours
Daily from 9 A.M. to 5 P.M.; closed New Year's, Thanksgiving, and Christmas
Admission
Free

General Grant National Memorial

Travelogue

Other Sites

Hall of Fame for Great Americans
Bronx, NY

See Sites Related to Multiple Presidents on page 258.

Old State Capitol State Historic Site
Springfield, IL

See Sites Related to Multiple Presidents on page 260.

Quartermaster Museum
Fort Lee, VA

See Sites Related to Multiple Presidents on pages 260–61.

Rutherford B. Hayes

Nineteenth President of the United States

Birthplace

Rutherford B. Hayes was born in his family's home on Williams Street in Delaware, Ohio, on October 4, 1822. The building no longer exists.

Home

Rutherford B. Hayes Presidential Center

Spiegel Grove
Fremont, OH 43420-2796
419-332-2081

Hayes retired following a single term as president, after which he and wife, Lucy, returned to Fremont. He died here on January 17, 1893, of a heart attack while in the arms of his son Webb. President-Elect Grover Cleveland attended funeral services here.

The Rutherford B. Hayes Presidential Center is the site of the nation's first presidential library and museum. The center opened May 30, 1916. It includes the two-story Hayes Museum and Library, which contains Hayes's diaries, presidential papers, books, and family possessions; Spiegel Grove, the president's 25-acre estate; the Hayes Home, a stately, 31-room brick house con-

taining original furnishings belonging to the president and his family; and the Hayes Tomb, the burial site of President and Mrs. Hayes. The center is surrounded by iron fencing that includes gates from the original White House.

Hours
Monday through Saturday from 9 A.M. to 5 P.M. and Sunday from noon to 5 P.M. The library is closed Sundays; the center is closed New Year's, Easter, Thanksgiving, and Christmas.

Admission
$5 for adults; $4 for guests over 60; $1.25 for ages six to 12; admission to the library is free

Rutherford B. Hayes Presidential Center

Travelogue

Rutherford B. Hayes Presidential Center
Photo by Gilbert Gonzalez

Education

Hayes learned the fundamentals from Daniel Granger in Delaware, Ohio, Jonah Chaplin in Norwalk, Ohio, and Isaac Webb in Middletown, Connecticut.

Kenyon College
Gambier, OH 43072
740-427-5000
www.kenyon.edu

Hayes was the valedictorian of Kenyon College's class of 1842. As a student, he occupied the "East Wing Bull's-Eye"—the front fourth-floor room of the east wing of Old Kenyon.

Old Kenyon, the first building on the Kenyon College campus, was designed by Charles Bulfinch and opened in 1829. The east and west wings were added in 1834 and

1836, respectively. Hayes's room, approximately 15 feet by 18 feet in size, was vacant and closed for many years. According to the *Gambier Weekly Argus* of September 21, 1876, adventurous students were known to sneak into the historic room by requesting permission to visit the belfry, then taking a detour through the long, dark attic. Eventually, the wall separating Hayes's room from the attic was broken.

Harvard University School of Law
Cambridge, MA

See Sites Related to Multiple Presidents on pages 246–47.

Marriage

Hayes married Lucy Ware Webb on December 30, 1852, at the bride's home in Cincinnati. The Hayeses celebrated their 25th anniversary by renewing their vows at a White

House celebration attended by many of the guests who had wished them well at the Cincinnati ceremony a quarter of a century earlier.

Inaugural Site

The Capitol
Washington, DC

March 5, 1877

Place of Death/Funeral/Burial Site

Spiegel Grove
Fremont, OH

See Rutherford B. Hayes Presidential Center on page 120.

Other Site

Blair House
Washington, DC

See Sites Related to Multiple Presidents on pages 251–52.

James A. Garfield
Twentieth President of the United States

Birthplace

The last of the log-cabin presidents, James A. Garfield was born November 19, 1831, in a cabin built by his grandfather in Orange, Ohio, just southeast of Cleveland. He spent most of his boyhood there. The cabin no longer exists.

Garfield's father died when the future president was 18 months old, leaving his mother to raise him.

Home

James A. Garfield National Historic Site
National Park Service
8095 Mentor Avenue
Mentor, OH 44060
440-255-8722
www.nps.gov.jaga

Garfield bought this estate in 1876 in order to accommodate his large family. It was here that he mounted his famous 1880 "front porch" campaign for the presidency. In fact, local reporters dubbed the place "Lawnfield."

Four years after Garfield's death, his widow had a memorial-library wing built, setting the stage for future presidential libraries. The home has recently been reopened following a $12 million renovation that restored it to its 1880s splendor. Throughout the visitor center are sensor-activated displays interpreting Garfield's life. The home is open for guided tours.

Hours
Monday through Saturday from 10 A.M. to 5 P.M. and Sunday from noon to 5 P.M.; closed major holidays
Admission
$6 for adults; $5 for seniors; $4 for ages six to 12

James A. Garfield National Historic Site

Travelogue

James A. Garfield National Historic Site
Courtesy of National Park Service

Education

Garfield dreamed of becoming a sailor and at age 16 went to the docks in Cleveland, where he tried to sign up with a ship. He wound up joining the crew of the *Evening Star*, a canal boat owned by a cousin. During his brief time aboard the vessel, which shuttled between Cleveland and Pittsburgh, he fell overboard 14 times. Never having learned to swim, Garfield took the advice of his mother and left the job in favor of returning to school.

During 1849 and 1850, he worked his way through Geauga Academy in Chester, Ohio, by doing carpentry work in nearby Solon.

Hiram College
P.O. Box 67
Hiram, OH 44234
330-569-3211
www.hiram.edu

Garfield studied at Hiram College (then called Western Reserve Eclectic Institute) for three years before finishing his studies at Williams College. During this time at Western Reserve, he held jobs as a janitor and teacher in the communities of Warrensville and Blue Rock, Ohio. Following his graduation from Williams, he returned to Western Reserve, where he joined the faculty and eventually became president. Garfield is credited with expanding the scope of the college to include the full range of the liberal arts and with dramatically raising the school's standards.

Williams College
Williamstown, MA 01267
413-597-3131
www.williams.edu

Garfield was much influenced by a speech by Ralph Waldo Emerson he heard at Williams and by the college's president, Mark Hopkins. In later years, Garfield expressed his admiration for Hopkins this way: "The ideal college is Mark Hopkins on one end of a log and a student on the other." Garfield might have admired a later Williams president even more. His son Harry Augustus Garfield held that title from 1908 until 1934.

As a student, Garfield was the school's debating champion and the president of the Philologian Society and the Mills Theological Society. He was also editor of the *Williams Quarterly*. He graduated with honors in 1856 and delivered the "Metaphysical Oration" at commencement.

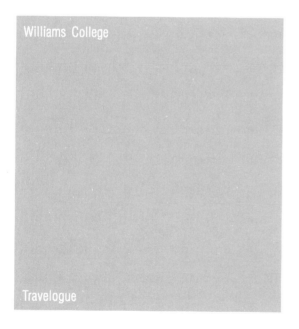

Williams College

Travelogue

Marriage

Garfield married Lucretia "Crete" Randolph on November 11, 1858, at the home of the bride's parents in Hiram, Ohio.

Inaugural Site

The Capitol
Washington, DC

March 4, 1881

Place of Death

On July 2, 1881, Garfield was in the Baltimore and Potomac Railroad Station in Washington when he was shot by Charles Guiteau. Guiteau was seeking revenge for not being appointed to a government position and believed his rejection was solely Garfield's fault.

Following the shooting, Garfield was treated at the White House by a team of doctors led by D. W. Bliss and including J. K. Barnes, J. J. Woodward, Robert Reyburn, D. W. Agnew, and F. H. Hamilton. In their efforts to locate and remove a bullet, the doctors repeatedly put their unwashed fingers and medical instruments into one of Garfield's wounds. As a result, the president became badly infected. That infection, combined with possible blood poisoning from the bullet, severely weakened Garfield's body. Thinking that the sea air would help him recover, he took a special train to the town of Elberon on the New Jersey shore, where he died on September 19.

Burial Site

Lakeview Cemetery
12316 Euclid Avenue
Clcveland, OH 44106
216-421-2665

Garfield's imposing monument sits atop a hill in this famous cemetery. Also included on the 285-acre grounds are the graves of United States senator Mark Hanna, John D. Rockefeller, and John Hay, who served as secretary of state under President McKinley.

Hours
Daily from 7:30 A.M. to 5:30 P.M.
Admission
Free

Chester A. Arthur

Twenty-First President of the United States

Birthplace

Chester A. Arthur Birthplace
Off VT 36 and VT 108
East Fairfield, VT 05448
802-933-8362

Chester A. Arthur was born October 5, 1829, in a temporary parsonage. The present structure is a replica that contains exhibits interpreting Arthur's life and presidency.

Arthur's father was a Baptist minister who was transferred from parish to parish throughout the future president's childhood. In Vermont, the family lived in Fairfield, Williston, and Hinesburg. The church the elder Arthur served in Fairfield is on a hillside near the presidential birthplace and is open to visitors. In New York, the family lived in Perry, York Union Village (now Greenwich), Schenectady, and Hoosick.

During Arthur's presidency, opponents claimed that he was actually born in Canada and was thereby ineligible to hold the office. The claim was dismissed by Arthur.

<u>Hours</u>
Wednesday through Saturday from 9 A.M. to 5 P.M. from June to Columbus Day
<u>Admission</u>
Free

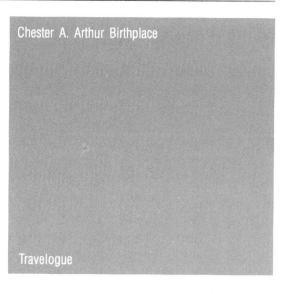

Chester A. Arthur Birthplace

Travelogue

Home

Arthur retired from the presidency to his home at 123 Lexington Avenue in New York City, now a private residence not open to the public.

Church

St. John's Lafayette Square
Washington, DC

See Sites Related to Multiple Presidents on pages 243–44.

Education

Arthur attended the Lyceum in Schenectady, New York. The school no longer exists.

Union College
Union Street
Schenectady, NY 12308
518-388-6000
www.union.edu

Arthur entered Union as a sophomore in 1845. Of modest financial means, he worked his way through college by teaching school in nearby Schaghticoke during winter vacations. He also accepted money from the college's indigent student fund to help defray his $28 tuition and $125 room-and-board fees.

During that time, there existed in Schenectady a strong town-and-gown rivalry that occasionally turned physical. Arthur, being a local resident, frequently found himself caught in the middle. On one occasion, he fought "like a tiger" in a brawl between townspeople and Union people, according to a local newspaper. There is no record of the fight's outcome.

At his graduation in 1848, Arthur gave an oration entitled "The Destiny of Genius."

While at Union, Arthur carved his initials into a library window sill. That portion of the sill was removed and is preserved in the college's archives. A popular site on campus today is a statue of Arthur located near the entrance to Jackson Gardens.

Statue of Chester A. Arthur on the campus of Union College
Courtesy of Union College

After his graduation from Union College, Arthur studied law in the New York office of E. D. Culver.

Union College

Travelogue

Marriage

Calvary Episcopal Church
61 Gramercy Park North
New York, NY 10010-5401
212-475-1216

Arthur married Ellen "Nell" Lewis Herndon here on October 25, 1859.

Calvary Episcopal Church in New York City
Photo by Ian Ferris

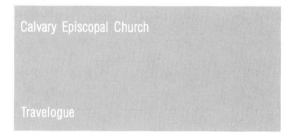

Calvary Episcopal Church

Travelogue

Inaugural Sites

New York Supreme Court judge John R. Brady administered the oath of office in Arthur's New York City home on September 9, 1881. The following day, Morrison Waite, the chief justice of the United States Supreme Court, administered the oath in the vice president's office in the Capitol in Washington.

Place of Death

Suffering from the then-fatal Bright's disease, Arthur was confined to his bed during his last few months. Although he assured visitors he would be fine, he ordered that all the personal and professional papers in his possession be burned. He suffered a stroke on the night of November 16, 1886, that left him partially paralyzed. He never regained consciousness. He died at his home on Lexington Avenue in New York—now a private residence not open to the public—on November 18.

Funeral

Church of the Heavenly Rest
Fifth Avenue at 90th Street
New York, NY 10128-0674
212-289-3400
www.metanoi.org/chr

The pallbearers at Arthur's funeral included Robert T. Lincoln, General Philip H. Sheridan, Charles L. Tiffany, and Cornelius Vanderbilt.

Church of the Heavenly Rest

Travelogue

Burial Site

Albany Rural Cemetery
Cemetery Avenue
Albany, NY 12204
518-463-7017

Arthur is buried beside his wife in the Arthur family plot. Albany Rural Cemetery is listed on the National Register of Historic Places.

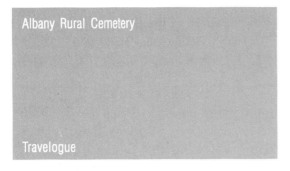

Other Sites

Arthur Cottage
Cullybackey, Ireland
011-44 (0) 1266-44111

The Arthur family's ancestral home, a country cottage atop Gourley's Hill, has been preserved as a historic site. The town's connection to Arthur is promoted locally.

Alan and Eliza Arthur (Chester's grandparents) were living here when William Arthur (Chester's father) was born December 5, 1797. William Arthur and numerous relatives came to the United States between 1816 and 1820.

The cottage may be visited Monday through Friday from 10:30 A.M. to 5 P.M. and Saturday from 10:30 A.M. to 4 P.M.

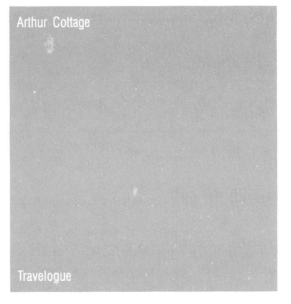

Blair House
Washington, DC

See Sites Related to Multiple Presidents on pages 251–52.

Grover Cleveland
Twenty-Second and Twenty-Fourth President of the United States

Birthplace

Grover Cleveland Birthplace State Historic Site
Grover Cleveland Park
207 Bloomfield Avenue
Caldwell, NJ 07066-5115
201-226-1810
caldwellnj.com/gcpark.htm

Grover Cleveland was born in this house, then a Presbyterian manse, in 1837 and lived here until 1840. The home contains many of his personal possessions. Adjacent is St. Aloysius Church, where Cleveland's father served as pastor.

Hours
Wednesday through Friday from 9 A.M. to 6 P.M., Saturday from 9 A.M. to 5 P.M., and Sunday from noon to 5 P.M.; closed major holidays. It is suggested that visitors call ahead.
Admission
Free

Grover Cleveland Birthplace State Historic Site

Travelogue

Homes

Cleveland, the son of a Presbyterian minister, moved frequently throughout his childhood. When he was four, his family moved to Fayetteville, New York. It moved to Clinton, New York, 10 years later and to Holland Patent, New York, a few years after that.

Westland
15 Hodge Road
Princeton, NJ 08540

During the last year of Cleveland's second term, he and his wife decided to settle in Princeton following his retirement from the presidency. Mrs. Cleveland selected this house, which had been built by Commodore Robert F. Stockton. Cleveland named it Westland in honor of his friend Andrew F. West, a Princeton professor.

Although Cleveland never attended college, he maintained an active involvement with Princeton throughout his retirement. He was elected to Princeton's board of trustees in 1901 and became board chairman three years later. In that position, he frequently fought with university president Woodrow Wilson over policy issues. Princeton students serenaded Cleveland at Westland every year on his birthday. After football games in which Princeton was the victor, a parade would often wind up at Westland. Cleveland's home hosted regular gatherings of what the former president called "The Poverty Club," a group of card-playing friends.

Westland is currently a private residence and may not be visited by the public.

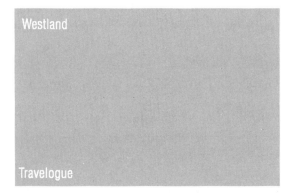

Westland

Travelogue

Church

National Presbyterian Church
Washington, DC

See Sites Related to Multiple Presidents on page 242.

Education

Cleveland was educated in public schools in Fayetteville and Clinton, New York. He did not attend college but studied law in the Buffalo offices of Rogers, Bowen, and Rogers. He was admitted to the New York Bar in 1859.

Marriage

The White House
Washington, DC

Cleveland, the only president to marry in the White House, wed Frances Folsom, the daughter of one of his original law partners, on June 2, 1886.

Inaugural Site

The Capitol
Washington, DC

March 4, 1885
March 4, 1893

Place of Death/Funeral

Westland
Princeton, NJ

Cleveland's health declined steadily during his last year. He was often bedridden for weeks at a time. On June 23, 1908, he suffered a heart attack. He died the following day. Simple funeral services were conducted by the Reverend Henry Van Dyke at Westland (see page 131).

Burial Site

Princeton Cemetery
Witherspoon and Wiggins Streets
Princeton, NJ 08540
609-924-1369

This historic cemetery contains the remains of Cleveland, John Witherspoon, Aaron Burr, and Paul Tulane.

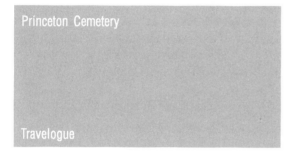

Princeton Cemetery

Travelogue

Other Sites

Hall of Fame for Great Americans
Bronx, NY

See Sites Related to Multiple Presidents on page 258.

Princeton University
Princeton, NJ

See Sites Related to Multiple Presidents on pages 247–48.

Benjamin Harrison

Twenty-Third President of the United States

Birthplace

Benjamin Harrison was born in 1833 on the 600-acre North Bend, Ohio, farm of his grandfather William Henry Harrison. At the time, the elder Harrison was briefly retired, having served in the United States House of Representatives and Senate and as minister to Colombia. Around the time of his 1840 election to the presidency, the elder Harrison deeded the farm to Benjamin's father.

The birthplace is off US 50 near William Henry Harrison's tomb. A historical marker at the side of the road is all that currently marks the spot.

Home

President Benjamin Harrison Home
1230 North Delaware Street
Indianapolis, IN 46202-2531
317-631-1898

Harrison moved from his home state of Ohio to Indianapolis in 1854 to pursue a successful law career. He lived in this house from the 1870s until his death in 1901. It was from this home that he initiated his "front porch" presidential campaign in 1888.

The restored house is operated as a historic site by the President Benjamin Harrison Home Foundation.

Hours
Monday through Saturday from 10 A.M. to 3:30 P.M. and Sunday from 12:30 to 3:30 P.M. Tours are conducted on the hour and half-hour.
Admission
$5 for adults; $4 for seniors; $1 for guests under 18; preschool children are free

President Benjamin Harrison Home

Travelogue

President Benjamin Harrison Home
Photo courtesy of the President Benjamin Harrison Home

Church

Southport First Presbyterian Church
1427 Southview Drive
Indianapolis, IN 46227-5027
317-788-5925

Harrison was elected a deacon in 1857 and an elder in 1861. He taught Sunday-school classes and organized adult Bible-study classes here.

Education

Harrison attended Farmers' College preparatory school from 1847 to 1850. The school no longer exists.

Miami University of Ohio
21 North Campus Drive
Oxford, OH 45056-1303
513-529-1541
www.muohio.edu

Harrison was admitted as a junior in 1850 and graduated in 1852. He was one of the speakers at his graduation, although his name was misspelled in the commencement program.

Harrison went on to study law in the Cincinnati offices of Storer and Gwynne and was admitted to the Ohio Bar in 1854.

Marriages

Harrison married Caroline Lavinia Scott in the bride's home in Oxford, Ohio, on October 20, 1853. She died in October 1892.

On April 6, 1896, Harrison wed Mary Scott Lord Dimmick in New York City.

Inaugural Site

The Capitol
Washington, DC

March 4, 1889

Place of Death

President Benjamin Harrison Home
Indianapolis, IN

In early 1901, Harrison caught the flu, which developed into pneumonia. Medications were ineffective, and he slipped into a coma on March 12. He died quietly at home (see pages 134–35) the following day.

Funeral

Southport First Presbyterian Church
Indianapolis, IN

After Harrison's body lay in state in the Indiana Statehouse, funeral services were held at Southport First Presbyterian (see page 135), where poet James Whitcomb Riley delivered the eulogy.

Burial Site

Crown Hill Cemetery
408 Short Street
Indianapolis, IN 47330-1053
317-855-2781

Crown Hill, the nation's third-largest cemetery, is on the National Register of Historic Places. Its self-guided tours are popular; call for details.

Hours
Open from dawn to dusk
Admission
Free

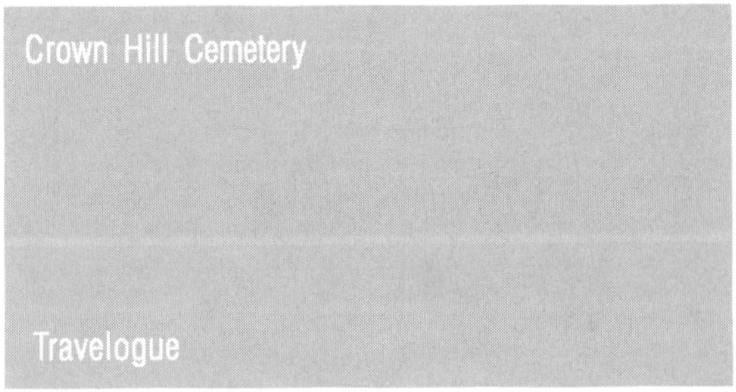

Crown Hill Cemetery

Travelogue

William McKinley

Twenty-Fifth President of the United States

Birthplace

National McKinley Birthplace Memorial

McKinley Memorial Library
40 North Main Street
Niles, OH 44446-5049
216-652-1704
www.mckinley.lib.oh.us/muse.htm

William McKinley was born in a small frame house a block south of this site on January 29, 1843. The current structure, designed by McKim, Mead, and White, was dedicated in 1917. The birthplace is marked by a 232-foot-by-136-foot monument of Georgian marble. The memorial has two wings, one containing the McKinley Memorial Library and the other a museum featuring McKinley memorabilia and Civil War and Spanish-American War artifacts.

Hours
Monday through Thursday from 9 A.M. to 8 P.M., Friday and Saturday from 9 A.M. to 5:30 P.M., and Sunday from 1 to 5 P.M.; closed Sundays from May through September
Admission
Free

National McKinley Birthplace Memorial

Travelogue

Home

In 1853, the McKinley family moved to Poland, Ohio, about 10 miles from the future president's birthplace. McKinley lived there for the remainder of his childhood.

Churches

Church of the Savior
120 Cleveland Avenue SW
Canton, OH 44702
330-455-0153

McKinley was superintendent of the Sunday school at First Methodist Church in Canton, which has since been renamed Church of the Savior.

Church of the Savior

Travelogue

Metropolitan Memorial United Methodist Church
3401 Nebraska Avenue NW
Washington, DC 20016-2759
202-363-4900
www.gbgm.umc.org/metromemdc

McKinley attended Metropolitan Memorial during his years in Washington.

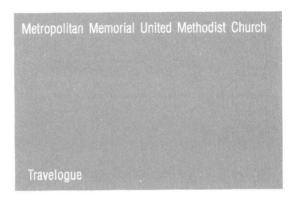
Metropolitan Memorial United Methodist Church

Travelogue

Education

Poland Seminary High School
3199 Dobbs Road
Poland, OH 44514
330-757-7018
www.polandbulldogs.com

One of the oldest secondary schools in the country, this institution began in 1802 as Poland Academy. McKinley graduated from Poland Seminary in 1857. In 1909, it became part of the Poland public schools.

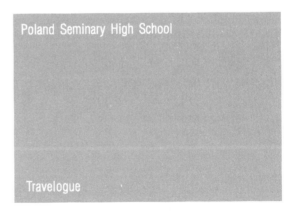
Poland Seminary High School

Travelogue

Allegheny College
520 North Main Street
Meadville, PA 16335-3903
814-332-3100
www.aleg.edu

McKinley entered Allegheny as a junior in 1860 but withdrew due to illness. However, tradition holds that he was thrown out for leaving a cow in the school's bell tower—hence the cow-shaped McKinley logo in the campus center. Family finances and McKinley's involvement in the Civil War precluded his returning to the college.

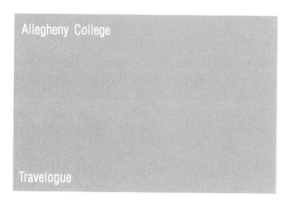

Albany Law School
80 New Scotland Avenue
Albany, NY 12208-3494
518-445-2311

McKinley attended Albany Law School in 1866 and 1867 but dropped out before graduation.

McKinley finished his law study in the Youngstown, Ohio, office of Judge Charles E. Glidden. He was admitted to the Ohio Bar in 1867.

Marriage

Christ Presbyterian Church
530 West Tuscarawas Street
Canton, OH 44702
330-456-8113

McKinley married Ida Saxton at First Presbyterian Church in Canton on January 25, 1871. The church has since been renamed Christ Presbyterian.

Inaugural Site

The Capitol
Washington, DC

March 4, 1897
March 4, 1901

Place of Death

McKinley was in Buffalo on September 6, 1901, when he was shot twice at point-blank range by Leon Czolgosz, an unemployed mill worker, during a public reception at the Pan-American Exposition's Temple of Music. Doctors removed one of the bullets but were unable to locate the other. Following surgery, he was taken to the home of his friend J. G. Milburn on Delaware Avenue in Buffalo. He died eight days later of the gangrene that developed in and around his wounds. The Milburn home no longer exists.

Burial Site

McKinley Museum and National Memorial
800 McKinley Monument Drive
Canton, OH 44708-4832
330-455-7043
www.mckinleymuseum.org

This 26-acre park features a monument to McKinley, who is buried here along with his wife and two children. The McKinley Mu-

seum includes McKinley Hall, which has items related to the McKinley presidency; Historical Hall, which features items from the Victorian era; Industrial Hall, which contains exhibits of the area's leading industries, Discover World, which has hands-on scientific displays; and the Hoover-Price Planetarium. A regular event at the park is "A Walk with the President," a walking tour that includes McKinley's home and the building in which he maintained his law office.

Hours
Monday through Saturday from 9 A.M. to 5 P.M. and Sunday from noon to 5 P.M.; the hours are extended to 6 P.M. during the summer; closed major holidays
Admission
$6 for adults; $5 for seniors; $4 for ages three to 18

McKinley Museum and National Memorial

Travelogue

Other Site

Antietam National Battlefield
National Park Service
MD 65
P.O. Box 158
Sharpsburg, MD 21782-0158
301-432-5124
www.nps.org/anti

On September 17, 1862, this was the site of the bloodiest day of fighting in the Civil War. More than 23,000 soldiers lost their lives on that single day in what was called the Battle of Antietam by the Union and the Battle of Sharpsburg by the Confederacy. One Union soldier who survived it was William McKinley.

The battle's outcome enabled Lincoln to issue the Emancipation Proclamation.

<u>Hours</u>
Daily from 8 A.M. to 6 P.M. during the summer and from 8 A.M. to 5 P.M. the rest of the year; closed New Year's, Thanksgiving, and Christmas
<u>Admission</u>
$2 per person; $4 per family

Antietam National Battlefield

Travelogue

Theodore Roosevelt

Twenty-Sixth President of the United States

Birthplace

Theodore Roosevelt Birthplace
National Historic Site

National Park Service
28 East 20th Street
New York, NY 10003
212-260-1616
www.nps.org/thrb

This reconstructed home is the only birthplace of an American president within New York City.

Theodore Roosevelt's grandfather Cornelius Roosevelt bought the homes at 28 and 26 East 20th Street and gave them to his sons, Theodore Sr. and Robert, as wedding gifts. Theodore Sr. and his wife, Martha Bulloch, moved into the home at 28 East 20th in 1854. Theodore Jr. was born here October 27, 1858. The family lived here until 1872.

In 1916, the home was demolished to make way for a two-story commercial building. Following the president's death in 1919, a group of prominent citizens bought the site, razed the commercial building, and reconstructed the birthplace as a memorial. The adjoining lot, once the home of Robert Roosevelt, includes galleries and other facilities. The entire complex was opened to the public in 1923. The home's four floors contain various exhibits related to Roosevelt's professional and recreational interests. A guided tour of five rooms is offered, as are occasional films and weekend concerts. A book and gift shop is on the premises.

Hours
Wednesday through Sunday from 9 A.M. to 5 P.M. except on federal holidays. Tours are given on the hour; the last tour starts at 4 P.M.

Admission
$2 for adults; guests under 17 are free

Theodore Roosevelt Birthplace
National Historic Site

Travelogue

The Parlor of the Theodore Roosevelt Birthplace National Historic Site
Photo courtesy of Theodore Roosevelt Birthplace National Historic Site

The Library of the Theodore Roosevelt Birthplace National Historic Site
Photo courtesy of Theodore Roosevelt Birthplace National Historic Site

Homes

Upon their return from an extended trip abroad in 1873, the Roosevelts moved into a home at 6 West 57th Street in New York City. It is currently owned by Arista Records and is not open to the public.

Sagamore Hill National Historic Site
National Park Service
20 Sagamore Hill Road
Oyster Bay, NY 11771-1899
516-922-4447
www.nps.gov/sahi

Roosevelt built this 23-room Victorian mansion in 1884 and 1885. It served as the "Summer White House" during his presidency. Adjacent is Old Orchard Museum, once the home of Roosevelt's son Ted; today, Old Orchard serves as the site's museum. The National Park Service has restored Sagamore Hill to the way it looked in the first decade of the 20th century. Exhibits and audiovisual programs interpret Roosevelt's life and career.

Hours
The mansion is open daily from 9 A.M. to 5 P.M. during spring and summer and Wednesday through Sunday from 9 A.M. to 4 P.M. during fall and winter; call for exact dates.
Admission
Tours of the home are $5 for adults; guests under 17 are free. Admission to the grounds is free.

Sagamore Hill National Historic Site

Travelogue

Churches

Madison Avenue Presbyterian Church
921 Madison Avenue
New York, NY 10021-3508
212-288-8920

Roosevelt attended this church as a child because no Dutch Reformed church was accessible.

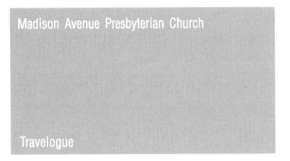

Christ Episcopal Church
61 East Main Street
Oyster Bay, NY 11771-2493
516-922-6377

The Roosevelts attended this church while on Long Island. It was built in 1878.

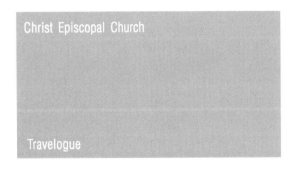

Grace Reformed Church
1405 15th Street NW
Washington, DC 20005-1920
202-387-3131

The Roosevelts regularly attended Grace while in Washington.

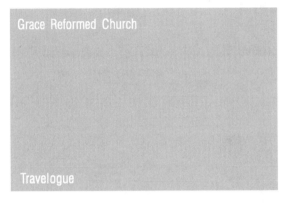

St. John's Lafayette Square
Washington, DC

See Sites Related to Multiple Presidents on pages 243–44.

Christ Church of Cambridge
Garden Street
Cambridge, MA 02138
617-876-0200

While a student at Harvard, Roosevelt taught Sunday school here until the rector discovered he was not Episcopalian. As a result, he was dismissed.

Roosevelt was a member of the Dutch Reformed Church but regularly worshiped at

Episcopal and Presbyterian churches when there was no convenient Reformed church.

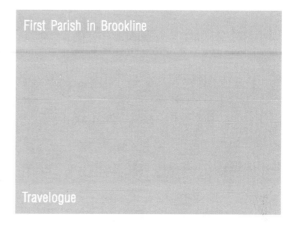
Christ Church of Cambridge

Travelogue

Education

Harvard University
Cambridge, MA

See Sites Related to Multiple Presidents on pages 246–47.

Columbia University
New York, NY

See Sites Related to Multiple Presidents on page 245.

Marriages

First Parish in Brookline
328 Walnut Street
Brookline, MA 02146
617-566-1933

Roosevelt married Alice Hathaway Lee

here on October 27, 1880. She died in New York on February 14, 1884.

First Parish in Brookline

Travelogue

St. George's Church
Hanover Square
London, England

Roosevelt married Edith Kermit Carow here on December 2, 1886.

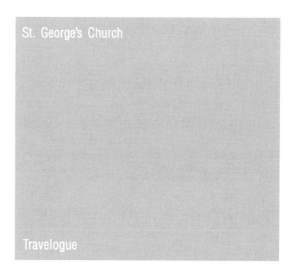
St. George's Church

Travelogue

Inaugural Sites

Theodore Roosevelt Inaugural National Historic Site

Theodore Roosevelt Inaugural National Historic Site
National Park Service
641 Delaware Avenue
Buffalo, NY 14202
716-884-0095

Only hours after the September 14, 1901, death of William McKinley, Roosevelt took the oath of office in the library of this 1838 Greek Revival house, the home of his friends Ansley and Mary Wilcox.

Items related to McKinley's assassination and Roosevelt's inauguration are featured at the site. An exhibition gallery and a gift shop are on the premises. Special events include the annual Teddy Bear Picnic, the Summer Victorian Camp for children, the Inauguration Anniversary Luncheon, and the Victorian Christmas Celebration.

Hours
Monday through Friday from 9 A.M. to 5 P.M. and Saturday and Sunday from noon to 5 P.M.; call to verify winter weekend hours; closed major holidays
Admission
$5.50 for families; $2 for adults; $1 for ages six to 12

Theodore Roosevelt Inaugural National Historic Site

Travelogue

The Capitol
Washington, DC

March 4, 1905

Place of Death

Sagamore Hill National Historic Site
Oyster Bay, NY

Feeling the effects of various ailments of previous years, Roosevelt was hospitalized numerous times during 1918. He suffered a fatal cardiac embolism early in the morning on January 6, 1919, while sleeping at Sagamore Hill (see page 143).

Funeral

Christ Episcopal Church
Oyster Bay, NY

Christ Episcopal (see page 144) was the site of the simple funeral service without music Roosevelt had requested.

Burial Site

Young Memorial Cemetery
Oyster Bay, NY

This cemetery is adjacent to Sagamore Hill (see page 143).

Other Sites

Hall of Fame for Great Americans
Bronx, NY

See Sites Related to Multiple Presidents on page 258.

Mount Rushmore National Memorial
Keystone, SD

See Sites Related to Multiple Presidents on pages 254–55.

Theodore Roosevelt Island
National Park Service
George Washington Memorial Parkway
Turkey Run Park
McLean, VA 22101
703-285-2600
www.nps.gov/this

This 91-acre island lies in the Potomac River between Virginia and Washington. It is accessible from the northbound lanes of George Washington Memorial Parkway immediately north of the Theodore Roosevelt Bridge. The large granite monument on the site includes a bronze statue of Roosevelt and four tablets inscribed with his ideas on nature, youth, manhood, and the state.

Hours
Open daily from dawn to dusk
Admission
Free

Theodore Roosevelt Island

Travelogue

Theodore Roosevelt National Park

National Park Service
Medora, ND 58645
701-623-4466
www.nps.gov/thro

Roosevelt first came to North Dakota's Badlands in 1883. He later established cattle ranches here, where he came to cultivate his interest in nature and conservation. The massive site features three visitor centers, a bookstore, interpretive exhibits, guided tours, campfire programs, cabin tours, and numerous outdoor activities. Overnight camping is available from May through September; no hookups are available, and reservations are not accepted.

Hours
Open all year; closed New Year's, Thanksgiving, and Christmas. Many roads in the park are closed during winter because of ice and snow. The Medora Visitor Center is open daily from 8 A.M. to 8 P.M. in summer and from 8 A.M. to 4:30 P.M. the rest of the year. The Painted Canyon Visitor Center is open daily from 8 A.M. to 6 P.M. in summer and from 8 A.M. to 4:30 P.M. most of the rest of the year; it may be closed during winter. The North Visitor Center is open daily from 9 A.M. to 5:30 P.M. year-round.
Admission
$5 per person or $10 per vehicle; seasonal passes are available

Theodore Roosevelt National Park

Travelogue

Roosevelt Bird Sanctuary and Trailside Museum

East Main Street at Cove Road
Oyster Bay, NY 11771
516-922-3200

A memorial to Roosevelt is featured at this museum, which also includes exhibits related to Long Island plant and animal life. The site is adjacent to Young Memorial Cemetery, where Roosevelt is buried.

Hours
Monday through Thursday from 8 A.M. to 4:30 P.M., Friday from 8 A.M. to 2 P.M., and Saturday and Sunday from 1 to 4:30 P.M.; closed New Year's, Thanksgiving, and Christmas
Admission
$1.50

Roosevelt Bird Sanctuary and Trailside Museum

Travelogue

William Howard Taft

Twenty-Seventh President of the United States

Birthplace

William Howard Taft National Historic Site
National Park Service
2038 Auburn Avenue
Cincinnati, OH 45219-3025
513-684-3262
www.nps.gov/htdocs4/wiho/index.htm

William Howard Taft was born here September 15, 1857. Four rooms of the home are furnished according to the period when the Tafts lived here (1857–77). The other rooms feature exhibits about the Taft family, the Taft presidency, and Taft's devotion to public service. Parking is available at Southern Avenue and Young Street.

Hours
Daily from 10 A.M. to 4 P.M.; closed New Year's, Thanksgiving, and Christmas
Admission
Free

William Howard Taft National Historic Site

Travelogue

William Howard Taft National Historic Site
Courtesy William Howard Taft National Historic Site

Home

Taft Apartments
265 College Street
New Haven, CT 06510-2420
203-495-8238

Taft lived in what was then the Taft Hotel for the eight years he was on the Yale faculty following his retirement from the presidency. The hotel, at College and Chapel Streets, was built in 1912 and was at the time a home for New Haven's notables. Its proximity to New Haven's theaters made it attractive to actors and musicians destined for Broadway. Al

Jolson and Katharine Hepburn were among those who stayed here while performing in town.

Today, the building includes rental apartments, retail outlets, and restaurants.

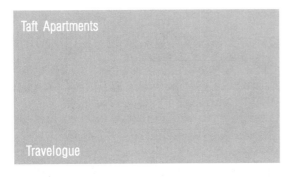

Taft Apartments

Travelogue

Education

Taft attended public schools in the Cincinnati area.

Yale University
New Haven, CT

See Sites Related to Multiple Presidents on pages 249–50.

University of Cincinnati
1 Edwards Center
Cincinnati, OH 45221-0091
513-556-1100
www.uc.edu

Taft worked his way through law school as a part-time courthouse reporter for the *Cincinnati Commercial*. He was admitted to the Ohio Bar in May 1880 and graduated later that spring.

University of Cincinnati

Travelogue

Marriage

Taft married Helen "Nellie" Herron on June 19, 1886, at the Cincinnati home of the bride's family.

Inaugural Site

The Capitol
Washington, DC

March 4, 1909

Place of Death

In his later years, Taft developed cardiac problems and high blood pressure. He resigned from the Supreme Court in February 1930 due to failing health. In early March, he began falling in and out of consciousness. He died in his sleep at his Washington home on the afternoon of March 8.

Funeral

All Souls Church (Unitarian)
Washington, DC

See Sites Related to Multiple Presidents on pages 241–42.

Burial Site

Arlington National Cemetery
Arlington, VA

See Sites Related to Multiple Presidents on page 240.

Other Site

United States Supreme Court
1 First Street NE
Washington, DC 20543-0002
202-479-3030
suptct.law.cornell.edu/suptct

Woodrow Wilson appointed Taft chief justice of the Supreme Court. Taft, the only president to serve on the nation's highest court, considered this the highlight of his career. As chief justice, he administered the oath of office to Presidents Calvin Coolidge and Herbert Hoover. He served from 1918 until 1930.

Tours and lectures are offered when the court is not in session; no tours are offered during the summer.

Hours
Daily from 9 A.M. to 4:30 P.M.
Admission
Free

United States Supreme Court

Travelogue

Woodrow Wilson

Twenty-Eighth President of the United States

Portrait of Woodrow Wilson from the
Woodrow Wilson Birthplace in Staunton, Virginia
Courtesy of Woodrow Wilson Birthplace Foundation, Inc.

Birthplace

Woodrow Wilson Birthplace

Woodrow Wilson Birthplace Foundation, Inc.
24 North Coatler Street
Staunton, VA 24401
540-885-0897 or 888-496-6376
xroads.virginia.edu/~VAM/WW/wwbma.htm

Wilson was born Thomas Woodrow Wilson on December 28, 1856, in the former manse of First Presbyterian Church, where his father, Joseph Ruggles Wilson, was pastor.

After graduating from college, Wilson used the name T. Woodrow Wilson, but he eventually dropped the first initial.

The site includes the house and an adjacent museum. The 1846 Greek Revival home is furnished as it was at the time of Wilson's birth. Many of the furnishings belonged to the Wilson family. In addition to interpreting Wilson's early life, the house presents an excellent picture of pre–Civil War life in Virginia's Shenandoah Valley. The museum, opened in 1990 in an adjacent chateau-style mansion, includes seven galleries depicting Wilson's early life, his career as a professor and university president, and his terms as governor of New Jersey and president. Displays interpret his roles in World War I, the Treaty of Versailles, and the League of Nations. An attached garage contains Wilson's beloved 1919 Pierce Arrow limousine.

Hours
Daily from 9 A.M. to 5 P.M. from March to October; Monday through Saturday from 10 A.M. to 4 P.M. and Sunday from noon to 4 P.M. from November to February; closed New Year's, Thanksgiving, and Christmas
Admission
$6 for adults; $5.50 for seniors; $4 for students; $2 for ages six to 12

*Woodrow Wilson Birthplace
in Staunton, Virginia*
Courtesy of Woodrow Wilson Birthplace Foundation, Inc.

Woodrow Wilson Birthplace

Travelogue

Homes

Boyhood Home of Woodrow Wilson

419 Seventh Street
Augusta, GA 30901
www.augusta.org/wilson.htm

From 1860 to 1870, while Wilson's father was pastor of First Presbyterian Church in Augusta, the family lived in its manse. Wil-son once said that his earliest recollection was "of standing at my father's gateway in Augusta, Georgia, when I was four years old, and hearing someone pass and say that Mr. Lincoln was elected and there would be war." He also recalled seeing General Robert E. Lee pass through the city under Union guard in 1865. Throughout his life, Wilson considered himself a Southerner, and he believed that the South was fully justified in seceding from the Union.

While living here, one of Wilson's playmates was Joseph Rucker Lamar, who in 1910 became an associate justice of the United States Supreme Court.

The home is currently being restored by Historic Augusta and is not yet open to the public. A historical marker in front of the house tells of Wilson's life here.

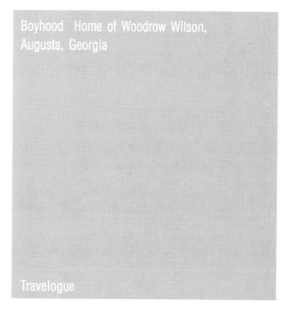

Boyhood Home of Woodrow Wilson, Augusta, Georgia

Travelogue

*Woodrow Wilson Boyhood Home
in Columbia, South Carolina*
Courtesy of Woodrow Wilson Boyhood Home

Tuesday through Saturday from 10 A.M. to 4 P.M. and Sunday from 1 to 5 P.M. All tours begin on the quarter-hour at the Robert Mills House gift shop at 1616 Blanding Street, located within walking distance. Tours include four historic homes operated by Historic Columbia: the Hampton-Preston Mansion at 1615 Blanding Street, the Robert Mills House, the Mann-Simons Cottage at 1403 Richland Street, and the Woodrow Wilson Boyhood Home.

Admission
$3

Woodrow Wilson Boyhood Home

Historic Columbia Foundation
1705 Hampton Street
Columbia, SC 29201
803-929-7693
www.midnet.sc.edu/histhous/wilson.htm

The Wilsons lived here from 1870 to 1874, moving in when Woodrow was 16. During that time, his father taught at Columbia Theological Seminary and preached at Columbia's First Presbyterian Church. Wilson's mother, Jessie Woodrow Wilson, received an inheritance that enabled her and her husband to build this, the only home they ever owned.

Today, the Victorian cottage includes the original mantels and remnants of the original gas lighting fixtures. Among the furnishings is the bed in which Woodrow Wilson was born. The Columbia Garden Club maintains Mrs. Wilson's gardens, which include magnolia trees she planted more than a century ago.

Woodrow Wilson Boyhood Home,
Columbia, South Carolina

Travelogue

Woodrow Wilson House

2340 S Street NW
Washington, DC 20008
202-387-4062

The only presidential house museum in Washington, this was Wilson's home from 1921 until his death in 1924. It is filled with possessions from Wilson's life and presidency

Woodrow Wilson House in Washington, D.C.
Courtesy of Woodrow Wilson House National Trust

Interior from the Woodrow Wilson House in Washington, D.C.
Courtesy of Woodrow Wilson House National Trust

and items representative of American life in the 1920s.

Hours
Tuesday through Saturday from 10 A.M. to 4 P.M.; closed major holidays
Admission
$5 for adults; $3.50 for guests over 62; $2.50 for students and children age seven and older

Education

Davidson College
P.O. Box 1719
Davidson, NC 28036
704-892-2000
www.davidson.edu

Wilson entered Davidson College in 1873 but was forced to drop out after one year due to poor health.

Princeton University
Princeton, NJ

See Sites Related to Multiple Presidents on pages 247–48.

University of Virginia
Charlottesville, VA

See Sites Related to Multiple Presidents on page 247.

Johns Hopkins University

3400 North Charles Street
Baltimore, MD 21218
410-516-8000
www.jhu.edu

The only president to earn a Ph.D., Wilson graduated in 1885 with a degree in political science. His thesis was a critically acclaimed work condemning congressional domination of the executive and judicial branches of the federal government.

Johns Hopkins University

Travelogue

Marriages

Wilson married Ellen Louise Axson on June 24, 1885, in the bride's home in Savannah, Georgia. She died during Wilson's first term in the White House.

On December 18, 1915, he married Edith Bolling Galt in Galt's Washington home. The widow Galt was a companion of Wilson's niece, who had assumed social responsibilities in the White House following the death of Wilson's first wife.

Inaugural Site

The Capitol
Washington, DC

March 4, 1913
March 5, 1917

Place of Death

Woodrow Wilson House
Washington, DC

Wilson never fully recovered from influenza he caught during the 1918 epidemic. In 1919, while in Paris, he suffered a stroke that left him partially paralyzed. His health declined steadily after that. He died in his Washington home (see page 154) on February 3, 1924.

Funeral/Burial Site

Washington National Cathedral
Protestant Episcopal Cathedral Foundation
Massachusetts and Wisconsin Avenues NW
Washington, DC 20016-5098
202-537-6200
www.cathedral.org/cathedral

After simple services for family and friends at Wilson's home, private services were held in the cathedral's Bethlehem Chapel. They were officiated by the Reverend James Taylor of Central Presbyterian Church, the Reverend

Sylvester Beach of Princeton University, and Bishop James Freeman of the cathedral.

Wilson, the only president buried within the District of Columbia, is interred in the Woodrow Wilson Bay, which is decorated with myriad images representing his life. The walls of the bay are inscribed with many of his quotes.

> Hours
> Daily from 10 A.M. to 4:30 P.M.; the hours are extended until 9 P.M. on weekdays from May through August
> Admission
> Free; guided tours cost $2 per adult and $1 per child

Washington National Cathedral

Travelogue

Other Sites

Bryn Mawr College
101 North Merion Avenue
Bryn Mawr, PA 19010-2899
610-526-5000
www.brynmawr.edu

Wilson took his first teaching job at Bryn Mawr in 1885, the year the college opened.

A small historical marker along New Gulph Road on the north side of the campus pays tribute to educator and statesman Wilson.

Bryn Mawr College

Travelogue

Hall of Fame for Great Americans
Bronx, NY

See Sites Related to Multiple Presidents on page 258.

Warren G. Harding

Twenty-Ninth President of the United States

Birthplace

Warren G. Harding was born in the family farmhouse in Blooming Grove (then Corsica), Ohio, on November 2, 1865. Though the building no longer exists, there is a historical marker at the site on OH 97 near Blooming Grove.

As a child, Harding lived in Blooming Grove and Caledonia. Neither of these homes exists today.

Home

President Harding Home and Museum

Ohio Historical Society
380 Mount Vernon Avenue
Marion, OH 43302
740-387-9630
www.oplin.lib/oh.us/OHS2/site/sites/central/hrdho.htm

This home was built for Harding and his future wife, Florence, during their engagement. They were married here July 8, 1891, and lived in the house until 1921, when they moved to the White House. While living here, Harding was editor of the *Marion Daily Star*, an Ohio senator, and the state's lieutenant governor. During the 1920 presidential election, he conducted his "front porch" campaign from this home.

The house has been authentically restored to the period of Harding's residence. A small museum chronicling his administration is in the former campaign press building, located behind the house. Harding and his wife are buried nearby. Guided tours of the home are offered.

Hours
Wednesday through Saturday from
9:30 A.M. to 5 P.M. and Sunday from noon
to 5 P.M. from Memorial Day to Labor Day;
Saturday from 9:30 A.M. to 5 P.M. and
Sunday from noon to 5 P.M. during
September and October; open by
appointment the rest of the year
Admission
$3 for adults; $1.25 for ages six to 12

President Harding Home and Museum

Travelogue

President Harding Home and Museum
Photo by Amanda B. Schaefer

Church

Calvary Baptist Church
928 Fifth Street NW
Washington, DC 20001-2501
202-347-8355

As a young man, Harding attended Seventh-Day Adventist services with his mother, but he challenged that church's doctrine while in college. As an adult, he settled on the Baptist tradition.

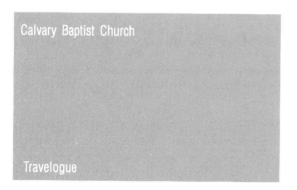

Education

Harding attended Blooming Grove's one-room schoolhouse and Ohio Central College, earning a B.S. degree in 1882. The college no longer exists, but a historical marker stands at its former location in Iberia.

Marriage

Harding married Florence "Flossie" Mabel Kling at the couple's home in Marion (see page 158) on July 8, 1891.

Inaugural Site

The Capitol
Washington, DC

March 4, 1921

Place of Death

Palace Hotel
Market Street
San Francisco, CA 94105
415-392-8600

In late June 1923, Harding began traveling cross-country on what he called his "Voyage of Understanding," during which he endeavored to talk to ordinary folks to explain his administration's policies. The rigors of the

The Garden Court of the Palace Hotel
Courtesy of the Palace Hotel

The Presidential Suite of the Palace Hotel
Courtesy of the Palace Hotel

Palace Hotel

Travelogue

trip weakened the president. He began to feel ill on July 27 while traveling south from Alaska, but Surgeon General Charles Sawyer dismissed it as a mild case of food poisoning. A few days later, Harding checked into the Palace Hotel in San Francisco and began to feel better. On the evening of August 1, his wife read a flattering review of him in the *Saturday Evening Post*. At one point, Harding said, "That's good. Go on, read some more." Those were the president's last words. He died later that evening in his sleep, though some historians believe he actually died August 2. The room in which he stayed is now called the Presidential Suite.

Burial Site

President Harding Home and Museum
Marion, OH

See page 158.

Other Site

Marion County Museum of History
169 East Church Street
Marion, OH
740-387-4255

This museum contains the Harding Room, which has an impressive collection of objects related to the Harding presidency.

Hours
Wednesday through Sunday from
1 to 4 P.M.
Admission
Free

Calvin Coolidge
Thirtieth President of the United States

Birthplace/Homes

President Calvin Coolidge State Historic Site
Vermont Division for Historic Preservation
Plymouth Notch Historic District
P.O. Box 247
VT 100A
Plymouth Notch, VT 05056
802-672-3773
www.cit.state.vt.us/dca/historic/hp_sites.htm

Plymouth Notch, the birthplace and boyhood home of Calvin Coolidge, is a gem of American history. The quaint Vermont village remains much as it was in August 1923, when Coolidge took the oath of office in the family homestead by the light of a kerosene lamp. The numerous buildings that comprise Plymouth Notch have been carefully restored, making this one of the nation's best-preserved presidential sites.

The village includes a visitor center built in 1972 in a style similar to the area's early stone structures. In the visitor center are a museum and a gift shop. An introductory exhibit outlines Coolidge's career. The visitor center is open year-round, although the balance of the community is closed from mid-October through mid-May.

The Wilder Barn is an 1875 pegged barn featuring an extensive collection of 19th-century farm equipment, horse-drawn vehicles, and equipment from the Plymouth Cheese Factory.

The Wilder House, built around 1830 and originally used as a tavern, was the childhood home of Coolidge's mother. The interior was remodeled into a coffee shop in 1956; the coffee shop continues to serve breakfast and lunch during the season.

The Coolidge Homestead was Coolidge's boyhood home. He was visiting this home in 1923 when he got the news of Warren Harding's death. His father, Colonel John Coolidge, a notary public, administered the oath of office at 2:47 A.M. on August 3, 1923. Many years later, when a visitor asked the elder Coolidge how he knew he could administer the oath to his own son, he quipped, "I didn't know that I couldn't." The home is furnished exactly as it was in 1923.

The Plymouth Cheese Factory, built in 1890 by Coolidge's father and three partners as an outlet for their milk, was reopened in the 1960s by Coolidge's son after nearly 30 years of inactivity. Today, the factory uses its original "granular curd" recipe to make cheese that can be purchased by the general public.

Also on the grounds is a one-room school-

Arthur Keller's painting, The Swearing In of Calvin Coolidge
by his Father
Courtesy of Vermont Division for Historic Preservation,
President Calvin Coolidge State Historic Site
Photo by Sherman Howe

house built around 1950 to replace the stone schoolhouse from which Coolidge graduated the eighth grade in 1885. The building is used by school groups and is not open to the public.

The Azro Johnson farm was built in 1845; it is not open to the public.

The Carrie Brown Coolidge Garden was started by Coolidge's teacher and stepmother. Some of the perennial flowers in the garden today are descended from original plants.

Union Christian Church was built in 1840 and redesigned in the 1890s. The Calvin Coolidge Memorial Foundation maintains offices in the basement.

The Calvin Coolidge Birthplace consists of modest living quarters attached to a general store. Coolidge was born here July 4, 1872. The family lived here until 1876, when it moved across the street. The residence has been restored to its 1872 appearance by the

state of Vermont. The Florence Cilley General Store, the main feature of the building, was operated by Coolidge's father from 1868 until 1877. In 1917, Coolidge sold the building to Florence Cilley—hence the store's name. Cilley operated it until 1945. The small post office in the store served Plymouth Notch until 1976. Above the store is Coolidge Hall, which was the town's social center for many years. The hall was the site of weekly dances and numerous family reunions well into the 20th century. In 1924, the hall became the summer White House. It has been restored to its appearance of that summer and features interpretive exhibits and original furnishings.

The Aldrich House was once the home of Coolidge's stepmother and is now the site's administrative office.

The Top of the Notch Cabins are three modest cabins that afforded visitors comfortable lodging during the 1920s. The middle cabin has been restored and is open for public viewing.

The Brown Family Farmhouse, built in 1869, was the centerpiece of one of the area's most productive farms. In 1879, for example, the farm produced 4,000 pounds of butter, 400 bushels of buckwheat, 350 bushels of oats, and 80 tons of hay. The farm is not open to the public.

Plymouth Cemetery is the steep hillside cemetery in which Coolidge and six generations of his family are buried. Upon leaving the White House, Coolidge said, "We draw our presidents from the people. . . . I came from them. I wish to be one of them again." True to this sentiment, Coolidge's grave is marked by a simple granite headstone.

The complex is on VT 100A six miles south of US 4 about midway across the state. Coolidge State Forest is nearby.

Hours
Daily from 9:30 A.M. to 5:30 P.M. from
mid-May through mid-October
Admission
$5; children under 14 are free

Coolidge and his wife retired to a two-family home in Northampton, Massachusetts, but soon thereafter moved into a larger and more secluded 12-room home on a cul-de-sac, so as to enjoy their privacy. Coolidge named the latter home "Beeches."

President Calvin Coolidge State Historic Site

Travelogue

Churches

Edwards Congregational Church
297 Main Street
Northampton, MA 01060-3106
413-584-5500

Coolidge attended this church after his retirement from the presidency.

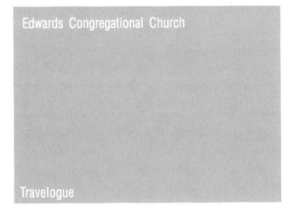
Edwards Congregational Church

Travelogue

First Congregational Church
10th Street NW
Washington, DC 20001
202-628-4317
www.erols.com/fccucc

Coolidge had reservations about joining a church, fearing that he could not live up to the high moral standards that members would require of him. But on his first Sunday as president, he accepted the invitation of the Reverend Jason Noble Pierce, extended to all in attendance, to take Communion. Deeming such participation to be a suitable public profession of faith, the church elected Coolidge a member.

The church's original building was replaced in 1959.

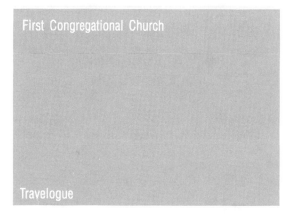

First Congregational Church

Travelogue

Education

Coolidge attended local public schools before enrolling in Black River Academy in Ludlow, Massachusetts. That school no longer exists.

St. Johnsbury Academy
7 Main Street
Ludlow, VT 05819-2699
802-748-8171
www.state.vt.us/schools/stj

After failing the entrance exam for Amherst College in 1891, Coolidge spent a year taking college preparatory courses at St. Johnsbury. The following year, he earned a college entrance certificate and was admitted to Amherst.

St. Johnsbury Academy

Travelogue

Amherst College
Amherst, MA 01002
413-542-2000
www.amherst.edu

Coolidge was a mediocre student his first two years but showed incredible improvement his junior and senior years and graduated *cum laude*. In his senior year, because of his reputation as the campus wit, he delivered the annual Grove Oration, a satirical address.

Coolidge studied law in the Northampton, Massachusetts, offices of John C. Hammond and Henry P. Field and was admitted to the Massachusetts Bar in 1897.

Amherst College

Travelogue

Marriage

Coolidge married Grace Ann Goodhue on October 4, 1905, in the home of the bride's family in Burlington, Vermont.

Inaugural Sites

President Calvin Coolidge State Historic Site
Plymouth Notch, VT

Coolidge was inaugurated in the Coolidge Homestead (see page 162) on August 3, 1923, following the death of Warren Harding.

The Capitol
Washington, DC

March 4, 1925

Place of Death

Coolidge died of coronary thrombosis at his home in Northampton, Massachusetts, on January 5, 1933. He was alone at the time; his wife discovered the body when she returned from a shopping trip.

Funeral

Edwards Congregational Church
Northampton, MA

Coolidge's funeral was held at Edwards Congregational Church (see page 164) in January 1933.

Burial Site

President Calvin Coolidge State Historic Site
Plymouth Notch, VT

Coolidge was buried simply in Plymouth Cemetery (see page 162).

Other Sites

Forbes Library
20 West Street
Northampton, MA 01060
413-587-1011
www.gazettenet.com/forbeslibrary

The Calvin Coolidge Memorial Room, located on the second floor of this library, is the repository for Coolidge's personal papers. The collection also includes microfilm copies of all Coolidge's presidential papers (the originals are in the Library of Congress) and a large assortment of memorabilia from his presidency.

Hours
The Calvin Coolidge Memorial Room is open Monday and Tuesday from 1 to 5 P.M., Wednesday from 2 to 4 P.M., and

other times by appointment.
Admission
Free

Forbes Library

Travelogue

Hotel Northampton

36 King Street
Northampton, MA 01060
413-584-3100
www.hotelnorthampton.com

In 1989, in tribute to Coolidge, this hotel hired a local artist to re-create the splendor of "Beeches," Coolidge's Northampton home, in its Coolidge Park Café. Coolidge was a frequent patron of the hotel's Wiggins Tavern Restaurant, which is adjacent to the café.

Hotel Northampton

Travelogue

Fitzwilly's Restaurant

23 Main Street
Northampton, MA 01060
413-584-8666
www.vitrual-valley.com/fitzwillys

Fitzwilly's is in the building that housed the law offices of Coolidge and Hemenway after Coolidge left the White House. A historical marker outside the structure identifies the spot. From time to time, Fitzwilly's offers a Calvin Coolidge special on its menu.

Fitzwilly's Restaurant

Travelogue

Herbert Hoover
Thirty-First President of the United States

Birthplace

Herbert Hoover National Historic Site

National Park Service
Downey Street
P.O. Box 607
West Branch, IA 52358
319-643-2541 (historic site)
or 319-643-5301 (presidential library)
www.nps.gov/heho.htm

Herbert Hoover birthplace cottage
Courtesy of Herbert Hoover National Historic Site, National Park Service

Hoover was born in his family's small cottage near midnight on August 10, 1874. Church records fixed the date as August 11, but in his memoirs, Hoover claimed August 10 to be his birthday.

The birthplace was captured in a painting by Grant Wood. Hoover complained that the painting made the place look too elaborate.

This site includes the birthplace cottage, a schoolhouse, Friends Meetinghouse, Hoover's boyhood neighborhood, the graves of President and Mrs. Hoover, a visitor center, a blacksmith shop, and the site of the Hoover family's second home; it also offers walking tours, cross-country skiing, and picnic facilities. The 44,500-square-foot Herbert Hoover Presidential Library and Museum, administered by the National Archives and Records Administration, is on the site. It includes seven galleries, a 180-seat auditorium, and numerous private meeting rooms.

Hours
Daily from 9 A.M. to 5 P.M.; closed New Year's, Thanksgiving, and Christmas
Admission
$2 for adults; $1 for guests 62 and over

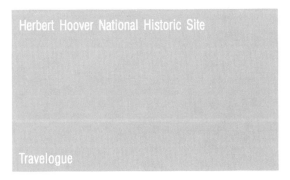

Herbert Hoover National Historic Site

Travelogue

Homes

Hoover-Minthorn House Museum

National Society of Colonial Dames in America
116 South Rivor Stroot
Newberg, OR 97132-3153
503-538-6629

Hoover lived his first few years with his immediate family in West Branch, Iowa. Following the death of his father in 1880, he and his sister and brother were frequently sent to live with relatives to ease life for their mother. Following his mother's death in 1883, Hoover was separated from his brother and sister, as each was sent to a different relative. Hoover initially lived with his uncle Allan Hoover on his West Branch farm. In 1885, he accepted an invitation to live in Oregon with another uncle, Dr. John Minthorn, the superintendent of Friends Pacific Academy. Minthorn and his wife had just lost their own son in a tragic accident and were prompted to invite Hoover in an attempt to overcome grief. Hoover registered in his uncle's school, where he was called "Bertie."

Minthorn's mansion was purchased and restored by friends of Hoover's during the 1950s. Many of the furnishings are original. In 1955, Hoover attended the opening of the museum on his 81st birthday.

Hours
Wednesday through Sunday from 1 to 4 P.M. from March to November; weekends from 1 to 4 P.M. during February and December; closed January

Admission
Free; donations are accepted

Hoover-Minthorn House Museum

Travelogue

Stanford University

Stanford, CA

See page 170.

Waldorf-Astoria Hotel

100 East 50th Street
New York, NY 10022-6805
212-872-4677
www.hilton.com/^467034169569847/hotels/
NYCWAHH/index

Hoover lived out his retirement in the residential portion of the Waldorf-Astoria, long considered one of New York's most elegant hotels and the flagship of the Hilton chain. In those years, he helped found both UNICEF and CARE, was honorary chairman of Boys'

Clubs of America, and wrote more than 40 books.

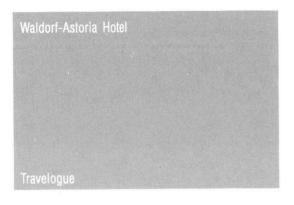

Waldorf-Astoria Hotel

Travelogue

Church

Religious Society of Friends
2111 Florida Avenue NW
Washington, DC 20008-1912
202-483-3310

Hoover was the first Quaker president.

Religious Society of Friends

Travelogue

Education

Hoover attended West Branch Free School before entering Friends Pacific Academy.

Stanford University
Stanford, CA 94305
650-723-2300
www.stanford.edu

Hoover was a member of the "pioneer class"—the first class of graduates—at Stanford, earning his bachelor's degree in geology in 1895. The "orphan from Iowa," as he was called, adopted Stanford as his surrogate family and maintained a lifelong relationship with the school.

Hoover was working in London in 1914 when World War I broke out. Seeing an opportunity to help humanity by collecting documents related to the war, he began building what eventually became the Hoover War Collection. In 1919, he gave Stanford $50,000 to establish a library for his collection, which has evolved into the Hoover Institute on War, Revolution, and Peace. In June 1941, Hoover dedicated the massive library. The Hoover Institute remains a vital part of Stanford today.

In 1920, Hoover and his wife built a sandstone home on the Stanford campus. Shortly thereafter, President-Elect Warren G. Harding nominated Hoover to be the nation's secretary of commerce. Hoover subsequently spent little time at his California home. Eventually, he gave it to the university for use as its president's residence. The home is not open to the public.

Stanford University

Travelogue

Marriage

Hoover married Lou Henry on February 10, 1899, in the Monterey, California, home of the bride's parents.

Inaugural Site

The Capitol
Washington, DC

March 4, 1929

Place of Death

During Hoover's last few years, while he was living in New York, he was plagued with various maladies that left him nearly blind and deaf. Following surgery for intestinal cancer in 1962, he had occasional gastrointestinal hemorrhages. On October 17, 1964, he suffered massive internal bleeding. Hoover fell into a coma two days later and died in a New York hospital on October 20 without regaining consciousness.

Funeral

St. Bartholomew's Episcopal Church
109 East 50th Street
New York, NY 10022-6804
212-751-1616

In keeping with Hoover's Quaker faith, there was no music at his funeral. Following the funeral, his body lay in state in the United States Capitol Rotunda.

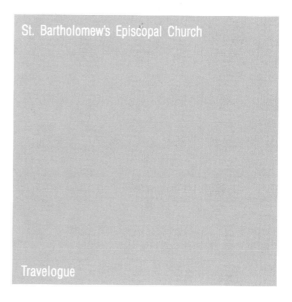
St. Bartholomew's Episcopal Church

Travelogue

St. Bartholomew's Episcopal Church
Photo by Ian Ferris

Burial Site

Herbert Hoover National Historic Site
West Branch, IA

See page 168.

Franklin D. Roosevelt

Thirty-Second President of the United States

Birthplace/Homes

Home of Franklin D. Roosevelt National Historic Site

National Park Service
519 Albany Post Road
Hyde Park, NY 12538
914-229-9115 or 800-FDR-VISIT
www.academic.marist.edu/fdr

Built in 1826, this was the birthplace and lifelong home of Franklin D. Roosevelt. Roosevelt was born here January 30, 1882. The home is preserved as it was at the time of his death in 1945.

Notable visitors to the Roosevelt home included King George VI and Queen Elizabeth, the first British monarchs to visit the United States. The home was called the "Summer White House" during Roosevelt's administration. It was here that he and Churchill signed the agreement that resulted in the development of the atomic bomb.

Franklin and Eleanor Roosevelt are buried in the estate's Rose Garden. The site also includes the Franklin D. Roosevelt Library and Museum (see page 177), a bookstore, and a tourist information center.

Hours
Daily from 9 A.M. to 5 P.M.; closed Thanksgiving and Christmas
Admission
$10 for adults; guests under 16 are free. The fee includes admission to the Franklin D. Roosevelt Library and Museum. Golden Age Passports are honored at a 50 percent discount. Golden Eagle and Golden Access Passports are also honored.

Home of Franklin D. Roosevelt National Historic Site

Travelogue

Campobello, Roosevelt's summer home
Courtesy of Roosevelt Campobello International Park

Service, the park is actually owned and operated by a joint United States/Canadian commission funded equally by both countries. The park was established by an agreement signed in 1964 by Lyndon Baines Johnson and Canadian prime minister Lester B. Pearson.

To reach the park from Maine, follow I-95 to Bangor, then take US 1A to Ellsworth, then US 1 to Whiting Village. From there, follow ME 189 to the Franklin Delano Roosevelt International Bridge at Lubec. Cross the bridge and continue about two miles to the park.

Roosevelt Campobello International Park

New Brunswick Route 774
Welshpool, Campobello
New Brunswick, Canada
United States mailing address:
National Park Service
P.O. Box 129
Lubec, ME 04652
506-752-2922
www.nps.gov.roca

Once Roosevelt's summer home, this site in southeastern Canada has been preserved as a monument to him and a symbol of the friendship between the peoples of the United States and Canada. The coastal home stands amidst rocky shores, fields, forests, and bogs that offer varied outdoor recreational opportunities. Tours of the Roosevelt Cottage and the Hubbard Cottage are offered. The visitor center has exhibits.

Although affiliated with the National Park

Hours
Daily from 9 A.M. to 5 P.M. EDT from the Saturday before Memorial Day through Columbus Day
Admission
Free

Roosevelt Campobello International Park

Travelogue

Little White House State Historic Site

Warm Springs, GA

See page 176.

Churches

St. James Church Episcopal
680 Albany Post Road
Hyde Park, NY 12538-1539
914-229-2820

Roosevelt was a lifelong member, vestryman, and senior warden of this church. His faith was a personal matter he rarely talked about.

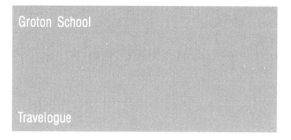
St. James Church Episcopal

Travelogue

St. John's Lafayette Square
Washington, DC

See Sites Related to Multiple Presidents on pages 243–44.

Education

Groton School
P.O. Box 991
Groton, MA 01450
978-448-3363
www.groton.org

Roosevelt attended Groton from 1896 to 1900. He was an above-average student whose extracurricular activities included singing soprano in the school choir, boxing, football, track and field (he set the school record in the high kick at more than seven feet), and playing the part of Uncle Bopaddy in Gilbert and Sullivan's *The Wedding March*. His uncle Theodore Roosevelt, then governor of New York, delivered the commencement address when Franklin graduated.

Groton School

Travelogue

Harvard University
Cambridge, MA

See Sites Related to Multiple Presidents on pages 246–47.

Columbia University
New York, NY

See Sites Related to Multiple Presidents on page 245.

Marriage

Roosevelt married Anna Eleanor Roosevelt, a fifth cousin once removed, on March 17, 1905, at the New York home of Mrs. E. Livingston Ludlow, the bride's aunt.

Inaugural Sites

The Capitol
Washington, DC

March 4, 1933
January 20, 1937
January 20, 1941

The White House
Washington, DC

January 20, 1945

Place of Death

Little White House State Historic Site
Georgia Department of State Parks and Historic Sites
401 Little White House Road
Warm Springs, GA 31830
706-665-5870
www.gastateparks.org

During the 1920s, a friend told Roosevelt, who suffered from polio, about the therapeutic waters of Warm Springs. Roosevelt first visited the area in 1924 and was immediately captivated by the springs, the pine-scented mountains, and the Southern hospitality. During the balance of his life, he made 41 trips here. In 1932, while he was governor of New

Little White House Museum
Photo by Mary F. Thrash

York, Roosevelt selected this site for a modest vacation home. As president, he developed many of his New Deal policies while visiting with his country neighbors here.

On April 12, 1945, Roosevelt was at the Little White House going over some papers when he suddenly put his hand to his temple and then his forehead before saying, "I have a terrific headache." Within moments, he was dead of a cerebral hemorrhage.

Hours
Daily from 9 A.M. to 5 P.M.
Admission
Free

Little White House State Historic Site

Travelogue

Burial Site

Home of Franklin D. Roosevelt National Historic Site
Hyde Park, NY

See page 173.

Other Sites

Eleanor Roosevelt National Historic Site
National Park Service
519 Albany Post Road
Hyde Park, NY 12538
914-229-9115
www.academic.marist.edu/fdr/val.htm

Val-Kill, the main cottage on this estate, was Eleanor Roosevelt's weekend and holiday retreat during her husband's presidency. It was also her home from the time of Franklin's death until her death in 1962.

The home has furniture made on the premises as part of a cottage industry that operated from 1927 to 1936. It features a film biography called *First Lady of the World*. The grounds include a pond, gardens, outbuildings, and woodland trails. The access road is narrow and unpaved.

Hours
Daily from 9 A.M. to 5 P.M. from May to October; weekends only from November to April
Admission
Free

Eleanor Roosevelt National Historic Site

Travelogue

Franklin D. Roosevelt Library and Museum
National Archives and Records Administration
249 Albany Post Road
Hyde Park, NY 12538
914-229-9115 or 800-FDR-VISIT
www.academic.marist.edu/fdr

The library and museum are housed in a building designed by Roosevelt for the purpose. The library contains Roosevelt's papers, collections, and family objects.

Hours
The library is open Monday through Friday from 8:45 A.M. to 5 P.M.; it is closed holidays and weekends. The museum is open daily from 9 A.M. to 6 P.M.; it is closed New Year's, Thanksgiving, and Christmas.
Admission
$10 for adults; guests under 16 are free.

The fee includes admission to Home of Franklin D. Roosevelt National Historic Site (see page 173). Golden Age Passports are honored at a 50 percent discount. Golden Eagle and Golden Access Passports are also honored.

Franklin D. Roosevelt Library and Museum

Travelogue

Franklin D. Roosevelt Memorial
National Park Service
West Potomac Park
900 Ohio Drive SW
Washington, DC 20242
202-376-6704
www.nps.gov/hydocs2/fdrm/index2.htm

At this memorial, bronze sculptures and bas-reliefs depict Franklin, Eleanor, and their dog Fala, as well as images of the Great Depression and the New Deal. The artwork is displayed in red-granite-walled, open-air rooms in a 7.5-acre park. The memorial is near the Cherry Tree Walk close to the Tidal Basin.

Hours
The memorial is open 24 hours per day and is staffed from 8 A.M. to midnight.
Admission
Free

Franklin D. Roosevelt Memorial
Ohio Drive, Washington, D.C.

Travelogue

Franklin D. Roosevelt Memorial
National Archives and Records Administration
Pennsylvania Avenue
Washington, DC 20408

Located in a park alongside the National Archives between Seventh and Ninth Streets, this modest block of Vermont marble commemorates Roosevelt, who established the presidential library system.

Hours
Open 24 hours per day
Admission
Free

Franklin D. Roosevelt Memorial
Pennsylvania Avenue, Washington, D.C.

Travelogue

Gold Coast Railroad Museum
Miami, FL

See Sites Relates to Multiple Presidents on page 257.

United States Air Force Museum
Dayton, OH

See Sites Related to Multiple Presidents on pages 261–62.

Harry S Truman
Thirty-Third President of the United States

Birthplace

Harry S Truman Birthplace State Historic Site
407 East 11th Street
Lamar, MO 64759-1956
417-682-2279
http://www.mobot.org/stateparks/trubirth_s.html

Truman was born May 8, 1884, in the small, tidy home that his parents had bought a few years earlier for $685. The family lived here until 1885. The house had six tiny rooms, no running water, no electricity, and no basement.

To celebrate the birth of his first son, John Truman planted a pine seedling in the front yard. That pine still shades the property. Period furnishings fill the house. Guided tours are available, and a museum store is on the premises.

Hours
Daily from 9 A.M. to 5 P.M.
Admission
Free

Harry S Truman Birthplace State Historic Site

Travelogue

Homes

Truman lived on a family farm in Harrisonville, Missouri, from 1885 to 1887 and at three homes in Independence—at 909 West Waldo Street, 619 South Chrysler Street, and 902 North Liberty Street—after 1890. Today, all of these properties are private homes and are not open to the public. Also of significance is the Independence Public Library. Legend holds that by the age of 14, Truman had read every one of its 2,000 books.

Truman Historic District
National Park Service
23 North Main Street
Independence, MO 64050
816-254-7199, 816-254-9929, or 816-254-2720
http://www.nps.gov/hstr/

Harry S Truman Home
Photo courtesy of the Harry S Truman Library

This site administers both the Truman Home in Independence and the Truman Farm Home in Grandview, located 20 miles away. The visitor center at the Independence site includes a museum, a shop, and rest rooms. There is no visitor center at Grandview; portable toilets are available. House tours are offered at both locations. Walking tours of the Independence neighborhood are conducted daily at 10 A.M. and 2 P.M. from June through August.

The Truman Home is located at 219 North Delaware Street in Independence. It is the centerpiece of the Truman Historic District, which leads north along North Delaware Street to the Truman Library. Following his service in World War I, Truman returned to Independence and married Bess Wallace. The couple "temporarily" moved into Bess's room, Harry arriving with little more than books and clothes. Although the newlyweds planned to move into their own house, they wound up making this their lifelong home. One of Independence's fashionable homes, it had been in Bess's family since 1867. During the Truman administration, the home served as the "Summer White House." The adjacent homes of two of Bess's brothers are included in the historic site, as is the home of Harry's beloved cousins Nellie and Ethel Noland across the street.

To reach the Truman Farm Home in Grandview, take I-435 south, then follow US 71 south to Blue Ridge Boulevard. Go west on Blue Ridge Boulevard; the farm is on the left after less than a mile. It was Truman's maternal grandparents, the Solomons, who acquired the land for this impressive 600-acre farm. The Truman family moved into the farmhouse in 1887. Truman later wrote that some of his fondest memories were of his childhood there. At one time, counting aunts, uncles, and servants, there were 14 people living in the house. Truman and his younger brother Vivian shared a tiny second-floor room that was oppressively hot in summer and unbearably cold in winter; Truman's mother once said that it was there that Harry got his common sense. In 1890, the Trumans moved to Independence so Harry could get a good education. But the farm remained important to the family. In 1892, Truman's grandfather died at the age of 72. Less than a year later, a servant accidentally ignited a fire that burned the home to the ground. The house that remains today is the small structure built as a temporary residence for Truman's grandmother. Several outbuildings also remain at the site. Harry Truman returned to the home in 1906 when he became a partner with his father in the family farm, an occupation he held until 1917, when he left to serve in World War I.

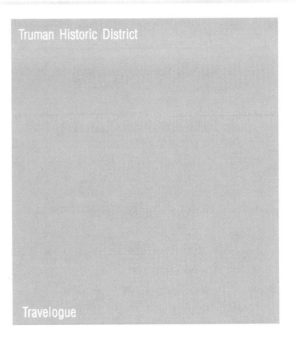

Truman Historic District

Travelogue

Hours

Daily from 8:30 A.M. to 5 P.M.; closed New Year's, Thanksgiving, and Christmas. Tours of the Truman Home are offered between 9 A.M. and 4:45 P.M.; no tours are given on Mondays from Labor Day to Memorial Day. Tours of the Truman Farm Home are offered between 9 A.M. and 4 P.M. on Friday, Saturday, and Sunday from May through August; guests may take self-guided tours at all other times.

Admission

$2 for adults; guests under 16 and over 62 are free. Tickets may be purchased at the ticket center on the corner of Truman Road and Main Street, adjacent to Independence Square.

Harry S Truman Little White House Museum

111 Front Street
Key West, FL 33041-6443
305-294-9911
www.artcom.com/museums/nv/gl/33041-64.htm

The Little White House, Truman's beloved vacation home, is Florida's only presidential home. Truman held frequent retreats here during his presidency. It was here that he spent what he called some of the happiest moments of his life—the times when, during retirement, he gathered his family and spent time with his four grandchildren. In 1964, the former president dedicated the Truman Bridge at nearby Duck Key.

The home is open for 30-minute guided tours and for special events such as the Annual Truman Poker Party, held on May 8, Truman's birthday. A museum store is on the premises.

Hours
Daily from 9 A.M. to 5 P.M.
Admission
Free

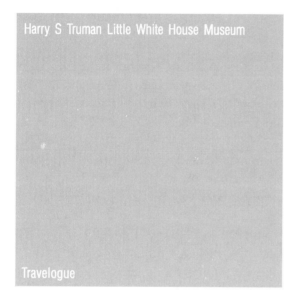
Harry S Truman Little White House Museum

Travelogue

Churches

First Presbyterian Church
100 North Pleasant Street
Independence, MO 64050-2654
816-252-3300

Although raised a Baptist, Truman attended church and Sunday school here as a child because of First Presbyterian's proximity to his home.

First Presbyterian Church

Travelogue

First National Baptist Church
Washington, DC

See Sites Related to Multiple Presidents on page 242.

See Sites Related to Multiple Presidents on page 242.

Trinity Episcopal Church
409 North Liberty Street
Independence, MO 64050-2701
816-254-3644

Truman married Elizabeth "Bess" Wallace here on June 28, 1919. His love for Bess went back to their days in school together. While a young farmer in Grandview, he proposed to her through the mail. She turned him down. He persisted and finally won her heart upon his return from World War I.

Truman attended this church—that of his wife's family—following their marriage. He became active in its men's group and other activities and gave an address at the 1959 dedication of the education wing. Truman's daughter Mary was baptized, confirmed, and married here. In October 1982, former first ladies Rosalynn Carter and Betty Ford and first lady Nancy Reagan attended Mrs. Truman's memorial service here.

There are numerous Truman memorials at Trinity Episcopal.

A plaque given by Truman's daughter Margaret marks the pew used regularly by the family.

The Bess Truman Memorial Library includes church books, Truman memorabilia, a series of Marvin Carlson photographs of the newly restored White House during the Truman administration, an entertainment center given to the Trumans by Jack Benny, and President Truman's record collection, which includes many albums autographed by the artists.

The wrought-iron fence along the west front of the walled garden was part of the original fence surrounding the Trumans' house.

A Bible in the lectern was given by friends in memory of President Truman.

The baptismal font was given by the Wallace family in memory of George Wallace, brother of Mrs. Truman.

Also on the premises are crosses made of cherry wood from a wardrobe that once belonged to Mrs. Truman's aunt.

Tours are offered Monday through Friday from 9 A.M. to 3 P.M. Sunday services are at 8 and 10:30 A.M.

Trinity Episcopal Church

Travelogue

Education

Truman attended Noland Elementary School and Columbia School in Independence. The schools no longer exist.

Truman High School
3301 South Noland Road
Independence, MO 64050
816-252-8233

In Truman's time, few boys attended high school. Truman was one of 11 young men in his class of nearly 50 in what was at the time Independence High School.

Truman wanted to attend either West Point or Annapolis but was prevented from doing so by his poor eyesight. His family's finances made enrolling in a civilian college difficult. From 1923 to 1925, he attended Kansas City Law School, which no longer exists.

Truman High School

Travelogue

Marriage

Trinity Episcopal Church
Independence, MO

See page 183.

Inaugural Sites

The White House
Washington, DC

Chief Justice Harlan F. Stone administered the oath of office for Truman's first term in the Cabinet Room on April 12, 1945. The room is not accessible to the public.

The Capitol
Washington, DC

January 20, 1949

Place of Death

Research Medical Center
2316 East Meyer Boulevard
Kansas City, MO 64132-1199
816-276-4000
www.healthmidwest.org/hospitals/rmc.shtm#history

Truman fell ill shortly before Christmas 1972 and was taken to the hospital by ambulance. On Christmas morning, he fell into a coma, from which he never awoke. He died in a sixth-floor room here on December 26 due to what was described as "organic failures causing a collapse of the cardiovascular system."

Burial Site

Harry S Truman Library and Museum
Independence, MO

See page 186.

Other Sites

Blair House
Washington, DC

See Sites Related to Multiple Presidents on pages 251–52.

Gold Coast Railroad Museum
Miami, FL

See Sites Relates to Multiple Presidents on page 257.

Harry S Truman Library and Museum
National Archives and Records Administration
US 24 and Delaware Street
Independence, MO 64050-1798
816-833-1225
Fax: 816-833-4368
http://www.lbjlib.utexas.edu/truman/
E-mail: library@truman.nara.gov.

Harry S Truman Library
Courtesy of the Harry S Truman Library

This library, which was built entirely with private funds raised from more than 17,000 donors, includes more than 18,000 square feet of exhibition space. Rotating and permanent exhibitions focus on the Truman presidency and related topics. Approximately 99 percent of the library's holdings are open to the public, in keeping with Truman's wish that "people may have these things available for study and research, and for their enjoyment and education." Truman himself did much to promote the library's mission. From its opening in July 1957 until 1966, he spent nearly every day in the library, where he greeted and talked with visitors and taught them about the history of our country.

The graves of Harry and Bess Truman are in the courtyard behind the library.

<u>Hours</u>
Daily from 9 A.M. to 5 P.M.

<u>Admission</u>
Free

Harry S Truman Library and Museum

Travelogue

Harry S Truman Office and Courtroom

Jackson County Courthouse
Main and Lexington Streets
Independence, MO 64052
816-881-4467

Truman served as an administrative judge for Jackson County following the closing of his haberdashery, Truman & Jacobson. His entry into politics came on the suggestion of his dear friend Jim Pendergast and with the support of the influential "Pendergast machine." Judge Truman spoke at the dedication of the new courthouse on September 17, 1933, a day he remembered as one of his proudest.

The Jackson County Courthouse is just one block from the visitor center for the Truman Home. A multimedia presentation called *The Man from Independence* is shown regularly.

Hours
Monday through Friday from 11 A.M. to 4 P.M., Saturday from 9 A.M. to 5 P.M., and Sunday from 1 to 5 P.M.
Admission
$2 for adults; $1 for ages five to 12

Harry S Truman Office and Courtroom

Travelogue

Kansas City Club

1228 Baltimore Avenue
Kansas City, MO 64105-1908
816-421-6789

Truman joined this fashionable private club in the early 1920s while operating Truman & Jacobson. Numerous photos of him decorate the walls today. The club is not open to the public.

Kansas City Club

Travelogue

Radisson Hotel

106 West 12th Street
Kansas City, MO 64105
816-221-7000
www.radisson.com

In November 1919, Truman and former army buddy Edward Jacobson opened Truman & Jacobson, a posh haberdashery, on the ground floor of what was then the Glennon Hotel. Capitalizing on the trendy location, the pair enjoyed initial success selling shirts, ties, hats, and other men's accessories. A downturn in the local economy, however, thrust the store into failure in 1921.

The hotel property, now on the National

Register of Historic Places, has been renovated as a Radisson Hotel. There is no marker indicating the Truman connection.

Radisson Hotel

Travelogue

Savoy Grill

Travelogue

Savoy Grill

Hotel Savoy
219 West Ninth Street
Kansas City, MO 64105-1689
816-842-3575
www.bbonline.com/mo/hotelsavoy/index.htm

During his years at Truman & Jacobson,

Truman regularly lunched here with friends Ted Marks and Jim Pendergast. The Hotel Savoy and the Savoy Grill date to the turn of the century. Both are listed on the National Register of Historic Places.

United States Air Force Museum
Dayton, OH

See Sites Related to Multiple Presidents on pages 261–62.

Dwight D. Eisenhower
Thirty-Fourth President of the United States

Birthplace

Eisenhower Birthplace State Historical Park
208 East Day Street
Denison, TX 75020
903-465-8908
www.eisenhowerbirthplace.org

Dwight D. Eisenhower was born October 14, 1890. He was the only one of the Eisenhower family's seven children to be born in Texas. Denison was a railroad town, and Eisenhower was born in a modest two-story house just yards away from three different railroad lines. That home, furnished in period style, is the focal point of this 10-acre park. Also on the premises are a visitor center, wooded areas, historic buildings, a creek, railroad trails, hiking paths, and picnic sites.

Hours
Daily from 10 A.M. to 4 P.M.; closed New Year's, Thanksgiving, and Christmas
Admission
$2

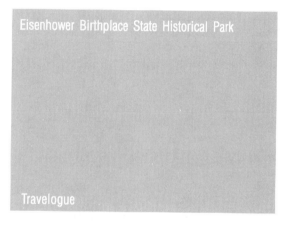

Eisenhower Birthplace State Historical Park

Travelogue

Homes

Dwight D. Eisenhower Library
Dwight D. Eisenhower Foundation
200 Southeast Fourth Street
Abilene, KS 67410
785-263-4751
redbud.lbjlib.utexas.edu/eisenhower/contents.htm

The Eisenhowers moved into a modest Abilene home when Dwight was one year old. He lived there until he left for West Point. The house, located within this site, is typical of late-18th-century homes of the area. It is furnished in period style. Also at the site are a museum with five major galleries, the Dwight D. Eisenhower Library, and the Place of Meditation. The museum interprets Eisenhower's life and career through exhibits and programs. The Place of Meditation is the site of the graves of Eisenhower, his wife, and their firstborn son.

Hours
Open daily from 9 A.M. to 4:45 P.M.; closed New Year's, Thanksgiving, and Christmas
Admission
There is a modest fee for the museum only.

Eisenhower home in Gettysburg, Pennsylvania
Courtesy of Eisenhower National Historic Site, National Park Service
Photo by Jim Voigt

Eisenhower National Historic Site
National Park Service
97 Taneytown Road
Gettysburg, PA 17325
717-338-9114
www.nps.gov/eise/

This is the only home ever owned by Eisenhower, a career army officer before his election to the presidency. The Eisenhowers bought the farm from Allen Redding in 1950, believing the original farmhouse well suited for their retirement. During renovation, however, they found that beneath the century-old brick veneer was a deteriorating 200-year-old log cabin that was in danger of collapse. The Eisenhowers then built a modified Georgian farmhouse, preserving as much of the original house as possible. The maid's room, the kitchen, and the pantry are in a portion of the original house that was salvaged. The fireplace and the oven in the den are from the original summer kitchen, which stood near the

Dwight D. Eisenhower Library

Travelogue

main house. On display at the 231-acre farm are Eisenhower's formal living room, his beloved sun porch, and many of his personal belongings. Dignitaries who visited Eisenhower here included Khrushchev, de Gaulle, and Churchill.

Access to the site is by shuttle bus from the visitor center at Gettysburg National Military Park. Those with physical disabilities should call for arrangements. Only 1,100 visitors are admitted daily.

Hours
Open daily from 9 A.M. to 4 P.M. from April to October; open Wednesday through Sunday during February, March, November, and December; closed January, Thanksgiving, and Christmas
Admission
Fees vary; call for details.

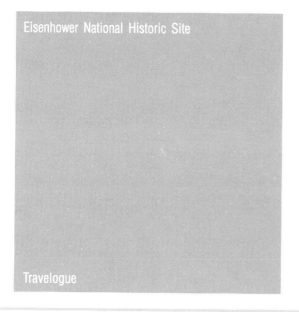

Eisenhower National Historic Site

Travelogue

Church

National Presbyterian Church
Washington, DC

See Sites Related to Multiple Presidents on page 242.

Education

Eisenhower attended public schools in Abilene, Texas.

United States Military Academy
West Point, NY

See Sites Related to Multiple Presidents on page 248.

Marriage

Eisenhower married Marie "Mamie" Geneva Doud on July 1, 1916, at the Denver home of the bride's parents.

Inaugural Site

The Capitol
Washington, DC

January 20, 1953
January 20, 1957

Place of Death

Walter Reed Army Medical Center
6900 Georgia Avenue NW
Washington, DC 20307-5001
202-782-3501 or 800-433-3574
www.wramc.amedd.army.mil

Eisenhower suffered numerous heart attacks—one while still in office, two in 1965, and three in 1968. Although he always rallied, his heart weakened each time. In February 1969, he contracted pneumonia following intestinal surgery. He continually deteriorated from that point until he died in the hospital of congestive heart failure on March 28.

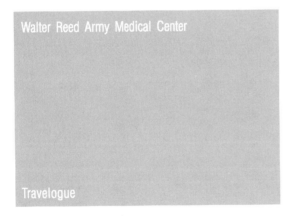

Walter Reed Army Medical Center

Travelogue

Burial Site

Dwight D. Eisenhower Library
Abilene, KS

See page 189.

Other Sites

Columbia University
New York, NY

See Sites Related to Multiple Presidents on page 245.

Gold Coast Railroad Museum
Miami, FL

See Sites Related to Multiple Presidents on page 257.

New York Avenue Presbyterian Church
Washington, DC

See Sites Related to Multiple Presidents on page 243.

Quartermaster Museum
Fort Lee, VA

See Sites Related to Multiple Presidents on pages 260–61.

United States Air Force Museum
Dayton, OH

See Sites Related to Multiple Presidents on pages 261–62.

John F. Kennedy
Thirty-Fifth President of the United States

Birthplace

John Fitzgerald Kennedy
National Historic Site

National Park Service
83 Beals Street
Brookline, MA 02146
617-566-7937

First home of John F. Kennedy
Courtesy of John Fitzgerald Kennedy National Historic Site
Photo by David F. Kratz

John F. Kennedy was the first president born in the 20th century. He lived here from his birth on May 29, 1917, until 1921. The humble house has been restored to its 1917 appearance and contains many of its original furnishings.

Hours
Wednesday through Sunday from 10 A.M. to 4:30 P.M. from mid-March to November 30. The house is shown by guided tour at 10:45 and 11:45 A.M. and 1, 2, 3, and 4 P.M.
Admission
$2 for adults; guests under 16 are free

John Fitzgerald Kennedy National Historic Site

Travelogue

Homes

The Kennedys lived in New York City in the late 1920s and in nearby Bronxville, New York, beginning in 1929. They also maintained a winter vacation home in Palm Beach, Florida.

Kennedy Compound
Irving and Marchant Avenues
Hyannisport, MA 02601

The compound consists of three homes on six acres of waterfront land. In 1929, Joseph P. Kennedy purchased the cottage he had rented over the preceding three years. After extensive renovation and expansion, it suited his family's needs. From then on, the Kennedys spent most of their summers here. In 1956, John F. Kennedy purchased a smaller residence on nearby Irving Avenue, after which Robert F. Kennedy acquired another adjacent to the first two.

The compound has remained pretty much unchanged since the assassination of John F. Kennedy. It is still owned and used by the Kennedy family and is not open to the public.

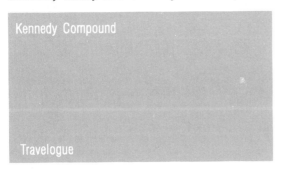

Kennedy Compound

Travelogue

Hammersmith Farm
Harrison Avenue
Newport, RI 02840
401-846-7346
visitrhodeisland.com/recreation.html

The childhood summer home of Jacqueline Bouvier, Hammersmith Farm was the site of the Kennedy-Bouvier wedding reception and was a "Summer White House" during the Kennedy administration. It is also the only working farm in Newport. The building is full of Kennedy and Bouvier memorabilia and offers spectacular water views. The gardens were designed by Frederick Law Olmsted.

Hours
Daily from 10 A.M. to 7 P.M. from Memorial Day to Labor Day and from 10 A.M. to 5 P.M. from March to Memorial Day and from Labor Day to November; special hours are in effect near Christmas. The mansion is available for private events.
Admission
$6.50 for adults; $3 for children

Hammersmith Farm

Travelogue

There are two former Kennedy residences in the nation's capital. In 1953, during his time as a Massachusetts senator, Kennedy lived at 3271 P Street NW. During the 1960 presidential election, he lived at 3307 N Street NW. Both of these homes are private residences and are not open to the public.

Church

St. Aidan's Roman Catholic Church
158 Pleasant Street
Brookline, MA 02146
617-277-0799

A small marker acknowledges this to be the church of Kennedy's baptism and boyhood.

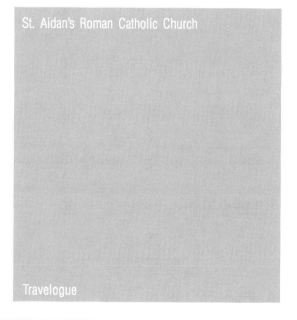

Education

Dexter School
20 Newton Street
Brookline, MA 02146-7498
617-522-5544
www.dexter.org

Kennedy attended Dexter from kindergarten through the third grade.

Riverdale Country School
5250 Fieldston Road
Bronx, NY 10471
718-549-8810
www.riverdale.edu

Kennedy studied at Riverdale from the fourth grade through the sixth grade.

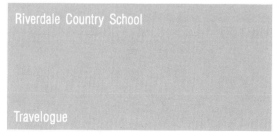

Choate Rosemary Hall
333 Christian Street
Wallingford, CT 06492
203-697-2000
www.choate.edu

John "Rat Face" Kennedy was a popular student about whom the headmaster once said, "Jack has a clever, individual mind. When he learns the right place for humor and learns to use his individual way of looking at things as an asset instead of a handicap, his natural gift of an individual outlook and witty expression are going to help him." His classmates voted Kennedy the student most likely to succeed.

In Kennedy's day, Choate was a boys' school. In 1974, it merged with Rosemary Hall, a girls' school, to form today's coeducational school.

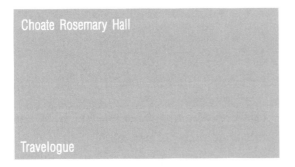

Choate Rosemary Hall

Travelogue

Harvard University
Cambridge, MA

See Sites Related to Multiple Presidents on pages 246–47.

Marriage

St. Mary's Roman Catholic Church
Spring Street
Newport, RI 02840
401-847-0475

Kennedy married Jacqueline L. Bouvier on September 12, 1953. The wedding was attended by an estimated 800 persons and was officiated by Archbishop Richard J. Cushing, who read a special blessing from Pope Pius XII.

Established April 8, 1828, St. Mary's is the oldest Roman Catholic parish in Rhode Island.

St. Mary's Roman Catholic Church

Travelogue

Inaugural Site

The Capitol
Washington, DC

January 20, 1961

Place of Death

Parkland Memorial Hospital
5201 Harry Hines Boulevard
Dallas, TX 75043
214-590-8000
www.swmed.edu/home_pages/parkland/txt/pmhtxt.html

Kennedy was pronounced dead shortly after being shot while traveling in a motorcade through Dallas (see below).

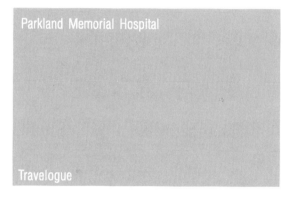

Parkland Memorial Hospital

Travelogue

Sixth Floor Museum at Dealey Plaza
Dallas County Historical Foundation
411 Elm Street
Dallas, TX 75202
214-747-6660 or 888-485-4854
www.jfk.org

On November 20, 1963, Kennedy and his wife were riding in an open limousine with Texas governor John Connally and his wife. Responding to the cheering crowds lining the streets, Mrs. Connally turned to Kennedy and said, "Mr. President, you can't say Dallas doesn't love you," to which the president responded, "That is very obvious." Moments later, Kennedy was shot twice as his motorcade passed through Dealey Plaza in front of the former Texas School Book Depository Building. It is believed that he was shot by Lee Harvey Oswald from the sixth floor of the building.

Since then, Dealey Plaza has become the most-visited site in Dallas. The museum was opened to interpret the events of that day, as well as the two investigations into the assassination. It has numerous exhibits and an extensive research library on the subject. Because of the significance of the events that happened there in 1963, the area has been designated the Dealey Plaza National Historic Landmark District.

Hours
Daily from 9 A.M. to 6 P.M.; closed Thanksgiving and Christmas
Admission
$5 for adults; $4 for seniors and guests ages six to 18

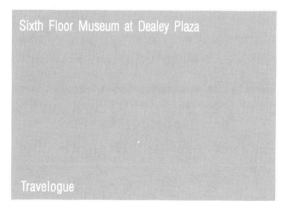

Sixth Floor Museum at Dealey Plaza

Travelogue

Funeral Site

St. Matthew's Cathedral
1725 Rhode Island Avenue NW
Washington, DC 20036-3005
202-347-3215

A marble marker within the cathedral commemorates Kennedy's funeral.

The Renaissance-style cathedral was designed by Grant LaFarge. The altar and baptismal font were gifts from India.

St. Matthew's is open daily from 6:30 A.M. to 6:30 P.M. Guided tours are offered on Sunday from 2:30 to 4:30 P.M.

St. Matthew's Cathedral

Travelogue

Burial Site

Arlington National Cemetery
Arlington, VA

See Sites Related to Multiple Presidents on page 240.

Other Sites

John F. Kennedy Hyannis Museum
397 Main Street
Hyannisport, MA 02601
508-790-3077

Located in the Hyannisport Town Hall, this museum features photos, oral histories, and a seven-minute video about Kennedy's summers on Cape Cod with family and friends.

Hours
Monday through Saturday from 10 A.M. to 4 P.M. and Sundays and holidays from 1 to 4 P.M.; the last video showing is at 3:30 P.M.
Admission
$3 for adults; guests under 16 are free

John F. Kennedy Hyannis Museum

Travelogue

John F. Kennedy Center for the Performing Arts

2700 F Street NW
Washington, DC 20566-0002
202-416-7910, 202-416-8340, or 800-444-1324
www.kennedy-center.org

This is known as the nation's premier performing house. Opened in 1971, the center actually traces its beginnings to 1958, when President Eisenhower signed the National Cultural Center Act for the design and construction of a major center to highlight American culture. Two months after the assassination in Dallas, Congress authorized that the center be developed as a memorial to Kennedy, long an advocate of the arts. President Johnson broke ground for the center in 1965.

A highlight of the center is the Robert Berks bust of Kennedy that stands in the grand foyer. Berks began sculpting the bust the night Kennedy was killed. The home of the National Symphony Orchestra, the Kennedy Center presents a wide variety of music, drama, and dance in its six theaters.

Hours
Daily from 10 A.M. to midnight; closed New Year's and Christmas. Tours are offered daily from 10 A.M. to 1 P.M. when the center is open.
Admission
The center may be visited free of charge, but tickets are required for most performances; prices vary depending on the event.

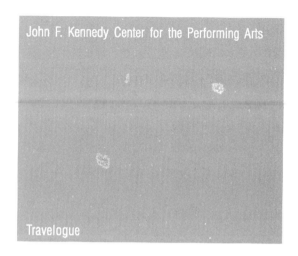

John F. Kennedy Center for the Performing Arts

Travelogue

John Fitzgerald Kennedy Library and Museum

National Archives and Records Administration
Columbia Point
Boston, MA 02125
617-929-4500
www.cs.umb.edu/jfklibrary/index.htm

This museum includes 21 exhibits highlighting the life and work of Kennedy. Popular exhibits include Kennedy's Oval Office desk, documents, and photos. A 17-minute introductory film is shown every 20 minutes. An expansive atrium overlooks Boston Harbor; one of Kennedy's personal sailboats is on display.

Hours
Daily from 9 A.M. to 5 P.M.; closed New Year's, Thanksgiving, and Christmas
Admission
$6 for adults; $4 for students and guests over 62; $2 for ages six to 16

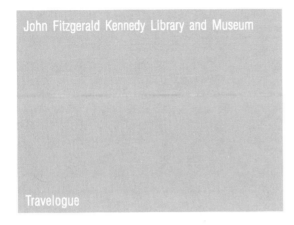

John Fitzgerald Kennedy Library and Museum

Travelogue

Quartermaster Museum
Fort Lee, VA

See sites related to Multiple Presidents on pages 260–61

United States Air Force Museum
Dayton, OH

See sites related to Multiple Presidents on pages 261–62.

Lyndon Baines Johnson

Thirty-Sixth President of the United States

Birthplace/Home

Lyndon B. Johnson National Historical Park

National Park Service
P.O. Box 329
Johnson City, TX 78636
830-868-7128
www.nps.gov/lyjo/index.html

This park has two components, one in Johnson City and the other in Stonewall. Both units are on US 290. Johnson City is 50 miles west of Austin; Stonewall is 15 miles west of Johnson City.

Guided and self-guided tours are offered at the Johnson City unit, which contains the LBJ Boyhood Home, the Johnson Settlement, and a visitor center. The focus at the Johnson Settlement, begun by Lyndon's grandfather in 1857, is on early Texas history. What is now the visitor center opened as a town hospital in 1969 with funds provided by the Johnson administration. Due to its failure to attract sufficient business, the hospital was closed. It was then converted to a visitor center, which opened in October 1994. The visitor center offers two exhibit galleries, three film presentations, and a book shop.

Bus tours are conducted at the Stonewall unit. The tours cost $3 and last about 90 min-

Lyndon B. Johnson National Historical Park's visitor center
Photo by Duane Lokken

utes. They operate throughout the day on no set schedule. The tours pass the one-room Junction School, which Johnson attended beginning at age four; the LBJ Birthplace, where the future president was born on August 27, 1908; the Johnson family cemetery; and the LBJ Ranch, where cattle are still raised.

Note that tours may be abbreviated or canceled due to high heat or other inclement weather.

Hours
Daily from 9 A.M. to 5 P.M.; closed New Year's and Christmas
Admission
Free

Lyndon B. Johnson National Historical Park

Travelogue

The school was renamed in his honor during the 1960s. In the school office is a photo of Johnson that he signed while president. Also on display are photos of his class. Visitors are welcome but should call ahead.

Lyndon B. Johnson High School

Travelogue

Southwest Texas University

601 University Drive
San Marcos, TX 78666-4604
512-245-2111
www.swt.edu

Education

Junction School
Johnson City, TX

See Lyndon B. Johnson National Historical Park on page 201.

Lyndon B. Johnson High School
400 East Ash Street
Johnson City, TX 78636
830-868-7410

Johnson graduated from what was then called Johnson City High School in 1924.

Johnson delayed going to college, preferring to work various jobs in Texas and California. Three years after he graduated from high school, his mother's prodding led him to enroll at what was then called Southwest Texas Teachers' College. He worked his way through college by being a trash collector, a janitor, and an assistant to the president's secretary. He graduated in 1930.

While a student, Johnson lived in the former Miller boardinghouse, which now houses the university's alumni association. Located on the corner of LBJ and University

Drives, the structure was awarded Texas Historical Landmark status in 1968 and was placed on the National Register of Historic Places in 1983. On display inside are items related to Johnson's time at the university. Visitors should call ahead for hours.

The university has recently completed the $14 million LBJ Student Center; numerous family members attended the dedication ceremony. The school also sponsors the annual LBJ Distinguished Lecture Series. Although not organized for public exhibition, the university has an LBJ Archive.

Southwest Texas University

Travelogue

Georgetown University
Washington, DC

See Sites Related to Multiple Presidents on page 246.

Marriage

St. Mark's Episcopal Church
315 East Pecan Street
San Antonio, TX 78205-1885
210-226-2426
www.stmarks-sa.org

Johnson met Claudia Alya "Lady Bird" Taylor in 1934 at the Austin home of mutual friend Eugene Lasseter. The morning after their meeting, he invited Lady Bird to breakfast, where he proposed marriage. She refused at first but later changed her mind on the advice of her father. On November 17, 1934, they were married here in an impromptu service with no music, no flowers, and only four or five attendees. The Johnsons remained members of St. Mark's; a bronze plaque in the narthex commemorates them.

The public is welcome to attend Sunday services, which are held at 7:45, 9, and 11 A.M. Call ahead to arrange for a visit during regular office hours.

St. Mark's Episcopal Church

Travelogue

Inaugural Sites

Johnson took the oath of office aboard a presidential Boeing 707 at Love Field in Dallas, Texas, on November 22, 1963, following the Kennedy assassination. That plane is now housed at the United States Air Force Museum (*see* Sites Related to Multiple Presidents on pages 261–62).

The Capitol
Washington, DC

January 20, 1965

Place of Death

Johnson suffered heart attacks in 1955 and 1972. In his book *Just As I Am*, evangelist Billy Graham wrote that in early 1972, Johnson told him in confidence that he expected he would soon die of heart disease, as relatives of his had done in their 60s. That, according to Graham, was the primary reason why Johnson decided against seeking reelection.

About 3:30 P.M. on January 22, 1973, Johnson awoke from a nap complaining of chest pains. He died less than an hour later while en route from the LBJ Ranch (*see* Lyndon B. Johnson National Historical Park on page 201) to the hospital in San Antonio.

Funeral Site

National City Christian Church
14th Avenue NW
Washington, DC 20005
202-232-0323

Dr. George Davis presided and Leontyne Price sang at Johnson's funeral. A historical marker commemorates the service.

National City Christian Church is open to the public during regular worship hours and office hours; call ahead to visit during office hours.

National City Christian Church

Travelogue

Burial Site

Johnson Family Cemetery
Stonewall, TX

Graveside services were conducted by the Reverend Billy Graham at the family cemetery (*see* Lyndon B. Johnson National Historical

Park on page 201). Anita Bryant sang "The Battle Hymn of the Republic."

Other Sites

Johnson City Bank
Court House Square
Johnson City, TX 78636
830-868-7131

Built in 1885 of limestone quarried in nearby Blanco County, this structure has remained a focal point of Johnson City. Commonly referred to as the "Rock Building," it has served as a courthouse, jail, retail store, restaurant, hotel, bus station, and nursing home. In 1916, the building was acquired by Sam Ealy Johnson, Lyndon's father. He sold it in 1920. At that time, the building had a dry-goods store on the first floor and a large open area called the "Opera House" on the second. The Opera House was the site of school graduations, social functions, movie showings, and dramatic presentations. Many Johnson family functions were held there through the years.

In 1944, Citizens State Bank opened in the building. In 1948, when the bank's board was expanded from five to six persons, Johnson was elected to the board. The bank's current name was adopted in 1965. In 1970, Johnson acquired ownership of the bank and the building, but he sold his interest the following year. The former president briefly maintained offices in the building's basement.

Today, the bank occupies the first floor and private offices are maintained on the second.

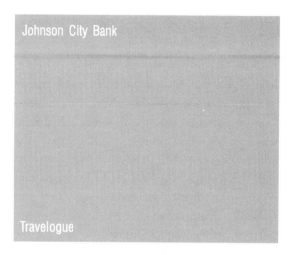

Johnson City Bank

Travelogue

Johnson City Historic District
c/o Lyndon B. Johnson National Historical Park
P.O. Box 329
Johnson City, TX 78636
830-868-7128
www.nps.gov/lyjo/index.html

The Johnson City Historical Review Board is working with Southwest Texas University and the National Park Service to identify and develop a historic district that would include most of Johnson City's downtown area. Below are a few of the sites within the proposed district.

Impeckible Aviaries on Nugent Street is a bird store occupying the space that once housed the Casparis Café, where Johnson is said to have developed his fondness for chili. "Bowl o' red, darlin'" is how he would order chili from "Miz Fannie" Casparis. In fact, he was so fond of Miz Fannie's chili—which he dubbed "Mexican T-bone"—that he brought her recipe to Washington. Johnson always kept a pot of chili on hand at the White House.

Rare Bird Antiques, across the street from Impeckible Aviaries, is the former site of the Maddox Barber Shop, where the young Johnson worked shining shoes. It was there, it is said, that he had his introduction to the adult world of politics and business. One day, the shop's regulars teased the future president by inviting him to sit on a chair they had secretly smeared with oil of mustard. Johnson subsequently ran in pain into the street. The original building burned in 1929 but was immediately replaced by the existing masonry structure.

The Pedernales Electric Cooperative (PEC), located on Ninth Street, was Johnson's first great achievement in politics. During his first term in Congress, he won the support of President Franklin D. Roosevelt for PEC's creation. It was at the time the largest rural electrification project in the country. In November 1939, Johnson threw the switch that energized the first section of the PEC system. Following that ceremony, he went to the porch of his boyhood home (see page 201), where he was serenaded by hundreds of residents ecstatic about their new electric power. The PEC remains one of the area's largest employers. Although greatly altered over time, the original building is still in use. Many of its original furnishings are in use in the council chamber of city hall.

Johnson City Historic District

Travelogue

Lyndon B. Johnson Memorial Grove on the Potomac

National Park Service
George Washington Parkway
McLean, VA 22101
703-285-2598

At this site, a megalith sculpted by Harold Vogel is surrounded by 500 white pine trees. The statue is made of rough-hewn red granite from a quarry near the LBJ Ranch. The 15-acre site features bike trails and picnic facilities and has an impressive view of Washington. The grove is near the Pentagon between the Arlington Memorial and 14th Street Bridges along the west bank of the Potomac.

Hours
Daily from dawn to dusk
Admission
Free

Lyndon B. Johnson Memorial Grove on the Potomac

Travelogue

Lyndon B. Johnson State Historical Park

US 290
P.O. Box 238
Stonewall, TX 78671
830-644-2252 or 800-792-1112
www.tpwd.state.tx.us/park/lbj/lbj.htm

To honor Johnson, friends raised money to purchase the 700-acre plot directly across the Pedernales River from the LBJ Ranch. The park opened in 1972. Famous for its wild-flower displays, it also includes exhibits of local culture and history, picnic areas, a pool, hunting trails, and tennis courts.

Hours
Daily from 8 A.M. to 5 P.M.
Admission
Free, although there are charges for various park activities

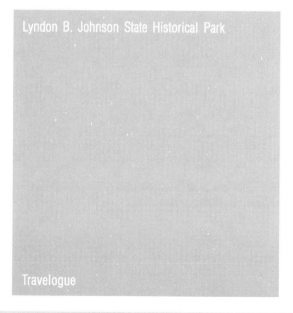
Lyndon B. Johnson State Historical Park

Travelogue

Lyndon Baines Johnson Library and Museum
Photo by Frank Wolfe

Lyndon Baines Johnson Library and Museum

National Archives and Records Administration
2313 Red River Street
Austin, TX 78705-5702
512-916-5136
www.lbjlib.utexas.edu

The library houses 40 million documents, including those from Johnson's entire public career. This massive collection dominates the Great Hall, from which the public can look through four stories of interior windows and see the red buckram boxes that hold the papers. The museum provides year-round public viewing of permanent and temporary exhibits, as well as a plethora of educational programming.

Shortly after assuming the presidency, Johnson asked his wife to take on the task of planning a presidential library and museum.

Although his alma mater and his birthplace were sentimental favorites, the regents of the University of Texas proposed building a new graduate school of public affairs, to be named in Johnson's honor. They also wanted to build a library and museum complex to the family's and the government's specifications, to be the focal point of the university's new East Campus.

At the May 1971 dedication, Johnson referred to the library and museum as "the story of our time—with the bark off."

Hours
Daily from 9 A.M. to 5 P.M.; closed
Christmas
Admission
Free

Lyndon Baines Johnson Library and Museum

Travelogue

Richard M. Nixon
Thirty-Seventh President of the United States

Birthplace

Richard M. Nixon Library and Birthplace

Richard M. Nixon Foundation
18001 Yorba Linda Boulevard
Yorba Linda, CA 92686-3903
714-993-3393
www.nixonfoundation.org

Richard M. Nixon was born in this small house on January 9, 1913. His father, Frank, had built it the year before. The Nixons lived here until 1922, when they moved to nearby Whittier. The property then passed through the hands of numerous owners before being acquired in 1948 by the Yorba Linda school district, which owned the adjacent property. Between 1948 and 1959, the home was nearly demolished numerous times. In 1959, the school district and the people of Yorba Linda finally designated it a historic site.

The site includes a 52,000-square-foot museum, 22 high-tech galleries, video theaters, the First Lady's Garden, and Nixon's birthplace and grave. Included in the museum is the 22-foot limousine that served Presidents Johnson, Nixon, Ford, and Carter. The 11,000-pound 1967 Lincoln has nearly two tons of armor, two-inch-thick bulletproof glass, and steel wheel inserts that would al-low the car to be driven at top speed for 50 miles with four flat tires. The birthplace home is original and includes the actual piano on which the future president learned to play and the bed in which he was born.

Hours
Monday through Saturday from 10 A.M. to 5 P.M. and Sunday from 11 A.M. to 5 P.M.
Admission
$5.95 for adults; $4.95 for active military; $3.95 for guests 62 and older; $2 for ages eight to 11; children seven and under are free

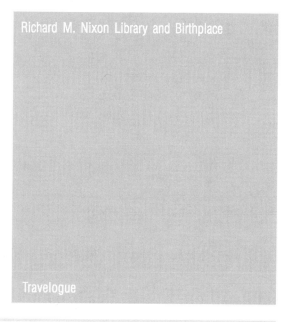

Richard M. Nixon Library and Birthplace

Travelogue

Homes

During the 1940s, Nixon lived at 14033 Honeysuckle Lane in Whittier. The property is now a private residence.

After retiring from the presidency, he settled in San Clemente, California. He later moved to New York City and finally to Saddle River, New Jersey. None of these former homes is open to the public.

Church

East Whittier Friends Church
15911 Whittier Boulevard
Whittier, CA 90603-2524
562-947-9441

Nixon attended this church. He rejected the Quaker belief in pacifism and enlisted in the navy during World War II. He also rejected the Quaker stance on taking oaths of office when he took the oath as vice president. He could have substituted the word *affirm* for *swear*, as had the only other Quaker president, Herbert Hoover.

East Whittier Friends Church

Travelogue

Education

Fullerton High School
201 East Chapman Avenue
Fullerton, CA 92832
714-870-3700

While a student at Fullerton, Nixon won the Constitutional Oratorical Contest and went on to represent the West Coast in the National Oratorical Contest. He transferred to Whittier High School in his junior year.

Nixon is included on Fullerton High's "Wall of Fame," a photographic tribute to about 75 graduates who have achieved some level of prominence. On display in the school office is a letter from Nixon during his presidency. The public is welcome to visit the school but should call ahead to make arrangements.

Fullerton High School

Travelogue

Whittier High School

Whittier Union High School District
9401 Painter Avenue
Whittier, CA 90605-2729
562-698-8121

Nixon graduated from Whittier High in 1930 and was presented the California Inter-scholastic Federation Gold Seal Award for scholarship and the Harvard Award for being the best all-around student.

Richard M. Nixon Memorial, Orthogonian Society, Whittier College
Photo courtesy of Whittier College

Whittier College

13406 Philadelphia Street
Whittier, CA 90601-4413
562-907-4200
www.whittier.edu

Nixon, a history major, was elected president of the student body during his senior year. He ran on a platform of "A Dance a Month." The college had banned dancing, but Nixon was able to convince administrators to reconsider their stance to keep students away from Los Angeles dance halls. He also founded the Square Shooters, a club for students of modest means. He was active in the glee and drama clubs and was founding president of the Orthogonian Society. A lover of football, he was second-string tackle for the college's team. At age 25, Nixon was named president of the Whittier Alumni Association; the following year, he became the college's youngest trustee.

The Orthogonian Society recently erected a Nixon monument on campus. The Nixon Room in the college's Bonnie Bell Wardman Library houses the second-largest collection of Nixon memorabilia and gifts in existence. The room was established in the 1970s when

Nixon donated a large collection of gifts he and his wife had received from world leaders. Whittier has assembled a list of Nixon experts and speakers ranging from scholars to former classmates.

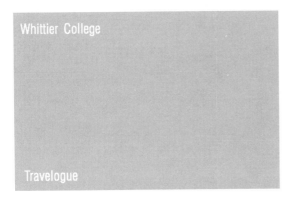

Duke University School of Law
Durham, NC 27708
919-684-8111
www.duke.edu

Nixon attended Duke on scholarships and earned income through a New Deal National Youth Administration program that brought him 35 cents an hour. He was known by friends as "Gloomy Gus" because of his demeanor. He graduated in 1937 and was admitted to the California Bar that same year.

Nixon never posed for an official presidential portrait. However, Duke owns a Nixon portrait done by Joseph Wallace King. It is currently on loan to the Speaker of the United States House of Representatives. It is then scheduled to be loaned to the National Portrait Gallery and eventually to the Richard M. Nixon Library and Birthplace. Duke's Perkins

Library has a small collection of Nixon's papers.

Marriage

Mission Inn
3649 Mission Inn Drive
Riverside, CA 92501
909-784-0300

Nixon married Thelma Catherine "Pat" Ryan on June 21, 1940, in this hotel's St. Francis of Assisi Chapel. Ryan had come to Whittier to teach typing and shorthand at Whittier High School. She continued her amateur acting career while in town. When a friend of Nixon's told him in 1938 that a pretty young teacher had come to town and gotten involved with a local theater group, Nixon auditioned for and won the male lead (opposite Ryan) in *The Dark Tower*. He proposed marriage that evening. She turned him down but changed her mind after two years of dating.

The Mission Inn is a National Historical

Landmark Hotel. Ronald and Nancy Reagan spent their honeymoon here.

Mission Inn
Photo by Bob Torrez

Mission Inn

Travelogue

Inaugural Site

The Capitol
Washington, DC

January 20, 1969
January 20, 1973

Place of Death

Mount Sinai Hospital
Fifth Avenue at East 101st Street
New York, NY 10029
212-241-6500

Nixon died here on April 22, 1994, after suffering a stroke at his New Jersey home.

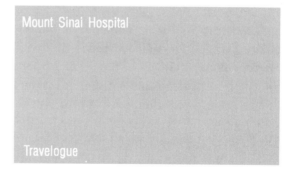

Mount Sinai Hospital

Travelogue

Funeral/Burial Site

Richard M. Nixon Library and Birthplace
Yorba Linda, CA

See page 209.

Other Sites

Nixon Presidential Materials Staff

National Archives and Records Administration
8601 Adelphi Road
College Park, MD 20740-6001
301-713-6950
sunsite.unc.edu/lic/president/nixon.html

During the Watergate investigation, Congress mandated that official Nixon administration papers not be removed from the Washington area, so that information could be readily accessed as necessary. As a result, the National Archives and Records Administration established the Nixon Presidential Materials Staff—the Nixon Project—in nearby College Park, Maryland. It is not associated with the Nixon Library and Birthplace.

The project's holdings include about 44 million pages of documents, 435,000 official photographs, 700 hours of film, 4,082 hours of "off-air" videotape, and 4,469 hours of audiotape. The 4,000 hours of White House audiotape include secret tapes recorded in the Oval Office, some of which were at the center of the Watergate investigation. Staff members are available to assist researchers during normal business hours; researchers should call ahead to make an appointment. The staff also maintains exhibitions of Nixon-related items and offers educational programs.

Hours
Monday and Wednesday from 8:45 A.M. to 5 P.M.; Tuesday, Thursday, and Friday from 8:45 A.M. to 9 P.M.; Saturday from 8:45 A.M. to 4:45 P.M.
Admission
Free

Nixon Presidential Materials Staff

Travelogue

Richard M. Nixon Center
1615 L Street NW, Suite 1250
Washington, DC 20036
202-887-1000
www.nixonfoundation.org

Founded in 1994, this is a public-policy institute that deals with issues such as United States–Russian relations, Chinese study, national security, and regional strategy. It offers a broad range of internships.

Richard M. Nixon Center

Travelogue

United States Air Force Museum
Dayton, OH

See Sites Related to Multiple Presidents on pages 261–62.

Gerald R. Ford

Thirty-Eighth President of the United States

Birthplace

Gerald R. Ford Birth Site and Gardens

Omaha Department of Parks,
Recreation, and Public Property
3202 Woolworth Avenue
Omaha, NE 68105
402-595-1180

Gerald R. Ford Birth Site and Gardens
Courtesy of Gerald R. Ford Birth Site and Gardens

Ford was born Leslie Lynch King, Jr., in Omaha on July 14, 1913. Soon afterward, his mother took him to Grand Rapids, Michigan, where they lived with her parents. In 1916, she and her husband divorced. She later remarried, at which time the future president was adopted by his stepfather and renamed Gerald Randolph Ford, Jr.

The home where Ford was born was razed in 1971 following a fire. In 1974, Omaha businessman James M. Paxon purchased the property to build a memorial. A proposed design by University of Nebraska architecture student Gary Dubas was selected. It called for a garden scene of walkways and plantings. A colonnade modeled after the south colonnade of the White House was added, as was a rose garden modeled after that at the White House. At the center of the park is a kiosk patterned after the original house's turret. It contains a model of the original house and Ford mementos. Paxon deeded the park to the city. In September 1977, the Fords attended the dedication ceremony.

Hours
Daily from 7:30 A.M. to 9:30 P.M.
Admission
Free

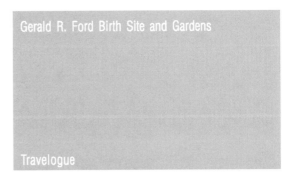

Gerald R. Ford Birth Site and Gardens

Travelogue

Homes

Ford lived in the Michigan communities of Grand Rapids, East Grand Rapids, and Ottawa Beach. None of his former homes is open to the public.

Churches

Grace Episcopal Church
1815 Hall Street SE
Grand Rapids, MI 49506-4099
616-241-4631

This is the Ford family's hometown church.

St. John's Lafayette Square
Washington, DC

See Sites Related to Multiple Presidents on pages 243–44.

Education

Job Corps of Grand Rapids
110 Hall Street SE
Grand Rapids, MI 49507
616-243-6877

Ford attended school in this building when it housed South High School, which no longer exists. He entered in grade seven and graduated in 1931. He was the star center of the South High Trojans football team. During his junior year, Ford was inducted into the National Honor Society. He graduated in the top 5 percent of his class.

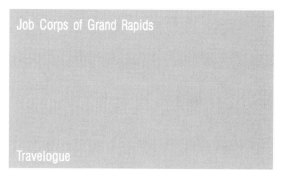

University of Michigan
Ann Arbor, MI 48109
734-764-1817
www.umich.edu

Ford attended the University of Michigan on a partial scholarship and earned money by busing tables in the university hospital and washing dishes in his fraternity house. He was voted outstanding freshman on the football team and was named most valuable player his senior year for his play as first-team center. On January 1, 1935, he played in the Shrine East-West all-star game in San Francisco. That August, he played in an all-star game against the Chicago Bears. Upon his graduation in 1935, Ford was offered contracts by both the Detroit Lions and the Green Bay Packers, but he decided to pursue a legal education.

Ford's football uniform and some photos of him are on display in Schembechler Hall, located at 1200 South State Street. The building is open to the public weekdays from 11 A.M. to 4 P.M. and Saturdays from 10 A.M. to 2 P.M. Admission is free.

University of Michigan
Travelogue

Yale University
New Haven, CT

See Sites Related to Multiple Presidents on pages 249–50.

Marriage

Grace Episcopal Church
1815 Hall Street SE
Grand Rapids, MI 49506-1099
616-241-4631

Ford married Elizabeth Ann "Betty" Bloomer here on October 15, 1948. Visitors are welcome to attend Sunday services, held at 8 and 10 A.M.

Inaugural Site

The White House
Washington, DC

Ford took the oath of office in the East Room just minutes after the resignation of Richard M. Nixon on August 9, 1974.

Other Sites

Gerald R. Ford Conservation Center
Nebraska State Historical Society
32nd Street at Woolworth Avenue
Omaha, NE 68105
402-595-1180

In 1995, James M. Paxon acquired the lot adjoining the Gerald R. Ford Birth Site and Gardens and constructed the Gerald R. Ford Conservation Center. A division of the Nebraska State Historical Society, the center

Gerald R. Ford Conservation Center
Courtesy of Gerald R. Ford Birth Site and Gardens

provides facilities for the conservation and preservation of museum artifacts, textiles, paper, rare books, manuscripts, and photographs. It serves museums, libraries, and private clients throughout the region. It also houses a permanent display of Ford artifacts.

Hours
The exhibition gallery is open Tuesday through Friday from 1 to 4 P.M.
Admission
Free

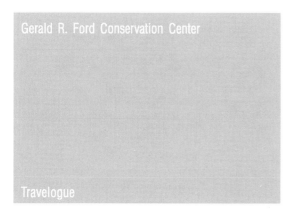
Gerald R. Ford Conservation Center

Travelogue

Gerald R. Ford Library
National Archives and Records Administration
1000 Beal Avenue
Ann Arbor, MI 48109
734-741-2218
www.lbjlib.utexas.edu/ford/homepage.html

The library, on the campus of the University of Michigan, contains 20 million documents related to the Ford presidency. Archivists use a wide range of aids to help researchers find, organize, and interpret documents. The focus of the library is the preservation and presentation of Ford's presidential papers; the majority of public programming is offered through the Gerald R. Ford Museum.

Hours
Weekdays from 8:45 A.M. to 4:45 P.M.;
closed federal holidays
Admission
Free

Gerald R. Ford Library

Travelogue

Gerald R. Ford Museum
Courtesy of Gerald R. Ford Museum

Gerald R. Ford Museum

Gerald R. Ford Foundation
303 Pearl Street NW
Grand Rapids, MI 49504-5353
616-451-9263
www.lbjlib.utexas.edu/ford/homepage.html

This museum overlooks downtown Grand Rapids. In early 1997, it reopened after a $5.3 million upgrade. Museum director Richard Norton Smith oversaw the renovation. Smith joined the museum's staff in 1996 after directing the presidential libraries of Hoover, Eisenhower, and Reagan.

The Gerald R. Ford Museum is considered one of the nation's best. Included are 10 exhibition galleries interpreting the Ford presidency, the 1970s, the Constitution, and other topics. A variety of exceptionally creative temporary exhibits are shown. For example, a recent exhibit on World War I included a 40-foot battlefield trench.

Hours
Daily from 9 A.M. to 5 P.M.; closed New Year's, Thanksgiving, and Christmas
Admission
$3 for adults; $2 for seniors; guests under 16 are free

United States Air Force Museum
Dayton, OH

See Sites Related to Multiple Presidents on pages 261–62.

Jimmy Carter

Thirty-Ninth President of the United States

Birthplace

Lillian G. Carter Nursing Center
225 Hospital Street
Plains, GA 31780-3432
912-824-7796

Jimmy Carter was the first president born in a hospital. He was born October 1, 1924, in what was then Wise Hospital. Since then, the nursing center has been renamed in honor of Carter's mother for her many years of community service.

Lillian G. Carter Nursing Center

Travelogue

Homes

Jimmy Carter National Historic Site
National Park Service
Route 1, Box 800
Andersonville, GA 31711-9707
912-924-0343
www.nps.gov/jica/

This site administers four properties in Plains that deal with Carter's life and typify rural Georgia. Here, life revolves around home, church, and school. As he grew, Carter was greatly influenced by these aspects of his life.

The visitor center is in the former Plains High School. Carter and his wife both attended grammar and high school here. Rosalynn Carter once told how she and her husband were influenced by their teacher and principal, Miss Julia Coleman, who told them that in such a great country, "any schoolboy, even one of ours, might be president of the United States." Jimmy Carter played on the school's basketball team. Rosalynn was valedictorian of the class of 1944. The school was built in 1921, integrated in 1966, and closed in 1979. It reopened in 1996 as the visitor center/museum.

The family moved into Carter's boyhood

The former Plains Depot, Carter campaign headquarters
Courtesy of the Jimmy Carter National Historic Site
Photo by M. Jolly

the former president by White House staff members. The residence is under constant protection by the Secret Service and is not accessible to the public.

The Plains Railroad Depot was built in 1888, when the community of Plains was relocated a few miles to its current spot to take advantage of a new railroad. During the 1976 presidential campaign, the depot was Carter's campaign headquarters. Today, it houses a small exhibit about that campaign.

A driving-tour audiotape and a self-guided driving-tour brochure are available at the visitor center.

<u>Hours</u>
Daily from 9 A.M. to 5 P.M.; closed New Year's, Thanksgiving, and Christmas
<u>Admission</u>
Free

home in 1928. On that day, his father forgot the key. They got into the home only after the four-year-old future president crawled through a window and unlocked a door. On the surrounding 360-acre farm, the Carters grew and sold cotton, peanuts, and corn and raised vegetables and livestock for their own consumption. Carter recalls the day in 1937 when "an unbelievable change took place in our lives." On that day, electricity was supplied to the house. The home is currently undergoing restoration, but visitors may view its exterior and walk around the grounds.

The Carter family residence on Woodlawn Drive is the only home Jimmy and Rosalynn have ever owned. They purchased the 2.4-acre plot in 1960 and built the current ranch-style home on it. They renovated the home in 1974 and again in 1981, at which time a wood shop was built with tools presented to

Former Plains High School
Courtesy of the Jimmy Carter National Historic Site
Photo by M. Jolly

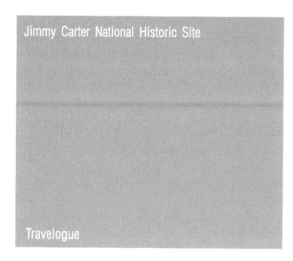

Jimmy Carter National Historic Site

Travelogue

Churches

Maranatha Baptist Church
Plains, GA 31780
912-824-7896

Carter is a lifelong member of this church and to this day teaches adult Sunday-school classes when he is in town. Visitors may call the church office to inquire about dates when he is scheduled to teach. Sunday-school classes are held at 10 A.M.

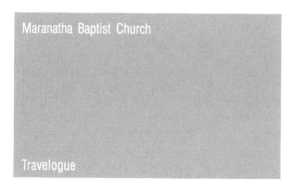

Maranatha Baptist Church

Travelogue

First National Baptist Church
Washington, DC

See Sites Related to Multiple Presidents on page 242.

Education

Plains High School
Plains, GA

See Jimmy Carter National Historic Site on page 221.

Georgia Southwestern College
800 Wheatley Street
Americus, GA 31709
800-338-0082
www.gsu.peachnet.edu

The library at this college is named in honor of Carter's father, James Earl Carter. The college is also home to the Rosalynn Carter Institute, an organization that supports caregivers.

Georgia Southwestern College

Travelogue

U.S. Naval Academy
Courtesy of U.S. Naval Academy

United States Naval Academy

Annapolis, MD 21402
410-293-2291
www.nadn.navy.mil

Carter transferred from Georgia Southwestern to the United States Naval Academy in 1942 after taking math courses at Georgia Institute of Technology. His constant grin and Southern accent brought him much torment from upperclassmen. Carter graduated 59th out of 820 midshipmen.

The academy has on display in the main rotunda of Bancroft Hall a small collection of memorabilia of distinguished alumni. Included are Carter's yearbook photo and a photo from his presidency. Bancroft Hall is included on the tour of campus given by the admissions office. Visitors should call ahead to make arrangements.

United States Naval Academy

Travelogue

Marriage

Plains United Methodist Church

305 West Church Street
Plains, GA 31780
912-824-7801

Carter married Eleanor Rosalynn Smith on July 7, 1946. Immediately after the wedding, they drove to Norfolk, Virginia, where Carter began his first tour of duty with the navy.

Plains United Methodist Church

Travelogue

Inaugural Site

The Capitol
Washington, DC

January 20, 1977

Other Sites

Carter Center
1 Copenhill
453 Freedom Parkway
Atlanta, GA 30307-1406
404-420-5100
www.emory.edu/CARTER_CENTER/homepage.html

Carter Center
Courtesy of Carter Center

The Carter Center, founded in 1982 by Jimmy and Rosalynn Carter, is a nonprofit organization whose aim is to advance peace and health worldwide. Located five miles from downtown Atlanta, the center has improved lives in more than 65 countries. It brings people and resources together to resolve conflicts; promotes democracy; fights disease, hunger, and poverty; and protects and promotes human rights. It houses the offices of Jimmy and Rosalynn Carter, the nondenominational Cecil B. Day Chapel, and conference facilities. Although separately chartered and independently governed, the center is part of Emory University.

Located next door to the center and open to the public is the Jimmy Carter Library and Museum. The museum offers visitors an intimate look at the American presidency and the Carter administration. Also open to the public are the 35-acre grounds, which include a rose garden, a wildflower meadow, and Japanese gardens.

Hours
For museum hours, call 404-331-3942.
Admission
Free

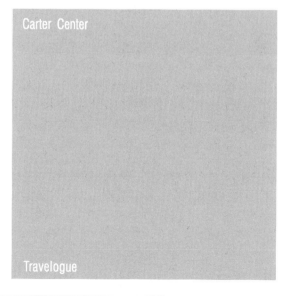

Carter Center

Travelogue

Jimmy Carter Library and Museum
Atlanta, GA

See Carter Center page 225.

Smiling Peanut Statue
Davis E-Z Food and Bottle Shop
GA 45 North
Plains, GA 31780
912-824-7701

This 13-foot statue of a smiling peanut honors Carter's trademark smile and his previous vocation as a peanut farmer. It was created for a presidential rally in Evansville, Indiana. At the rally, Carter was heard to say, "I want that" (although, according to campaign worker Maxine Reese, he does not recall uttering those words). The people of Evansville shipped the statue to Georgia following the rally. It stood on the platform of the Plains Railroad Depot (Carter's campaign headquarters) for some time before being moved to its current spot. It remains one of the area's most popular attractions today. The statue is available 24 hours per day for those wishing to take photos.

Smiling Peanut Statue

Travelogue

United States Air Force Museum
Dayton, OH

See Sites Related to Multiple Presidents on pages 261–62.

Ronald Reagan
Fortieth President of the United States

Birthplace

Ronald Reagan's Birthplace
Tampico Area Historical Society
111 Main Street
Tampico, IL 61283
815-438-2130

Ronald Reagan was born February 6, 1911, in a five-room apartment above a bakery in the Graham Building. The family lived here until May 1911. Later that year, First National Bank moved into the first floor of the building. The building changed hands a number of times before being purchased by Mr. and Mrs. Paul Nicely in 1968. The Nicelys lived in the former Reagan apartment and still own the building. Mrs. Nicely recently moved from the property, which is being developed into a Reagan museum.

Adjacent to the birthplace are Reagan Park and the former W. H. Harrison General Store, now the Tampico Historical Society. The historical society offers a walking-tour brochure.

Hours
Daily from 10 A.M. to 4 P.M.
Admission
Free; donations are requested

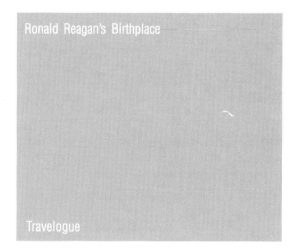

Ronald Reagan's Birthplace

Travelogue

Homes

In May 1911, the Reagans moved to a large single-family home on Glassburn Street less than two blocks from Ronald's birthplace. To see this home, follow Main Street south from the birthplace to Glassburn. Turn right onto Glassburn; the house is on the south side of the street in the middle of the block. It is a private residence not open to the public.

When Reagan was two, the family moved to Chicago. It later moved to the Illinois towns of Galesburg and Monmouth before returning to Tampico in 1919. At that time, the family lived above the Pitney Store, located across the street from Reagan's birthplace. In late 1920, the family moved to Dixon (*see* Ronald Reagan's Boyhood Home below).

Ronald Reagan's Boyhood Home
Courtesy of Ronald Reagan Boyhood Home
Photo by Eldon Glick

Ronald Reagan's Boyhood Home
Ronald Reagan Home Preservation Foundation
816 South Hennepin Avenue
Dixon, IL 61021-3646
815-288-3404

Although his family rented five homes while living in Dixon, this house is the only one mentioned in Reagan's autobiography. The Reagans lived here from 1920 to 1923. Ronald and his brother, Neil, shared one of the three second-floor bedrooms. Another was shared by their parents, and the third was used by Mrs. Reagan as a sewing room so she could supplement the family's income.

A single-family rental home in the 1920s, it was remodeled into a two-family home sometime thereafter. In the summer of 1980, following the Republican National Conven-

tion, a local postal carrier noticed that the house was for sale. He put $250 down as a deposit and then set about raising funds to purchase the $31,500 home. In the fall of that year, the house was opened to the public, although it was completely empty. Funds were raised for its renovation as a museum in time for Reagan's visit to the site on his birthday in 1984.

The home is furnished in period style. Guided tours are available.

<u>Hours</u>
Monday through Saturday from 10 A.M. to 4 P.M. and Sunday from 1 to 4 P.M. from April to November; Saturday from 10 A.M. to 4 P.M. and Sunday from 1 to 4 P.M. during February and March; closed January, Thanksgiving, and December
<u>Admission</u>
Free

Ronald Reagan's Boyhood Home

Travelogue

Churches

Church of Christ
201 Fremont Street
Tampico, IL 61283
815-438-6805

Reagan and his mother attended this church. His father and brother attended the local Roman Catholic church.

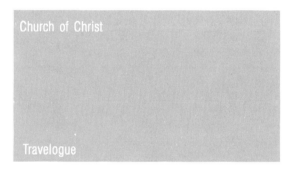

First Christian Church (Disciples of Christ)
123 South Hennepin Avenue
Dixon, IL 61021
815-288-1222

Reagan and his mother attended this church and were Sunday-school teachers here. The two Reagan boys were baptized at First Christian on June 21, 1922.

Education

Dixon Historical Center
Hennepin Avenue
Dixon, IL 61021

Reagan attended South Side School—later called South Central School—from 1920 to 1923. The red-brick building in which the school was housed is being renovated and will become the Dixon Historical Center. The center will feature Reagan-related displays. An opening date has not yet been announced.

Dixon High School
415 South Hennepin Avenue
Dixon, IL 61020
815-284-7723

Reagan played right guard on this school's football team and also played on the basketball and track teams. He was student body president, wrote for the yearbook, and was in school plays. He graduated in 1928. During Reagan's senior year, his yearbook caption read, "Life is just one grand sweet song, so start the music."

Dixon High School

Travelogue

Eureka College
300 East College Avenue
Eureka, IL 61530-0280
309-467-6407 (Reagan exhibit)
or 800-322-3756 (college)

Reagan, a mediocre student, graduated in 1932 with a degree in sociology and economics. He was on the football, swimming, and track teams and was active in other campus activities. He attended Eureka on a partial football scholarship and made up the balance of his tuition and fees by washing dishes in a fraternity house and a female dormitory. In 1982, while serving as president, he returned to campus to deliver the commencement address; it was also the occasion of his 50th reunion.

The Ronald Reagan Exhibit at Eureka's Cerf College Center includes about 3,000 items, nearly 1,000 of which are on display at any given time. The collection consists of artifacts and manuscripts from Reagan's days at Eureka, his movie and television career, his years as governor of California, his presidential campaigns, and both his terms as president. The collection was established in 1975.

Hours
The Ronald Reagan Exhibit is open weekdays from 9 A.M. to 8 P.M., Saturdays from 10 A.M. to 6 P.M., and Sundays from noon to 8 P.M. during the school year; it is open Monday through Saturday from 10 A.M. to 4 P.M. from June to August.
Admission
Free, although there is a charge for special tours; call for details

Eureka College

Travelogue

Marriages

Reagan and actress Jane Wyman played opposite each other in the 1938 film *Brother Rat*. On January 26, 1940, during the filming of the sequel, *Brother Rat and a Baby*, they married at the Wee Kirk O'Heather Wedding Chapel in Hollywood, California. When the couple parted ways in 1948, Reagan became the first president to divorce. The chapel no longer exists.

Little Brown Church
Church of the Valley
4418 Coldwater Canyon Avenue
Studio City, CA 91604-1498
818-761-1127

Reagan met actress Nancy Davis in 1949 after she sought help from film director Mervyn Leroy about left-wing mailings she had been receiving. Leroy referred her to Reagan, who was serving as president of the Screen Actors Guild. They married on March 4, 1952. Actor William Holden was best man at the wedding. The Reagans spent their honeymoon at the Mission Inn, where Richard and Pat Nixon were married.

Little Brown Church has since merged with the Church of the Valley in Van Nuys. Wednesday-evening Bible study is held at Little Brown Church.

Little Brown Church

Travelogue

Inaugural Site

The Capitol
Washington, DC

January 20, 1981
January 21, 1985

Other Sites

Loveland Community Center
513 West Second Street
Dixon, IL 61021
815-284-2741

As a teenager, Reagan was a lifeguard at nearby Lowell Park, where he is credited with saving 77 lives. Following each rescue, he made a notch on a log near the swimming area. After the log washed away, the community presented him with a bronze plaque commemorating his lifesaving accomplishments. That plaque and other community artifacts are on display in a small museum within the center. Call for museum hours.

Loveland Community Center

Travelogue

Ronald Reagan Presidential Library and Museum

National Archives and Records Administration
40 Presidential Drive
Simi Valley, CA 93065-0699
805-522-8444 or 800-410-8354
www.webportal.com/reaganlibrary/lobby.html

The library and museum cover 153,000 square feet spread over 100 acres. In the library are 49 million pages of documents, more than 1.6 million photographs, and 100,000 gifts. Among the most popular artifacts are a section of the Berlin Wall, a Cossack saddle from Mikhail Gorbachev, a nuclear missile, and mementos of first lady Nancy Reagan. One of the exhibits is an exact replica of the Oval Office. Videos on Reagan's life and presidency are shown throughout the museum.

Hours
Daily from 10 A.M. to 5 P.M.; closed New Year's, Thanksgiving, and Christmas

Admission
$4 for adults; $2 for guests over 62; children under 15 are free

Ronald Reagan Presidential Library and Museum

Travelogue

United States Air Force Museum
Dayton, OH

See Sites Related to Multiple Presidents on pages 261–62.

George Bush
Forty-First President of the United States

Birthplace

Bush was born in his family's Victorian home in Milton, Massachusetts, on June 12, 1924. The house is now a private residence and is not open to the public.

Homes

The Bush family also lived on Grove Lane in Greenwich, Connecticut. That home is not open to the public.

Walker's Point
Kennebunkport, ME

Walker's Point was purchased by George Herbert Walker, Bush's grandfather, in 1902. The main house was built shortly thereafter. Bush once commented that his fondest childhood memories were of family vacations on Walker's Point. He has spent part of every summer of his life in Kennebunkport—with the exception of one year. That was 1944, when he was unable to visit due to his involvement in World War II.

He purchased the property shortly after becoming vice president. Today, Bush main-

tains *Fidelity II*, his 31-foot powerboat, here. While in Kennebunkport, he spends time fishing, boating, golfing, and enjoying his 14 grandchildren.

Walker's Point is not open to the public.

The Bushes currently reside in Texas. Their home is not open to the public.

Churches

St. Anne's Episcopal Church
Ocean Avenue
Kennebunkport, ME 04043
207-967-8043

Bush is a member of the St. Anne's vestry. He and Mrs. Bush attend services here during their stays in Maine. Bush's mother and father were married here.

St. Anne's is open Memorial Day through Labor Day.

St. Anne's Episcopal Church

Travelogue

St. Martin's Episcopal Church
717 Sage Road
Houston, TX 77056-2199
713-621-3040

The Bushes attend this church when they are in residence in Texas.

St. Martin's Episcopal Church

Travelogue

Education

Greenwich Country Day School
Old Church Road
P.O. Box 623
Greenwich, CT 06836-0623
203-622-8500
www.gcds.pvt.k12.ct.us:4080

Bush was the first baseman on this school's baseball team and a running back on the football team. He also played soccer and tennis. In 1997, he was presented the school's distinguished alumni award.

Greenwich Country Day School

Travelogue

Phillips Academy
Main Street
Andover, MA 01810-4161
508-749-4000

At Phillips Academy, Bush was senior class president, president of the Society of Inquiry, and editor of the school newspaper. He was also involved in baseball, soccer, and basketball. He was voted the second-most-influential student with the faculty, the school's third-best athlete, and its third-most-handsome student. He graduated on his 18th birthday, June 12, 1942.

Phillips Academy

Travelogue

Yale University
New Haven, CT

See Sites Related to Multiple Presidents on pages 249–50.

First Presbyterian Church
Photo by Ian Ferris

Marriage

First Presbyterian Church
Boston Post Road
Rye, NY 10580
914-967-0842

Bush met Barbara Pierce at a Christmas dance at Greenwich Country Club in 1942. They married on January 6, 1945. The Bushes have never managed to put down community roots, living in as many as 29 homes in 17 different cities through their 53 years of marriage.

First Presbyterian Church

Travelogue

Inaugural Site

The Capitol
Washington, DC

January 20, 1989

Other Sites

George Bush Presidential Library and Museum
National Archives and Records Administration
1000 George Bush Drive West
College Station, TX 77845
409-260-9552
www.csdl.tamu.edu/bushlib

This facility was dedicated on November 6, 1997. It was financed with $43 million in private contributions, including a large sum from Kuwaiti rulers, whose country was spared in the Persian Gulf War during the Bush administration. The complex spans 90 acres on the West Campus of Texas A & M University. The library contains 38 million documents and can accommodate 20 researchers at once. The museum has 60,000 objects, including a TBM Avenger plane like the one Bush flew and crashed during World War II and the first baseman's glove he wore while playing for Yale. Most of the 17,000 square feet of permanent exhibition space is dedicated to foreign affairs during the Bush administration. Also included is a classroom—the first in any presidential library. It is available to school groups as both a traditional and an electronic classroom.

<u>Hours</u>
Monday through Saturday from 9:30 A.M. to 5 P.M. and Sunday from noon to 5 P.M.
<u>Admission</u>
$3 for adults; $2.50 for seniors and those attending in groups; guests 16 and under are free

George Bush Presidential Library and Museum

Travelogue

United States Air Force Museum
Dayton, OH

See Sites Related to Multiple Presidents on pages 261–62.

William J. Clinton
Forty-Second President of the United States

Birthplace

Julia Chester Hospital
Hope, AR

Clinton was born William Jefferson Blythe IV on August 19, 1946. At the age of 16, he legally changed his last name to that of his stepfather. The hospital where he was born was subsequently converted into an apartment building, which was later destroyed by fire.

Homes

Clinton Center and Birthplace
Clinton Birthplace Foundation, Inc.
117 South Hervey
P.O. Box 1925
Hope, AR 71801
870-777-4455
www.clintonbirthplace.com

Following his birth, the future president was brought from Julia Chester Hospital to this, the home of his maternal grandparents, Eldridge and Edith Grisham Cassidy. Clinton lived the first four years of his life in this 1917 American Foursquare house.

House in Hope, Arkansas, where Clinton lived the first four years of his life
Courtesy of Clinton Birthplace Foundation, Inc.

Today, the site features the restored home, the Virginia Clinton Kelley Memorial Garden, and a visitor center with a gift shop. On display in the visitor center is a replica of the carpet that Clinton had installed in the newly decorated Oval Office; designed by Kaki Hockersmith, the carpet features the presidential seal. For $25, individuals may purchase a brick to be placed in the memorial garden; the brick may bear the name of the donor or any other person as a tribute.

Hours
Tuesday through Saturday from 10 A.M. to 4:30 P.M.; the site is also open Sunday from 1 to 5 P.M. during spring and summer
Admission
$5 for adults; $4 for seniors; $3 for ages six to 18

Clinton Center and Birthplace

Travelogue

Clinton grew up in Hope and Hot Springs, Arkansas. He lived briefly with his grandparents, who ran a grocery store in Hope. From 1950 to 1953, he lived at 321 13th Street in Hope.

Church

Immanuel Baptist Church
1000 Bishop Street
Little Rock, AR 72202-4699
501-374-7464

Immanuel Baptist Church

Travelogue

This is the church Clinton attends when in Arkansas.

Education

St. John's Catholic School
583 West Grand Avenue
Hot Springs, AR 71901
501-624-3171

After attending Miss Mary Purkins' School for Little Folks through grade one, Clinton was enrolled here in the second grade because his mother thought he was not ready for a large public school. Although a good student, he got poor marks in conduct because of his habit of yelling out answers to questions without giving other children a chance.

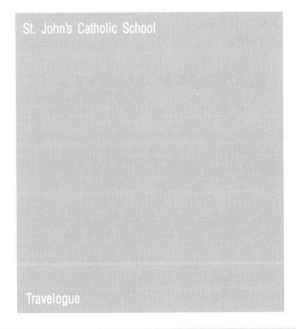
St. John's Catholic School

Travelogue

William Jefferson Clinton Cultural Campus

801 Central Avenue
Hot Springs, AR 71901
501-624-1964

Clinton entered the Hot Springs public schools in the fourth grade, enrolling at Ramble Elementary School. He then studied at Central Junior High School and Hot Springs High School. He was an exceptional student in high school, earning an Academically Talented Student Award, membership in the National Honor Society, and a spot in the semifinals of the National Merit Scholarship Contest. He was also junior class president, a member of the student council, and drum major of the school band. He graduated fourth in his class in 1964.

In 1997, some of the president's friends undertook to develop a cultural campus in the building where Clinton attended high school. The complex is scheduled to open in 2000.

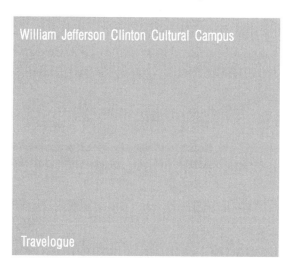

William Jefferson Clinton Cultural Campus

Travelogue

Georgetown University
Washington, DC

See Sites Related to Multiple Presidents on page 246.

Yale University
New Haven, CT

See Sites Related to Multiple Presidents on pages 249–50.

Marriage

Clinton married Hillary Rodham on October 11, 1975, in a house the couple had recently purchased in Fayetteville, Arkansas.

Inaugural Site

The Capitol
Washington, DC

January 20, 1993
January 20, 1997

Other Site

United States Air Force Museum
Dayton, OH

See Sites Related to Multiple Presidents on pages 261–62.

Appendix 1
Sites Related to Multiple Presidents

Cemeteries

Arlington National Cemetery
Arlington, VA 22211
703-695-3250
www.mdw.army.mil/cemetery.htm

There are more than 100 national cemeteries in the United States, but this is one of only two administered by the United States Army, the other being the United States Soldiers' and Airmen's Home National Cemetery in Washington.

The site was once part of the 1,100-acre plantation of Mary Ann Randolph Custis, a relative of George Washington's who married Robert E. Lee. In 1861, seeing the approach of civil war, Lee resigned his commission with the Federal military so he would not have to fight against his home state of Virginia. Shortly thereafter, the Union's Army of the Potomac marched across the river and established its headquarters in Arlington House, the palatial former home of the Lees. In 1864, the estate was confiscated and sold to the government when Lee failed to pay property taxes of $92.07 in person. The army built three fortifications on the grounds and set aside 200 acres as a national cemetery.

On June 15, 1864, some 65 soldiers were buried here; by the end of the Civil War, 16,000 were interred. Eventually, veterans from the Revolutionary War and the War of 1812 were reinterred at Arlington. Today, the 612-acre cemetery is the final resting place of about 250,000 military heroes. It averages 20 funerals per day and welcomes 4 million visitors annually. The best-known site in the cemetery is the Tomb of the Unknowns. The new visitor center includes exhibits.

William Howard Taft is buried in Arlington beneath a 14-foot granite monument designed by James Earl Frazer.

Early in 1963, John F. Kennedy visited Arlington House and commented that the view of Washington was so spectacular that he could stay there forever. Following his assassination later that year, he was buried in a plot in Arlington marked by an eternal flame. Although speculation at the time was that he would be buried in the family plot in Massachusetts, his widow preferred that he be interred on federal property, saying her late husband belonged to the people. She desired that his funeral be modeled after that of Abraham Lincoln. Library of Congress director David Mearns and Professor James Robertson, executive director of the United

States Civil War Centennial Commission, researched Lincoln's funeral using copies of *Frank Leslie's Illustrated* and *Harper's Weekly* from 1865. Meanwhile, Secretary of Defense Robert McNamara and Attorney General Robert Kennedy selected the burial site and oversaw preparation of the grave. Because of heavy visitor traffic, Kennedy and his two deceased children were reinterred in the current grave, which is marked with Cape Cod stones selected by family members. Kennedy's widow was interred here in 1994.

Hours
The visitor center is open daily from 8 A.M. to 7 P.M. from April to September and from 8 A.M. to 5 P.M. the rest of the year.
Admission
Free

Arlington National Cemetery

Travelogue

Hollywood Cemetery
412 South Cherry Street
Richmond, VA 23220-6214
804-648-8501

The History Channel called Hollywood Cemetery "the most impressive and gorgeously landscaped cemetery." It is named for the holly planted throughout it. In addition to the side-by-side graves of Presidents James Monroe and John Tyler, Hollywood is the site of the graves of Confederates Jefferson Davis, J. E. B. Stuart, Fitzhugh Lee, and 18,000 soldiers.

Hours
Daily from 8 A.M. to 6 P.M.
Admission
Free

Hollywood Cemetery

Travelogue

Churches

All Souls Church (Unitarian)
2835 16th Street NW
Washington, DC 20009
202-332-5266
www.all-souls.org

John Quincy Adams was among the

founders of All Souls Church, which was established in 1821.

William Howard Taft's funeral, held at All Souls in March 1930, was the first presidential funeral broadcast over radio. At Taft's request, it was a simple service that included his favorite hymns, "Lead Kindly Light" and "Abide with Me." Also included were readings of Tennyson's "Ode on the Death of the Duke of Wellington" and Wadsworth's "Happy Warrior."

All Souls Church (Unitarian)

Travelogue

First National Baptist Church
5400 D Street NW
Washington, DC 20019-6133
202-582-3058

While in Washington, Harry S Truman and Jimmy Carter frequently attended services here. Carter occasionally taught adult Sunday school.

First National Baptist Church

Travelogue

National Presbyterian Church
4101 Nebraska Avenue NW
Washington, DC 20016
202-537-0800
www.natpresch.org

Included in this, the national church for Presbyterians, is the Chapel of the Presidents.

Grover Cleveland, the son of a Presbyterian minister, regularly attended services here.

Dwight D. Eisenhower did not join a church until becoming president. In 1948, he said, "I am the most intensely religious man I know. Nobody gets through six years of war without faith." In 1953, he was baptized here.

Tours are offered by appointment from Monday to Saturday between 10 A.M. and 4 P.M. and Sunday at 12:30 P.M. Sunday services are at 9 and 11 A.M.

National Presbyterian Church

Travelogue

New York Avenue Presbyterian Church

1313 New York Avenue NW
Washington, DC 20005-4701
202-393-3700
www.nyapc.org

This church traces its history to 1793, when the Scottish stonemasons building the White House erected a temporary church on the grounds. Following the completion of the White House, worship services were held in the Treasury Building. Eventually, a church was built at 14th and F Streets.

In 1819, another group organized Second Presbyterian Church at this location. John Adams was a member of Second Presbyterian, and John Quincy Adams, then secretary of state, was a trustee. Andrew Jackson was a member while president.

In the mid-1800s, F Street and Second Presbyterian Churches merged. Dr. Phileas D. Gurley, a close friend of Abraham Lincoln, was the first pastor of the combined church. Lincoln never joined the church but regularly attended Sunday and midweek services; the Lincoln Chapel and Parlor, located on the street level, commemorate his attendance. On display today are the pew Lincoln rented from 1861 to 1863 and the manuscript of his proposal to abolish slavery.

The current Federal-style building was constructed in 1951 and dedicated by Harry S Truman. The 1954 "Lincoln Day" sermon, delivered by Dr. George Docherty with Dwight Eisenhower in attendance, was the inspiration for the addition of the words "one nation under God" to the Pledge of Allegiance.

Guided tours of the church are offered weekly following Sunday worship and by appointment.

New York Avenue Presbyterian Church

Travelogue

St. John's Lafayette Square

1525 H Street NW
Washington, DC 20005-1005
202-347-8766
www.us.net/edow/1/stjls

Established in 1815 as a place of worship for residents of the area surrounding the White House, St. John's has come to be known as "the Church of the Presidents." Its architect was Benjamin Henry Latrobe, the man who rebuilt the Capitol and the White House after their destruction during the War of 1812.

When the church opened, the vestry postponed offering the sale and rental of pews until the president responded to its invitation for a pew. President James Madison asked that a pew be assigned for him and his White House successors. Since then, every president has attended regularly or occasionally. Pew 54 is regarded as the President's Pew; in fact, an 1858 prayer book in the archives is inscribed "President's Pew." However, many presidents have elected to sit elsewhere in the church.

Abraham Lincoln visited the church on at least one occasion, as reported by Constance McLoughlin Green in her book, *The Church on Lafayette Square, 1815–1970:* "On an anxious Sunday morning eight days before the inauguration of Abraham Lincoln, Senator [William] Seward accompanied by a tall gaunt man 'in plain black clothes, with black whiskers, and hair well trimmed' occupied Pew #1 at St. John's. Nobody recognized the stranger. Dr. Pyne preached on a text from I Corinthians 7:31, 'And they that use this world, as not abusing it: for the fashion of this world passeth away,' a theme that permitted allusions to the perilous state of the nation and the impending change in administration. Not until the service was over and Senator Seward introduced his guest did the rector and congregation learn that the President-elect had been listening attentively to the sermon."

Chester A. Arthur never formally joined the church but attended regularly. Mrs. Arthur was a member of the choir. Following her death, the president donated a stained-glass window and dedicated it to his wife's memory. The window was visible to the president from the White House.

Theodore Roosevelt's family regularly occupied the President's Pew, although Roosevelt himself usually attended Dutch Reformed services.

Franklin D. Roosevelt divided his church visits between St. John's and Baptist and Methodist churches in Washington. He attended a special service here every year on the anniversary of his first inauguration. He once complained about tourists ogling him in church, saying that he could do just about anything "in the fishbowl of the president's life" except pray.

In the church's north transept, one stained-glass window honors Presidents Madison, Monroe, and Van Buren and another honors Presidents William Henry Harrison, Tyler, and Taylor. Other presidents who regularly attended were Andrew Jackson, James Buchanan, and Gerald R. Ford.

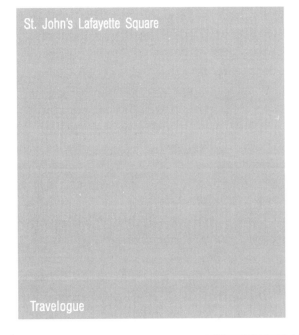

St. John's Lafayette Square

Travelogue

Colleges and Universities

College of William and Mary

P.O. Box 8795
Williamsburg, VA 23187-8795
757-221-4000
www.wm.edu

Thomas Jefferson spent two years at William and Mary, graduating in 1762. He studied under Dr. William Small, a man Jefferson said "probably fixed the destinies of my life." Jefferson is known to have studied 15 hours per day. He was also a member of the Flat Hat Club, a social fraternity. In 1779, while serving as governor of Virginia and a member of the college's board, he was instrumental in a major curricular revision that came to be known as the Jeffersonian Reorganization. A statue of Jefferson was given to the college by the University of Virginia in 1992. It stands between Washington and McGlothlin-Street Halls.

James Monroe enrolled at William and Mary at age 16. However, after two years of study, he left to take up arms in the Revolutionary War. He and other former students raided the arsenal at the Governor's Palace and used the seized munitions to arm the Williamsburg militia. Monroe never returned to college, although he studied law under Thomas Jefferson from 1780 to 1783.

John Tyler entered the college's preparatory division at age 12 and continued through graduation in 1807.

Columbia University

Broadway at 16th Street
New York, NY 10027
212-854-4902

Theodore Roosevelt had a lifelong ambition of becoming a naturalist, but in 1880 he instead entered Columbia Law School on the advice of some of his Harvard professors and his girlfriend. He left the school after one year in order to run for the New York State Assembly. He never completed his law studies and never sought admission to the bar.

Franklin D. Roosevelt entered Columbia Law School in 1904 but failed two courses (one covering contracts and the other pleading and practice). He dropped out once he passed the bar exam in 1907 and never earned a degree from the school.

Dwight D. Eisenhower became the 13th president of Columbia in 1948 but stepped down in 1953 when he became the 34th president of the United States.

Columbia University

Travelogue

Georgetown University

37th and O Streets NW
Washington, DC 20057
202-687-3596
www.georgetown.edu

Lyndon Baines Johnson studied law at Georgetown in 1934 and 1935 but did not graduate.

William J. Clinton chose Georgetown because of its excellent foreign-service program and its location. He was president of his freshman and sophomore classes and worked part-time in the office of his state's junior senator, J. William Fulbright. Fulbright, then the chairman of the Senate Foreign Relations Committee, greatly influenced Clinton's view of the Vietnam War. In April 1968, in the wake of the assassination of Martin Luther King, Georgetown student Clinton delivered food to burned-out sections of Washington as an American Red Cross volunteer. The large red crosses he put on his white Buick were his only protection in the racially tense neighborhoods he served.

Georgetown University

Travelogue

Harvard University

Harvard Square
Cambridge, MA 02138
617-495-1000

Six presidents graduated from Harvard: John Adams, John Quincy Adams, Rutherford B. Hayes, Theodore Roosevelt, Franklin D. Roosevelt, and John F. Kennedy.

John Adams ranked 15th among the 24 entering students when he came to Harvard in 1751; in those days, rankings at the school were dependent upon the social status of students' families, not on academics. It was at Harvard that Adams developed his love of books and his ambition to become a trial lawyer. He graduated in 1755.

Phi Beta Kappa graduate John Quincy Adams was second in his class in 1787. He gave the senior oration. Having spent his early years overseas, he had few friends in this country and did not participate in many extracurricular activities, except to play flute in the Harvard band.

Rutherford B. Hayes studied law at Harvard under Supreme Court justice Joseph Story, Simon Greenleaf, and Jared Sparks. He graduated in 1845.

Theodore Roosevelt graduated Phi Beta Kappa in 1880. He was runner-up in Harvard's lightweight boxing division. The school's Houghton Library maintains the Theodore Roosevelt Collection, a large repository of papers and artifacts. For information on the collection, call the curator at 617-495-2449.

Franklin D. Roosevelt graduated in 1904. He was a member of the Hasty Pudding Club, Alpha Delta Phi, the Newell Boating Club, and the glee club. He claimed his most enjoyable activity was serving as editor in chief of the *Harvard Crimson*.

John F. Kennedy entered Harvard after one semester at Princeton. He was a member of the Hasty Pudding Club and worked for the *Harvard Crimson*. He donated the $40,000 in royalties he received from the publication of his senior thesis, "Why England Slept," to the bombed-out city of Plymouth, England. In 1966, Harvard renamed its school of public administration the John F. Kennedy School of Government.

Harvard's only notable campus monuments to United States presidents are a Randolph Rogers sculpture of John Adams and a portrait of Abraham Lincoln, both of which are on display in Memorial Hall. Public access to Memorial Hall is limited.

Princeton University
Princeton, NJ 08544
609-258-3000
www.princeton.edu

James Madison completed his course of study at Princeton in two years but remained at the college following his 1772 graduation to study Hebrew under the Reverend John Witherspoon, who would later sign the Declaration of Independence.

Woodrow Wilson entered Princeton in 1875. He did well academically and maintained an active extracurricular life. He wrote frequently for campus periodicals and was editor of *The Princetonian*. He was also active in the American Whig Society, the Liberal Debating Club, the school's baseball association, and its football association. He graduated in 1879. Throughout the remainder of his life, he maintained strong ties to the university and to his classmates. Before entering politics, the highlight of Wilson's career was his appointment to the Princeton faculty and eventually to the presidency there. As university president, he frequently bickered with the university's board chair, retired United States president Grover Cleveland, over policy issues. As president of the United States, Wilson once held a White House reception for Princeton's class of 1879.

Grover Cleveland established a home—Westland—in the town of Princeton following his presidency. Although he never attended Princeton or any other college, he was elected to Princeton's board of trustees in 1901 and became board chairman three years later.

Princeton's library holds some papers of both Wilson and Cleveland.

Princeton University

Travelogue

United States Military Academy
West Point, NY 10996
914-938-3520
www.usma.edu

Ulysses S. Grant was horrified to learn of his acceptance to West Point, fearing he would fail there. He was also extremely squeamish and feared the sight of blood. Grant once said of those times, "A military life had no charms for me, and I had not the faintest idea of staying in the army even if I should be graduated, which I did not expect." Grant

graduated 24th out of 39 cadets in 1843. Because of his modest class standing, he was assigned to the infantry with the brevet rank of second lieutenant.

Dwight D. Eisenhower graduated 61st in a class of 164 in 1915. Not an outstanding student, he ranked 75th out of 212 cadets during his first year. He blamed his mediocre academic performance on his preoccupation with athletics. As he was on his way to becoming the starting quarterback on the school's football team, his career was stymied when he severely hurt his knee during a 1912 game against Tufts. While at West Point, Eisenhower was once busted from sergeant to private for ignoring the admonition to stop whirling his partner so vigorously about the dance floor.

The West Point Museum includes a wide range of military exhibits and artifacts related to Grant and Eisenhower.

Hours
The West Point Museum is open daily from 10:30 A.M. to 4:15 P.M.; it is closed New Year's, Thanksgiving, and Christmas.
Admission
Free

United States Military Academy

Travelogue

University of Virginia

Charlottesville, VA 22903
804-924-0311
www.uva.edu

Thomas Jefferson founded the University of Virginia. He bought the land, raised the money for the buildings, and designed the campus. His innovative concept of "the Academical Village" placed the principal buildings around a central lawn. At one end of the lawn, he built the Rotunda, which was completed the year he died. The opposite end of the lawn was left open, offering students and faculty a contemplative vista of the Virginia mountains.

Woodrow Wilson entered the university's law school in 1879 but withdrew after one year due to health reasons. He is said to have been bored with the study of law, enduring it only as a means to entering politics. While recuperating at home in North Carolina, he continued to read the law. He was admitted to the bar in 1882.

University of Virginia

Travelogue

Yale University Visitor Center

149 Elm Street
New Haven, CT 06520-1942
203-432-8469
www.yale.edu

William Howard Taft graduated second in Yale's class of 1878. Taft was active in few extracurricular activities. He won the junior-class math prize and won composition prizes during his senior year. Throughout the rest of his life, he visited Yale frequently. As president, he donated an extra-large seat in the first row of the balcony of Yale's theater, so he could sit comfortably during performances; the seat still exists. Taft returned to Yale as Kent Professor of Law following his retirement from the presidency. He taught here from 1913 to 1921.

Gerald R. Ford accepted a full-time position as assistant football coach and head boxing coach at Yale, for which he earned an annual salary of $2,400. Although he wanted to enroll immediately in Yale's law school, administrators denied his request because of his full-time work load. By the fall of 1938, Ford convinced the university to admit him to its law school on a trial basis. He graduated in 1941 and was admitted to the Michigan Bar that same year.

George Bush rejected the advice of Phillips Academy's 1942 commencement speaker, Secretary of War Henry Stimson, who told graduates to earn a bachelor's degree before joining the armed forces. Upon his discharge from the navy, Bush, by then a married man, entered Yale's accelerated two-and-a-half-year program; he graduated Phi Beta Kappa and with honors in 1948. Bush was the captain of Yale's baseball team. In his senior year, he participated in a pregame ceremony during which Babe Ruth made his last public appearance. Bush kept his Yale first baseman's glove in the drawer of his Oval Office desk throughout his term as president.

After graduating from Georgetown, William J. Clinton spent two years on a Rhodes Scholarship at Oxford University in England. Instead of completing his third year there, he returned to the United States and accepted a scholarship to Yale's law school. To earn money, he taught community college and did investigative work for a New Haven lawyer. It was at Yale that he met fellow law student Hillary Rodham. Clinton earned his law degree in 1973.

Hours
The visitor center is open weekdays from 9 A.M. to 4:45 P.M. and weekends from 10 A.M. to 4 P.M.
Admission
Free

Yale University Visitor Center

Travelogue

Homes

Anderson House
United States Sailors' and Airmen's Home
2118 Massachusetts Avenue NW
Washington, DC 20008
202-785-2040

The original building on this site—known as "Corn Riggs" or the Anderson House—was used as a retreat by Presidents Buchanan, Lincoln, Hayes, and Arthur. Since that time, it has served numerous functions as a military facility. Today, it houses the Society of the Cincinnati, a group of descendants of officers of the Continental Army. Exhibits include artifacts from the Revolutionary War.

Hours
Tuesday through Saturday from 1 to 4 P.M.
Admission
Free

Anderson House

Travelogue

Belle Grove Plantation
Photo by Elizabeth A. McClurg

Belle Grove Plantation

336 Belle Grove Road
Middleburg, VA 22645
540-869-2028
www.globecom.net/wfcedc/tourism/ent_att/
entmuse4.htm

This house was built by Major Isaac Hite, brother-in-law of James Madison; Madison asked Thomas Jefferson for advice on the house plans.

Belle Grove is now a historic house museum and working farm. The Shenandoah Heritage Festival is held here each June and an antique show each Labor Day weekend.

Hours
Monday through Saturday from 10 A.M. to 4 P.M. and Sunday from 1 to 5 P.M. from March 15 to November 15
Admission
$7 for adults; $6 for guests over 65; $3 for ages 13 to 17; fees for special events vary

Blair House

704 Jackson Place NW
Washington, DC 20006-4904
202-652-9586

The main part of this structure was built by Dr. Joseph Lovell in 1824. In 1948, it was attached to the adjacent Lee House, built in the 1850s by Francis P. Blair for his daughter and her husband, Samuel P. Lee.

Blair House has long been used as a guest residence for visiting dignitaries. It served as a temporary residence for President Andrew Johnson in 1865 while President Lincoln's widow was preparing to leave the White House. It was used by President Truman in 1945 while Mrs. Franklin D. Roosevelt was likewise preparing to leave the White House, and again beginning in 1948 while the White House was being renovated.

An attempt on Truman's life occurred here on November 1, 1950, when Puerto Rican nationalists Oscar Collazo and Griselio Torresola tried to shoot him from the street. White House guard Leslie Coffelt was killed in the exchange of gunfire, as was Torresola.

Collazo was convicted and sentenced to death. Truman commuted the sentence to life imprisonment in 1951, and Jimmy Carter released Collazo in 1979. A plaque on the fence in front of Blair House commemorates Coffelt.

Blair House is not open to the public.

Blair House

Travelogue

The White House
1600 Pennsylvania Avenue NW
Washington, DC 20500-0003
202-456-7041
www.whitehouse.gov

Designed by James Hoban in 1792, the White House has been the home of every president except George Washington. It was burned by the British during the War of 1812. After its restoration, it was painted white to hide burn stains, hence its name. The West Wing, which includes the Oval Office, was built in 1902. The White House was completely renovated between 1948 and 1952.

Rooms open to the public include the East, Red, Green, and Blue Rooms on the State Floor and the Vermiel Room and the library on the ground floor.

Hours
Guests may take self-guided tours Tuesday through Saturday from 10 A.M. to noon.
Admission
Free; tickets are required from mid-March through September and may be obtained from the White House Visitor Center at E and 15th Streets beginning at 8 A.M.

The White House

Travelogue

Libraries

Library of Congress
101 Independence Avenue SE
Washington, DC 20540
202-707-6590
www.loc.gov

In April 1800, as the federal government was preparing for its move from Philadelphia to its new home along the Potomac, President John Adams authorized $5,000 for the purchase of "such books as may be necessary for the use of Congress." The initial order consisted of 740 volumes and three maps. In 1802, President Thomas Jefferson greatly expanded this repository by creating the Library of Congress and moving it to its own building.

Jefferson's constant involvement with the library paved the way for its development as the federal government's official library. Following his retirement from the presidency, he offered to sell his personal collection of 6,487 books to the library for $23,940. At the time, Jefferson's collection was twice the size of the library's.

In 1897, the current main structure, known as the Thomas Jefferson Building, was opened. It exists today as a memorial to Jefferson and his philosophy. Subsequent buildings were named for John Adams and James Madison. Among the library's holdings are the papers of 23 presidents.

Hours
Daily from 9 A.M. to 5 P.M.; closed major holidays
Admission
Free

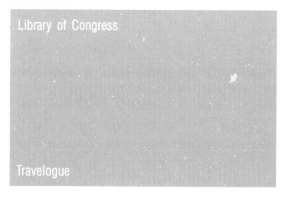

Library of Congress

Travelogue

Office of Presidential Libraries
National Archives and Records Administration
8601 Adelphi Road
College Park, MD 20740-6001
301-713-6050
www.nara.gov

Prior to the establishment of the presidential library system, presidential papers were dispersed following the close of each administration. Although many early collections are held by the Library of Congress, others were passed to historical societies or other institutions. As a result, many valuable presidential documents have been lost over the years.

In 1955, Congress passed the Presidential Libraries Act, enabling presidents to establish their own libraries. These libraries, built at separate sites with private funding, are operated and maintained by the National Archives and Records Administration's Office of Presidential Libraries, which has its headquarters in College Park. The libraries of Hoover, Franklin D. Roosevelt, Truman, Eisenhower, Kennedy, Lyndon Baines Johnson, Nixon, Ford, Carter, Reagan, and Bush are overseen by this office.

During the Watergate investigation, Congress mandated that a great number of Nixon's presidential papers be maintained close to Washington. As a result, the National Archives and Records Administration (NARA) also maintains the Nixon Presidential Materials Staff at College Park.

NARA offers behind-the-scenes tours of its College Park facility weekdays at 10:15 A.M.

and 1:15 P.M. These tours give visitors insight into the buildings and operations of NARA. Small, changing exhibits are open to the public.

Hours
Monday and Wednesday from 8:45 A.M. to 5 P.M.; Tuesday, Thursday, and Friday from 8:45 A.M. to 9 P.M.; Saturday from 8:45 A.M. to 4:45 P.M.
Admission
Free

Office of Presidential Libraries

Travelogue

Monuments

Lincoln Monument State Memorial
Lincoln State Drive between
Galena and Hennepin Avenues
Dixon, IL

This small park has a statue of Lincoln and is located on the site of the Dixon Blockhouse, where Abraham Lincoln, Jefferson Davis, and Zachary Taylor met during the Black Hawk War of 1832.

Lincoln Monument State Memorial

Travelogue

Mount Rushmore National Memorial
National Park Service
SD 244
P.O. Box 268
Keystone, SD 57751
605-574-2523
www.nps.gov/moru

Symbolizing the trials of our nation's first 150 years, the faces of George Washington, Thomas Jefferson, Abraham Lincoln, and Theodore Roosevelt are carved onto this granite mountain face. The site features the floodlit monument, a visitor center, and a gift shop. The Lincoln Borglum Visitor Center opened in June 1998. It offers 20 exhibits dealing with the sculptor, the sculpture, the workers, and the presidents. An interpretive film is shown in two theaters. During summer, numerous evening programs, interpretive exhibits, and audiovisual programs are offered. Wildlife watching and bird-watching are also popular activities here.

Hours
Daily from 8 A.M. to 10 P.M. from Memorial
Day through Labor Day and from 8 A.M. to
5 P.M. the rest of the year; closed
Christmas
Admission
Free, although there is a fee for parking

Mount Rushmore National Memorial

Travelogue

Museums

William Howard Taft (second from left in front row) and Woodrow Wilson (center) at the dedication ceremony of the Red Cross headquarters in Washington in 1915
Courtesy of the American Red Cross

The Three Presidents Statue
North Carolina State Capitol
Union Square
Raleigh, NC

President Harry S Truman dedicated this statue on October 19, 1948. The Charles Keck bronze piece features the three presidents born in North Carolina. Andrew Jackson is depicted on horseback; James Knox Polk is seated holding a map; and Andrew Johnson is seated holding the United States Constitution.

The Three Presidents Statue

Travelogue

American Red Cross Visitor Center
1730 E Street NW
Washington, DC 20006
202-639-3300
www.redcross.org

Since its founding in 1881, the American Red Cross has had as its honorary chairman the president of the United States. The Red Cross's archives thus contain numerous documents and artifacts related to the presidents.

The visitor center showcases the art of Red Cross posters and some of the more than 20,000 art objects and collectibles held at the site. It also provides a preview of the American Red Cross History and Education Center, which is scheduled to open in the next century. The adjacent national headquarters building was dedicated in 1915; both

Woodrow Wilson and William Howard Taft participated in the ceremony. The visitor center and two other Red Cross buildings together form Red Cross Square, a tranquil setting of gardens, sculpture, and greenery just west of the Ellipse near the White House.

Hours
The visitor center is open weekdays from 9 A.M. to 4 P.M. Red Cross Square is open during daylight hours.
Admission
Free

American Red Cross Visitor Center
Travelogue

Dumbarton House
National Society of the Colonial Dames of America
2715 Q Street NW
Washington, DC 20007-3071
202-337-2288

This Federal-style house features furnishings in the Sheraton and Heppelwhite styles, 18th- and 19th-century decorative arts, Chinese objects, and documents signed by George Washington, Thomas Jefferson, and James Madison.

The former home of Joseph Nourse, the first registrar of the United States Treasury, the house is now the headquarters of the National Society of the Colonial Dames of America.

Hours
Tours are offered Tuesday through Saturday at 10:15 and 11:15 A.M. and 12:15 P.M. from September to July; the house is closed on federal holidays.
Admission
A small donation is requested.

Dumbarton House
Travelogue

Famous Hall of Presidents
Baltimore Street
Gettysburg, PA 17325
717-334-5717

This is a commercially operated wax museum featuring representations of the presidents and first ladies.

Hours
Daily from 9 A.M. to 5 P.M. during spring and fall and from 9 A.M. to 9 P.M. during summer

Admission
$5.25 for adults; $3.25 for children;
guests under five are free

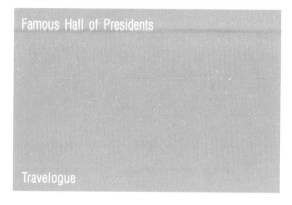

Famous Hall of Presidents

Travelogue

Gold Coast Railroad Museum

12450 SW 152nd Street
Miami, FL 33177-1402
305-253-0063 or 888-60-TRAIN
www.elink.net/goldcoast

The Gold Coast Railroad Museum has a collection of more than 300 pieces of railroad equipment and offers numerous public programs dealing with railroads. Included in its collection is the Ferdinand Magellan, a Pullman car custom-made for the president in 1928. Franklin D. Roosevelt authorized reconstruction of the car in 1942. For greater security, steel plates were riveted to all the exterior surfaces, and bullet-resistant glass was installed. At Roosevelt's request, the train was also made more comfortable.

When first put into service, the car was one of seven private Pullmans—all bearing the names of famous explorers—used by the presidents. Until 1942, presidents were not assigned any one particular car. The Ferdinand Magellan was used by Roosevelt, Truman, and Eisenhower on a regular basis. It was from the platform of the Ferdinand Magellan that Truman held up a newspaper declaring Dewey the winner of the 1948 election.

The car was retired from presidential use in the late 1950s, when air travel began replacing rail travel. During his 1984 reelection campaign, Ronald Reagan used the Ferdinand Magellan for one day of whistle-stop campaigning in Ohio.

Hours
Weekdays from 11 A.M. to 3 P.M. and weekends from 11 A.M. to 4 P.M.
Admission
$5 for adults; $3 for children

Gold Coast Railroad Museum

Travelogue

Hall of Fame for Great Americans
Bronx Community College
University Avenue at 181st Street
Bronx, NY 10453
718-289-5100
www.bcc.cuny.edu/hallfame/hallfame.htm

Thirteen presidents are honored in the Hall of Fame for Great Americans: Washington, John Adams, Jefferson, Lincoln, Grant, Madison, John Quincy Adams, Jackson, Monroe, Cleveland, Wilson, Theodore Roosevelt, and Franklin D. Roosevelt. The hall was established in 1900 by Dr. Henry Mitchell McCracken, then chancellor of New York University. His concept was to create a national shrine to people of greatness from a variety of backgrounds. In all, there are 102 honorees. Their larger-than-life sculptures are displayed in niches along the promenade surrounding what was New York University's Gould Memorial Library. The Neoclassical structure was designed by Sanford White.

Hours
Daily from 10 A.M. to 5 P.M.
Admission
Free

Hall of Fame for Great Americans

Travelogue

Independence Hall, one of the twenty buildings of Independence National Historic Park

Independence National Historic Park
313 Walnut Street
Philadelphia, PA 19106
215-597-8974
www.nps.gov/inde

This park has about 20 buildings on 45 acres in the center of Philadelphia and is truly the birthplace of our nation. It was here that both the Declaration of Independence and the Constitution were written and adopted. The park's main attractions include Independence Hall, the Liberty Bell Pavilion, the Second Bank Portrait Gallery, the Todd House, and the Graff House. A large visitor center offers interpretive exhibits and films. Numerous tours originate at the center.

Independence National Historic Park

Travelogue

Museum of American Political Life

University of Hartford
200 Bloomfield Avenue
West Hartford, CT 06117
860-768-4090
www.hartford.edu/polmus/polmus.htm

This museum's collection of artifacts related to the campaigns of the presidents ranks second only to that held by the Smithsonian Institution. The nucleus of its 60,000-artifact collection was donated by J. Doyle Dewitt.

Hours
Tuesday through Friday from 11 A.M. to 4 P.M.
Admission
Free

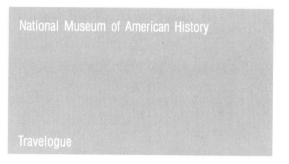

National Museum of American History

Smithsonian Institution
14th Street and Constitution Avenue NW
Washington, DC 20560
202-357-2700
www.si.edu

Established in 1964, this museum collects and interprets objects significant to the history and people of the United States. Included in its collection are numerous items related to the presidents. Recent exhibits have included White House china, presidential gifts, and inaugural ball gowns of the first ladies.

Founded in 1846, the Smithsonian Institution is one of the most extensive and comprehensive museums in the world. Most of its individual museums are centered on the National Mall in Washington.

Hours
Daily from 10 A.M. to 5:30 P.M.; closed Christmas
Admission
Free

National Portrait Gallery

Smithsonian Institution
8th and F Streets NW
Washington, DC 20002
202-357-2700
www.npg.si.edu

Originally the Patent Office Building, this structure was used as a Civil War hospital and was the site of Lincoln's second inaugural ball. Among its permanent collections is the Hall of Presidents, which features portraits of all the presidents. Other galleries highlight heroes of the Civil War and figures from sports, the arts, and literature.

Hours
Daily from 10 A.M. to 5:30 P.M.; closed
Christmas
Admission
Free

National Portrait Gallery

Travelogue

Old State Capitol State Historic Site
Illinois Historic Preservation Agency
Sixth and Adams Streets
Springfield, IL 62701
217-785-7961
www.state.il.us/HPA/OLDCAP1.HTM

This building served as the Illinois State Capitol from 1839 to 1876, after which it became the Sangamon County Courthouse. Ulysses S. Grant served as an assistant adjunct general here. It was also here that Abraham Lincoln served his last term in the state legislature before accepting the Republican nomination to the United States Senate with his "House Divided" speech. Following Lincoln's assassination, his body lay in state in the House chamber on the second floor of this building. The structure was dismantled in 1966 and then reconstructed with a new physical plant and expanded staff areas.

Hours
Daily from 9 A.M. to 5 P.M.
Admission
Free; donations are accepted

Old State Capitol State Historic Site

Travelogue

Quartermaster Museum
Building 5218, A Avenue and 22nd Street
1201 22nd Street
Fort Lee, VA 23801-1601
804-734-4203
www.lee.army.mil/quartermaster/museum/index.html

Founded in 1957, this museum collects and interprets artifacts related to the United States Army Quartermaster Corps, a military unit that traces its history to 1775. The museum has 26,000 artifacts and 30,000 documents. Among its holdings are Dwight D. Eisenhower's uniforms, the catafalque that carried Eisenhower's casket, saddles that belonged to Franklin Pierce and Ulysses S. Grant, the muffled drum used in John F. Kennedy's funeral, and a large collection of presidential flags.

Hours

Tuesday through Friday from 10 A.M. to 5 P.M. and weekends from 11 A.M. to 5 P.M.; closed New Year's, Thanksgiving, and Christmas

Admission

Free

Quartermaster Museum

Travelogue

United States Air Force Museum

United States Air Force Museum Foundation
Old Wright Field
Springfield Pike
Dayton, OH 45433-7102
513-255-3284
www.wpafb.af.mil/museum/

The United States Air Force Museum offers a close-up view of more than 300 aircraft from this nation and others. Included is a fleet of nine presidential aircraft. It should be noted that there is not one specific Air Force One aircraft. That designation is used for any aircraft with the president aboard.

One presidential aircraft in the collection is a Douglas VC-54C Sacred Cow. This plane was put into service in 1944 for Franklin D. Roosevelt, the first president to travel by air. The plane was equipped with an elevator to enable Roosevelt to board in his wheelchair. Its most notable mission came in February 1945, when it took Roosevelt to Yalta; for security reasons, its tail number was changed for that mission. On July 26, 1947, Harry S Truman signed the National Security Act while aboard; this act called for the creation of the United States Air Force. This plane, therefore, is considered the birthplace of the nation's air force.

The Douglas VC-118 Liftmaster on display was put into service in 1947, replacing the Sacred Cow. It was equipped with a state-room and could accommodate 24 seated passengers or 12 in modified sleeping berths. It was named the *Independence* in honor of Harry S Truman's hometown. Its most notable trip was in October 1950, when it took Truman to Wake Island to meet with General Douglas MacArthur about Korea.

Also on display is a Bell UH-13J Sioux. In March 1957, the air force put two helicopters into service for Dwight D. Eisenhower, the first president to travel by helicopter. When they were retired in 1967, one was sent to the Smithsonian Institution and the other here.

The collection's Lockheed VC-121E Constellation was Eisenhower's personal plane from 1954 to 1961. Mrs. Eisenhower named it *Columbine III*, after the state flower of Colorado, her adopted state. This plane was retired in 1966.

The Aero Commander U-4B, the smallest plane in the museum's presidential fleet, was used by Eisenhower between 1956 and 1960.

The museum's North American T-39A Sabreliner was put into air force service in Europe in 1963 and was damaged in a minor crash in 1966. From 1968 until 1973, it was used by Lyndon Baines Johnson for his trips to and from Texas.

The Beech VC-6A dubbed the *Lady Bird Special* was used to transport Johnson between Bergstrom Air Force Base in Texas and the LBJ Ranch.

The Lockheed VC-140B Jetstar was put into service in the 1960s. It served Presidents Richard M. Nixon, Gerald R. Ford, Jimmy Carter, and Ronald Reagan, though it was not the president's primary plane. It was retired in 1987.

The Boeing 707 retired from the presidential fleet in 1998 will soon become part of the museum's presidential collection. This aircraft was put into service in 1962 as John F. Kennedy's primary plane and served seven presidents while amassing 13,000 hours in the air. Lyndon Baines Johnson took his first oath of office aboard this plane at Love Field in Dallas just hours after Kennedy's death. In order that Kennedy's casket not travel back to Washington in the cargo hold on the flight that brought the newly inaugurated Johnson to Washington, two rows of passenger seats were removed from the main cabin to accommodate it. The plane took Kennedy to Berlin in 1963, Secretary of State Henry Kissinger to Paris in 1970 for secret talks with the North Vietnamese, and Richard M. Nixon to China in 1972. In 1981, it took former presidents Nixon, Ford, and Carter to Egypt for Anwar Sadat's funeral. Retired master sergeant Stan Goodwin, a radio operator on that trip, told the press that it was the only time he ever saw three presidents and two secretaries of state standing in line to use the men's room. The plane's final official use came in early 1998, when William J. Clinton's Boeing 747 became stuck in mud in Illinois.

Hours
Daily from 9 A.M. to 5 P.M.
Admission
Free

United States Air Force Museum

Travelogue

Park

Camp David
Catoctin Mountain Park
National Park Service
6602 Foxville Road
Thurmont, MD 21788-1518
301-663-9388
www.nps.gov/cato

Catoctin Mountain Park was developed

during the 1930s by the Civilian Conservation Corps as a camp for federal employees. In 1942, President Franklin D. Roosevelt directed the National Park Service to designate one of the park's camp areas a presidential retreat, so he could escape Washington's oppressive summer heat without traveling to his New York State home. Roosevelt named the presidential camp "Shangri-La," the main cottage "The Bear's Den," the laundry facility "The Soap Dish," the Secret Service quarters "The Baker Street Urchins," and the stewards' cabin "The Little Luzon." The retreat was seldom used by Truman, Kennedy, and Lyndon Baines Johnson but was frequently used by other presidents, most notably Nixon. Eventually, its name was changed to Camp David.

The camp has undergone extensive expansion and renovation and now includes nearly a dozen residential cabins. The main lodge is now called "Laurel" and the nearby presidential office cabin "Birch"; most new buildings are named for tree species. Camp David is closed to the public, but the rest of the park is available for use. Included are two overnight camps, Camp Misty Mount and Owens Creek Campground. Call the park ranger at the above number for information on overnight accommodations.

Hours
The visitor center is open Monday through Thursday from 10 A.M. to 4:30 P.M., Friday from 10 A.M. to 5 P.M., and weekends from 8:30 A.M. to 5 P.M.; it is closed federal holidays.

Admission
Free, although there is a fee for overnight camping

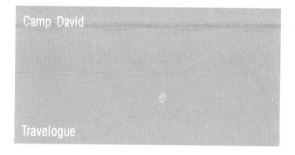
Camp David

Travelogue

Public Buildings and Sites

The Capitol
National Mall
Washington, DC 20510
202-224-3121
www.house.gov

It is in the Capitol that all presidents officially win election, when the joint houses meet to count the electoral votes. The Capitol generally serves as the inaugural site for presidents and is the location where State of the Union addresses are given.

Visitors wanting to take guided or self-guided tours should enter at the East Plaza, across from the Supreme Court. Guided tours leave from the Central Rotunda every 15 minutes from 9 A.M. until 3:45 P.M. and include the Rotunda, Statuary Hall, the Old Supreme Court Chamber, and the chambers of the House and Senate when they are not in session; those wishing to visit the chambers when Congress is in session need to call one of their senators or their representative for tickets. Statuary Hall, established in 1864, features statues honoring two residents of each state. The presidents honored in Statuary Hall include Garfield from Ohio, Jackson from Tennessee, and Washington from Virginia.

Hours
Daily from 9 A.M. to 4:30 P.M.
Admission
Free

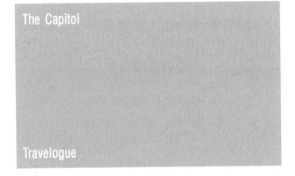

The Capitol

Travelogue

Pennsylvania Avenue National Historic Site
Pennsylvania Avenue Development Corporation
National Park Service
331 Pennsylvania Avenue NW
Washington, DC 20004-1703
202-426-6720
www.nps.gov/paav

This site includes the section of Pennsylvania Avenue between the Capitol and the White House. Intended by the city's designer, Pierre L'Enfant, as an official ceremonial route, Pennsylvania Avenue was the first Washington street to be paved and remains the city's widest. With few exceptions, it has served as a parade route following presidential inaugurations since Thomas Jefferson's historic horseback procession. Of the eight presidents who died in office, the processions of seven—William Henry Harrison, Tyler, Lincoln, Garfield, McKinley, Harding, and Kennedy—followed Pennsylvania Avenue; Franklin D. Roosevelt's funeral procession followed Constitution Avenue instead.

The site also includes many individual attractions of historic or architectural significance. The nonprofit educational organization Architour offers tours of the site; call 202-265-6454 for information.

Hours
Open 24 hours per day
Admission
Free, although fees may be charged for individual attractions and activities within the site

Pennsylvania Avenue National Historic Site

Travelogue

Appendix 2
Presidential Birth Dates

Many presidential sites hold special programming to coincide with presidential birthdays. In order to assist you in planning your travels, a list of presidential birth dates follows. Please call the individual sites to inquire about special events, especially in quinquennial years.

January 7, 1800, Millard Fillmore
January 9, 1913, Richard M. Nixon
January 29, 1843, William McKinley
January 30, 1882, Franklin D. Roosevelt

February 6, 1911, Ronald Reagan
February 9, 1773, William Henry Harrison
February 12, 1809, Abraham Lincoln
February 22, 1732, George Washington
Presidents' Day is the third Monday in
February.

March 15, 1767, Andrew Jackson
March 16, 1751, James Madison
March 18, 1837, Grover Cleveland
March 29, 1790, John Tyler

April 13, 1743, Thomas Jefferson
April 27, 1822, Ulysses S. Grant
April 23, 1791, James Buchanan
April 28, 1758, James Monroe

May 8, 1884, Harry S Truman
May 29, 1917, John F. Kennedy

June 12, 1924, George Bush

July 4, 1872, Calvin Coolidge

July 11, 1767, John Quincy Adams
July 14, 1913, Gerald R. Ford

August 10 or 11, 1874, Herbert Hoover
August 19, 1946, William J. Clinton
August 20, 1833, Benjamin Harrison
August 27, 1908, Lyndon Baines Johnson

September 15, 1857, William Howard Taft

October 1, 1924, Jimmy Carter
October 4, 1822, Rutherford B. Hayes
October 5, 1829, Chester A. Arthur
October 14, 1890, Dwight D. Eisenhower
October 28, 1858, Theodore Roosevelt
October 30, 1735, John Adams

November 2, 1795, James Knox Polk
November 2, 1865, Warren G. Harding
November 19, 1831, James Garfield
November 23, 1804, Franklin Pierce
November 24, 1784, Zachary Taylor

December 5, 1782, Martin Van Buren
December 28, 1856, Woodrow Wilson
December 29, 1808, Andrew Johnson

Bibliography

The American Heritage Pictorial History of the Presidents of the United States. New York: American Heritage Publishing Company, 1968.

Boller, Paul F., Jr. *Presidential Campaigns*. Oxford, England: Oxford University Press, 1984.

Degregorio, William A. *The Complete Book of U.S. Presidents*. New York: Barricade Books, 1993.

Durant, John, and Alice Durant. *The Presidents of the United States*. New York: Gaché Publishing, 1966.

Graff, Henry F. *The Presidents: A Reference History*. New York: Simon & Schuster/ Macmillan, 1997.

Graham, Billy. *Just As I Am*. New York: HarperCollins Publishers, 1997.

Kane, Joseph Nathan. *Facts about the Presidents*. New York: H. W. Wilson Company, 1985.

McCullough, David. *Truman*. New York: Simon & Schuster, 1992.

McQueen, Jane Bangley. *The Complete Guide to America's National Parks*. Washington: National Park Service, 1994.

Weems, Mason L. *The Life of Washington*. Cambridge, MA: Harvard University Press, 1962.

Wiencek, Henry. *Smithsonian Guide to Historic America: Southern New England*. New York: Stewart, Tabori & Chang, Publishers, 1989.

Geographic Index

Metropolitan Memorial United Methodist Church, 138
Monroe-Adams-Abbe House, 45
National City Christian Church, 204
National Museum of American History, 259
National Museum of Health and Medicine, 105
National Portrait Gallery, 259–60
National Presbyterian Church, 242
New York Avenue Presbyterian Church, 243
Octagon, The, 40
Pennsylvania Avenue National Historic Site, 264
Religious Society of Friends, 170
Richard M. Nixon Center, 214–15
Smithsonian Institution, 105, 259
St. John's Lafayette Square, 243–44
St. Matthew's Cathedral, 198
Thomas Jefferson Memorial and Tidal Basin, 35
United States Capitol. *See* District of Columbia: Capitol, the
United States Supreme Court, 151
Walter Reed Army Medical Center, 105, 192
Washington Monument, 24
Washington National Cathedral, 156–57
White House, the, 61, 62, 72, 98, 132, 185, 218, 252
Woodrow Wilson House, 154–55, 156

Florida

Key West: Harry S Truman Little White House Museum, 182–83
Miami: Gold Coast Railroad Museum, 257

Georgia

Americus: Georgia Southwestern College, 223
Atlanta: Carter Center, 225; Jimmy Carter Library and Museum, 226
Augusta: Boyhood Home of Woodrow Wilson, 153–54
Fort Oglethorpe: Chickamauga and Chattanooga National Military Park, 116
Plains: Jimmy Carter National Historic Site, 221–23; Lillian G. Carter Nursing Center, 221; Maranatha Baptist Church, 223; Plains United Methodist Church, 224; Smiling Peanut Statue, 226
Warm Springs: Little White House State Historic Site, 176

Illinois

Beardstown: Beardstown Courthouse, 94
Bement: Bryant Cottage State Historic Site, 104
Dixon: Dixon High School, 229–30; Dixon Historical Center, 229; First Christian Church (Disciples of Christ), 229; Lincoln Monument State Memorial, 254; Loveland Community Center, 231; Ronald Reagan's Boyhood Home, 228
Eureka: Eureka College, 230
Galena: Ulysses S. Grant Home State Historic Site, 112
Harristown: Lincoln Trail Homestead State Park, 90
Lerna: Lincoln Log Cabin State Historic Site, 93–94
Lincoln: Postville Courthouse State Historic Site, 96–97

Canada

United Kingdom

General Index

Harrison Tomb, 62

Harry S Truman Birthplace State Historic Site, 180

Harry S Truman Library and Museum, 185, 186

Harry S Truman Little White House Museum, 182–83

Harry S Truman Office and Courtroom, 187

Harvard University, 246–47

Herbert Hoover National Historic Site, 168, 172

Herbert Hoover Presidential Library and Museum, 168

Hermitage, the, 50–51

Hillsborough Historical Society, 78

Hiram College, 124

Historic Columbia Foundation, 154

Historic Gettysburg-Adams County, Inc., 103

Hollywood Cemetery, 241

Home of Franklin D. Roosevelt National Historic Site, 173, 177

Hoover-Minthorn House Museum, 169

Horseshoe Bend National Military Park, 53

Hotel Northampton, 167

Illinois Historic Preservation Agency, 95, 96, 97, 112, 260

Immanuel Baptist Church, 238

Independence Hall, 17, 27

Independence High School. *See* Truman High School

Independence National Historic Park, 17, 27, 258

Jackson County Courthouse. *See* Harry S Truman Office and Courtroom

James A. Garfield National Historic Site, 123—24

James Buchanan Foundation, 83–84

James Buchanan Memorial, 87

James K. Polk Ancestral Home, 67–68

James K. Polk Memorial State Historic Site, 67

James Madison Museum, 39

James Monroe Museum and Memorial Library, 44

Jefferson National Expansion Memorial, 33–34

Jimmy Carter Library and Museum, 226

Jimmy Carter National Historic Site, 221–23

Job Corps of Grand Rapids, 217

John Adams Birthplace. *See* Adams National Historic Site

John F. Kennedy Center for the Performing Arts, 199

John F. Kennedy Hyannis Museum, 198

John Fitzgerald Kennedy Library and Museum, 199–200

John Fitzgerald Kennedy National Historic Site, 193

John Kane House, 13–14

John Quincy Adams Birthplace. *See* Adams National Historic Site

Johns Hopkins University, 156

Johnson City Bank, 205

Johnson City High School. *See* Lyndon B. Johnson High School

Johnson City Historic District, 205–6

Johnson Family Cemetery, 204–5

Julia Chester Hospital, 237

Meridian Hill Park, 87

Metamora Courthouse State Historic Site, 95

Metropolitan Memorial United Methodist Church, 138

Miami University of Ohio, 135

Millard Fillmore Birthplace, 74–75

Millard Fillmore House, 75

Mission Inn, 212–13, 231

Monroe-Adams-Abbe House, 45

Monticello, 31

Montpelier, 37, 39

Mordecai Historic Park, 107

Morris-Jumel Mansion, 9

Morristown National Historical Park, 14–15

Mount Pulaski Courthouse State Historic Site, 96

Mount Rushmore National Memorial, 254–55

Mount Sinai Hospital, 213

Mount Vernon, 4, 18

Mount Vernon Ladies' Association, 4

Museum of American Architectural Foundation. *See* Octagon, The

Museum of American Political Life, 259

Museum of Western Expansion. *See* Jefferson National Expansion Memorial

National Archives and Records Administration sites: Dwight D. Eisenhower Library, 189–90, 192; Franklin D. Roosevelt Library and Museum, 177–78; Franklin D. Roosevelt Memorial, 178–79; George Bush Presidential Library and Museum, 235–36; Gerald R. Ford Library, 219; Harry S Truman Library and Museum, 185, 186;

Herbert Hoover Presidential Library and Museum, 168; John Fitzgerald Kennedy Library and Museum, 199–200; Lyndon Baines Johnson Library and Museum, 207–8; Office of Presidential Libraries, 253–54; Richard M. Nixon Materials Staff, 214; Ronald Reagan Presidential Library and Museum, 232

National City Christian Church, 204

National McKinley Birthplace Memorial, 137

National Museum of American History, 259

National Museum of Health and Medicine, 105

National Park Service sites: Abraham Lincoln Birthplace National Historic Site, 88–89; Adams National Historic Site, 26–27, 46–47; Andrew Johnson National Historic Site, 108–9; Antietam National Battlefield, 141; Appomattox Court House National Historical Park, 117–18; Camp David, 262–63; Catoctin Mountain Park, 262–63; Chickamauga and Chattanooga National Military Park, 116; Colonial National Historical Park, 15; Deshler-Morris House, 6; Eisenhower National Historic Site, 190–91; Eleanor Roosevelt National Historic Site, 177; Federal Hall National Memorial, 16–17; Ford's Theatre National Historic Site, 97–98; Fort Donelson National Battlefield, 115; Fort Necessity National Battlefield, 19; Franklin D. Roosevelt Memorial, 178; General Grant National Memorial, 118–19; George Washington Birthplace National Monument, 3; Gettysburg National Military Park, 100; Graff House, 32–33;

Herbert Hoover National Historic Site, 168, 172; Home of Franklin D. Roosevelt National Historic Site, 173, 177; Horseshoe Bend National Military Park, 53; Independence National Historic Park, 17, 27, 258; James A. Garfield National Historic Site, 123–24; Jefferson National Expansion Memorial, 33–34; Jimmy Carter National Historic Site, 221–23; John Fitzgerald Kennedy National Historic Site, 193; Lincoln Depot, 102; Lincoln Home National Historic Site, 91–92; Lincoln Memorial, 99; Lincoln's Boyhood Home National Memorial, 90; Longfellow National Historic Site, 8; Lyndon B. Johnson Memorial Grove on the Potomac, 206; Lyndon B. Johnson National Historic Site, 201–2; Martin Van Buren National Historic Site, 56; Morristown National Historical Park, 14–15; Mount Rushmore National Memorial, 254–55; Palo Alto Battlefield, 73; Pennsylvania Avenue National Historic Site, 264; Petersburg National Battlefield, 116–17; Roosevelt Campobello International Park, 174; Sagamore Hill National Historic Site, 143, 146–47; Shiloh National Military Park, 115–16; Theodore Roosevelt Birthplace National Historic Site, 142–43; Theodore Roosevelt Inaugural National Historic Site, 146; Theodore Roosevelt Island, 147; Theodore Roosevelt National Park, 148; Thomas Jefferson Memorial and Tidal Basin, 35; Todd House, 37–38; Truman Historic District, 181–82; Ulysses S. Grant National Historic Site, 111–12;

Valley Forge National Historical Park, 12–13; Vicksburg National Military Park, 114; Washington Monument, 24; William Howard Taft National Historic Site, 149
National Portrait Gallery, 259–60
National Presbyterian Church, 242
National Society of Colonial Dames of America, 169, 256
National Trust for Historic Preservation, 37, 55
Natural Bridge, 34
Nebraska State Historical Society, 218–19
New Salem. *See* Lincoln's New Salem
New Windsor Cantonment State Historic Site, 16
New York Avenue Presbyterian Church, 243
North Carolina Department of Cultural Resources, 67

Oak Ridge Cemetery. *See* Lincoln's Tomb State Historic Site
Octagon, The, 40
Office of Presidential Libraries, 253–54
Ohio Historical Society, 111, 158–59
Old House. *See* Adams National Historic Site
Old North Cemetery, 81
Old Orchard Museum. *See* Sagamore Hill National Historic Site
Old Presbyterian Meeting House, 18
Old St. Louis Courthouse. *See* Jefferson National Expansion Memorial
Old State Capitol State Historic Site, 260
Omaha Department of Parks, Recreation, and Public Property, 216